God Save the Queen

God Save the Queen

The Spiritual Heart of the Monarchy

IAN BRADLEY

continuum

Continuum International Publishing Group
The Tower Building, 11 York Road, London SE1 7NX
80 Maiden Lane, Suite 704, New York, NY 10038

www.continuumbooks.com

First published by DLT in 1999.
This revised and expanded edition published by Continuum 2012.

British Library Cataloguing-in-Publication Data
A catalogue record for this book is available from the British Library.

ISBN: 978-1-4411-9367-4 (paperback)

Typeset by Fakenham Prepress Solutions Ltd, Fakenham, NR21 8NN
Printed and bound in India

Contents

Acknowledgements

I have derived considerable help from conversations and correspondence with Marion Bowman, James Bradby, Kevin McGinnell, Gordon McPhate, Anne Rowbottom, Anne Stallybrass, Ray Simpson, Timothy Strauss, Geo Cameron, Paul Weller, Andrew Rutherford, Tom Wright, Tariq Modood and Archimandrite Alexis of the Saint Edward Brotherhood. June Boyce-Tillman kindly allowed me to quote her Golden Jubilee hymn. Gordon McConville and Richard Bauckham kindly read and commented on my chapters on the Old and New Testaments respectively. I am also grateful for the support and encouragement of Caroline Chartres and Robin-Baird Smith at Continuum.

Introduction

In the weeks leading up to the coronation of 1953, Geoffrey Fisher, the Archbishop of Canterbury, reflected in a series of sermons on the spiritual significance of the institution of monarchy. He argued that reduced temporal power enhanced rather than diminished its importance, bringing about 'the possibility of a spiritual power far more exalted and far more searching in its demands: the power to lead, to inspire, to unite, by the Sovereign's personal character, personal convictions and personal example'.[1]

Throughout the past 60 years, Queen Elizabeth II has exemplified that spiritual power and calling of monarchy. It would be hard to think of any Head of State in the world who has more consistently and faithfully embodied the principle of selfless, even sacrificial devotion to duty. Guided by a firm conviction in her calling and anointing by God, she has represented and articulated the spiritual feelings of her people in the most solemn and consecrated moments of the nation's life. Although naturally reserved and undemonstrative over what she quite rightly regards as a personal matter, she has made no secret of her own strong Christian faith and her belief in the positive reconciling power of religion as a force for good and in the continuing validity of the teachings of the world's major faiths. In a period that has seen a sea change in so many aspects of morality and culture, she has stood as an exemplar of probity, decency and incorruptibility while in other respects moving with the times and never appearing stuffy or censorious.

This book, which is published to coincide with the Diamond Jubilee of the Queen's accession and coronation, is both a celebration and an examination of the spiritual heart of monarchy. While it has a particular focus on the reign of Elizabeth II, the writings of the Prince of Wales and current debates about the religious character of the monarchy and the state, it ranges widely historically, looking back to the origins of sacred monarchy in primal religion and the Old and New Testaments of the Bible, and on the way the religious character of monarchy has been shaped in British history. It also looks forward to the future, specifically to the shape and form of the next coronation and the role of the monarch in a multicultural and multi-faith society.

Although this book is primarily about the institution and purpose of monarchy, there is inevitably much in it about the beliefs and practices of individual kings and queens. Christian monarchy involves responsibility and duty on the part of rulers as much as loyal service on the part of their subjects. It is about the example that monarchs set as disciples of Christ. In this respect there is much to celebrate and for which to give thanks down the centuries.

It is worth giving a brief tally of some of the contributions that have been made to the Christian life of the British Isles by our kings and queens. Westminster Abbey was the brainchild of Edward the Confessor, and was rebuilt and added to by Henry III and Henry VII. St George's Chapel, Windsor, was built on the initiative of Edward III and Dunfermline Abbey by David I of Scotland. The first English Prayer Book owed much to Edward VI's personal support of Thomas Cranmer. The Authorized Version of the Bible came out of the Hampton Court Conference convened by James VI of Scotland and I of England. Recent scholarship has suggested that the king took a strong personal interest in the making of the Bible which he saw as an *irenicon*, an instrument of peace to bring together both the divided factions in the Church and the nations of Scotland and England into a single United Kingdom. The practice of standing for the Hallelujah chorus in Handel's *Messiah* was begun by George III who rose to his feet during its first London performance in 1743. The entire audience followed his example, initiating a tradition that has continued ever since. Queen Victoria's personal intervention in defence of the national Kirk almost certainly played a decisive role in preventing the disestablishment of the Church of Scotland. There have, of course, been sinners as well as saints among those who have worn the crown down the centuries but, in common with other countries across Europe, Britain is not without its sainted and saintly kings and queens. At least two monarchs have been officially canonized – Edward the Confessor in 1161 and Margaret of Scotland in 1250 – and two officially recognized as martyrs – the Anglo-Saxon king Edward, who ruled from 962 to 979, and Edmund, King of East Anglia from 841 to 869. Several others have received unofficial recognition for their sanctity. Both Oswald and his cousin Oswy, who between them ruled Northumbria from 633 to 651, were venerated as saints soon after their deaths. Charles I is regarded as a martyr by many Anglicans, and is commemorated as such in several church dedications and in services on 30 January, the anniversary of his execution. King David I of Scotland, who earned the sobriquet of 'the Saint' from the number of his religious foundations, is commemorated in the Church of England's calendar as a confessor.

Many monarchs have left us their prayers. Several are quoted in the pages that follow and others may be found in two recently published collections, *All Majesty and Power*, an anthology of royal prayers compiled by Donald Gray (Hodder & Stoughton, 2000) and *Royal Prayer: A Surprising History* by David Baldwin (Continuum, 2009). A recent and unexpected addition to the stock of royal prayers was the one personally written by Prince William and Catherine Middleton for their wedding in Westminster Abbey in April 2011. It did not appear in the Order of Service and was read out by the Bishop of London at the end of his address:

> God our Father, we thank you for our families; for the love that we share and for the joy of our marriage. In the busyness of each day keep our eyes fixed on what is real

and important in life and help us to be generous with our
time and love and energy. Strengthened by our union help
us to serve and comfort those who suffer. We ask this in
the spirit of Jesus Christ. Amen.

Some monarchs have made significant theological statements
which still speak to us today. I have been struck in the context
of recent controversies both within and between different
Christian denominations about the precise meaning of the
Eucharist by how several of those seeking a common ground
have commended the 'mystical ambiguity' contained in words
spoken by Elizabeth I when questioned about her own opinion
of Christ's presence in the sacrament of communion:

'Twas God the word that spake it,
He took the Bread and brake it;
And what the word did make it;
That I believe, and take it.[2]

Our present Queen has contributed in several ways to the
spiritual life of the nation. She has taken very seriously her
role as Supreme Governor of the Church of England and her
relationship with the Church of Scotland, which she swore a
solemn oath to preserve at the meeting of the Privy Council
immediately following her accession. She has led the nation in
a particularly dignified way in the public services of thanksgiving and commemoration marking the great triumphs and
disasters that have taken place during her reign. She has been
a faithful and regular churchgoer and, while making no secret
of the importance and depth of her own Protestant Christian
faith, has reached out particularly warmly and generously to
those of other denominations and religious traditions.

In this devotion and attachment to the spiritual dimension
of her role as sovereign, the Queen has had the strong and
active support of her husband and eldest son, both of whom
have in their own right made a significant impact on religious
life and thought. Prince Philip, the Duke of Edinburgh, has a

similarly strong Christian faith, an impressive knowledge and understanding of the Bible, and a lively theological mind which has been especially applied to the relationship between religion and the environment and has given rise to several projects and writings, including his 1989 booklet *Survival or Extinction: A Christian Attitude to the Environment*, co-authored with Michael Mann. Prince Charles has made a notable contribution to the religious life of Britain with his consistent call for more emphasis to be given to the spiritual and holistic dimension, his particular interest in Islam and inter-faith dialogue, which has borne practical fruit in the Respect for Faith initiative, and his passionate championship of causes ranging from the Book of Common Prayer to sacred geometry. These and other themes are brought together in *Harmony: A New Way of Looking at Our World*, a book published in 2010 which he co-authored with two of his advisers, Tony Juniper and Ian Skelly. It mounts a powerful attack on post-Enlightenment modernism, materialism and rationalism, and argues for the innate harmony and deep interconnectedness of all things and for the re-enchantment of humanity through a greater sense of the sacred, a re-connection with the beauty and spirit of nature, and a deeper awareness of the presence of God.

For me, the Queen's most distinctive and significant contribution to the spiritual life of the nation has been her annual broadcast at 3 p.m. on Christmas Day, watched live by an audience of around nine million. Over recent years this has become noticeably more personal and more overtly Christian in tone. The royal Christmas broadcasts have always contained clear and obviously heartfelt expressions of the essence of the Christian Gospel and the Nativity story but in the 1980s and 1990s they were often essentially glorified travelogues reflecting the places which the Queen and other members of the royal family had visited during the year. A radically new tone was introduced in the 2000 Christmas broadcast when the Queen, speaking directly to camera, made testimony both to the importance of her own personal faith and to her sense of the continuing importance of the spiritual:

Whether we believe in God or not, I think most of us have a sense of the spiritual, that recognition of a deeper meaning and purpose in our lives, and I believe that this sense flourishes despite the pressures of our world.

This spirituality can be seen in the teachings of other great faiths. Of course religion can be divisive, but the Bible, the Koran and the sacred texts of the Jews and Hindus, Buddhists and Sikhs, are all sources of divine inspiration and practical guidance passed down through the generations.

To many of us our beliefs are of fundamental importance. For me the teachings of Christ and my own personal accountability before God provide a framework in which I try to lead my life. I, like so many of you, have drawn great comfort in difficult times from Christ's word and example. I believe that the Christian message remains profoundly important to us all.

This message, which ended with the words of the blessing in the Book of Common Prayer which begins 'Go forth into the world in peace', attracted 25 times more letters to Buckingham Palace than any previous Christmas broadcast. It was widely and rightly commended both for its strong and direct expression of personal faith and for its emphasis on the spiritual dimension in life, while acknowledging that not everyone was a believer and that not every believer was a Christian. For the *Daily Telegraph*, the broadcast showed the Queen 'speaking as a religious leader rather than a head of state', while for the ever-perceptive religious journalist and commentator Clifford Longley, 'it seemed the beginning of the reshaping of Christian monarchy to suit a more plural society, one without an Established Church of England as such but with an Anglican faith, alongside others alive within it'.[3]

Perhaps as a result of this warm reception but more, I suspect, through following her own instincts and those of her husband, the Queen has maintained the strong religious tone through many of her Christmas broadcasts in the 2000s and has continued to make frequent allusions to her own faith. In 2002, reflecting on a year that had seen the death of her mother and sister as well as the celebrations of her Golden Jubilee, she said:

> I know just how much I rely on my own faith to guide me through the good times and the bad. Each day is a new beginning, I know that the only way to live my life is to try to do what is right, to take the long view, to give of my best in all that the day brings, and to put my trust in God. Like others of you who draw inspiration from your own faith, I draw strength from the message of hope in the Christian gospel.

In 2004 she movingly retold the parable of the Good Samaritan and made a powerful plea for greater understanding and respect between those of different faiths and cultures. She cited the example of London and the experience of a visitor from abroad who was impressed on his tube journey from Heathrow Airport into the city centre by the way in which children from diverse ethnic and religious backgrounds were at ease with and trusted one another. Her 2008 and 2009 messages drew direct inspiration from the teachings of Jesus and in 2010 she began with a lengthy commendation of the King James Bible with its aim of bringing agreement between different parties within the Church and harmony to the kingdoms of England and Scotland. Increasingly, the Queen's Christmas messages have been filmed in a church or a chapel rather than in the drawing-room setting that was long the norm, and their sermonic style has been further enhanced by their tendency to end with a prayer or a quotation from the Bible. The 2010 message came from the chapel of Hampton Court and concluded with Jesus' statement of the so-called golden rule as recorded in Matthew 7.12: 'All things whatsoever ye would that men will do to you, do ye even so to them.'

Christmas Day is not the only time when millions of her subjects see the Queen in a religious setting. A very high proportion of the occasions when the sovereign and other members of the royal family are most visible and have their highest public profile are essentially religious in character – the annual Act of Remembrance at the Cenotaph, the Royal Maundy service, the Garter service at Windsor, and royal weddings and funerals and services of national thanksgiving and remembrance at St Paul's Cathedral and Westminster Abbey. Christmas Day television brings not only the Queen's annual message but pictures on all the news bulletins of her and other members of the royal family leaving morning worship at St Mary's Church, Sandringham. It is hardly surprising, given the ubiquity of these images of the Queen coming into or out of places of worship, and indeed kneeling in prayer with her husband in a church service, that so many people identify the monarchy strongly with the Church and with religious values. Nor is it surprising that for many people encounters with royalty often take on the character of a religious experience and that words like 'reverence' and 'blessing' are commonly used to describe them. This is confirmed in recent studies by social anthropologists. It has also been remarked upon by perceptive foreign observers, such as the American travel writer Paul Theroux, who while journeying round the coast of Britain arrived in the Fife coastal town of Anstruther just after it had been visited by the Queen.

> There was a heightened hum, a vibration racing in the air, the equivalent in sound of a twinkling light, something electric and almost visible. It was genuine. I felt it as soon as I entered the cobbled streets. It was as if the town had been refreshed with a blessing. In a way it had, for that atmosphere was the spirit left by the progress of the Royal visit.[4]

There is a strange reluctance in official and court circles and even in the higher echelons of the Church to acknowledge this spiritual aspect of the monarchy. It would be unthinkable today to hear a bishop mouthing the kinds of sentiments that Geoffrey Fisher expressed in 1953. I have been surprised to find among both church leaders close to the Crown and senior courtiers a determination to play down the spiritual significance of monarchy and a seeming embarrassment about affirming its Christian dimension. One senior member of the ecclesiastical household told me that he regarded my emphasis on the spiritual dimension of monarchy as 'eccentric'. A similar unease seems to underlie the comment made by a senior courtier to a journalist interested in Prince Charles' strong spiritual leanings: 'I think we've had rather too much of the sacred, don't you? He needs to be seen as a good bloke.'[5]

Official pronouncements on the purpose and value of the British monarchy are devoid of any religious references. The standard line presented in Central Office of Information pamphlets, and repeated in the report of the Royal Trustees to Parliament, speaks simply of the Queen providing 'a focus for national identity, unity and pride'. Search the word 'religion' in the official website of the British monarchy and you come up with just 41 matches. The word 'church' fares better with 115 matches but is still way behind 'government' with 262 or 'armed forces' with 251. This hardly seems a fair or accurate representation of the importance of the religious dimension in both the public and private life of the Queen.

It is, of course, the case that this aspect of the monarchy is profoundly counter-cultural and at odds with the prevailing secularism of modern Britain, and this may be why courtiers (though surely not clerics) are keen to play it down. The Queen is a considerably more devout and faithful Christian than the vast majority of her subjects, increasingly few of whom are to be found, as she is, voluntarily in church every Sunday morning. Her reign has seen a steady erosion of belief. The British Social Attitudes Survey first asked a representative sample of the British population about their religious allegiance in 1985. At the time, 63 per cent said that they were Christian and 34 per cent that they had no religious faith. Twenty-five years later, in 2010, the respective figures were 42 per cent and 51 per cent. It was the first time that any survey in Britain registered a majority of the population as having no religious belief. The *Guardian* took this finding as marking a cultural watershed and heralding 'the era of non-religious ascendancy beginning in Britain'.[6]

In this context, is the religious devotion of the Queen, the Duke of Edinburgh and other members of the Royal Family, so often found on their knees in prayer not just at great state occasions but Sunday after Sunday in the quiet and simple surroundings of the Royal Lodge Chapel in Windsor Great Park or Crathie Parish Church near Balmoral, an anachronism? Are the courtiers and advisers right to be embarrassed about it and keen to play it down? I think they are profoundly wrong. This is not just because I find the quiet, understated but clearly evident and sincere faith of the sovereign and her consort profoundly moving and inspirational. It is because I believe in the spiritual and religious heart of the monarchy, expressed institutionally and constitutionally in terms of its relationship with the Church as well as in its more personal aspects. I believe further that the monarchy has a potentially important role to play in healing, uniting and, indeed, re-sacralizing our increasingly fractured and secular nation. Something of this was evident in the Golden Jubilee celebrations of 2002, not least in the wonderfully exuberant carnival procession that snaked down the Mall led by a mass gospel choir. It may no longer be the case, as polls suggest that it was 40 years ago, that one-third of the United Kingdom population believe the Queen to have been specially chosen by God. At the popular level, however, there is clear evidence that royalty still inspires essentially spiritual feelings of reverence, respect and affection.

This contrasts with the prevailing secularism among many of those surrounding and supporting the monarchy – politicians, courtiers, public relations experts, image consultants and the 'gliterrati' of the media and showbusiness world – who seem to view it in wholly secular terms. Their emphasis is either on the 'people's monarchy', a definition which is essentially populist rather than popular and denies its derivation from and accountability to God, or on its celebrity superstar status. Both of these perspectives were evident among those who attended the service in Westminster Abbey in November 1997 to mark the fiftieth anniversary of the marriage of the Queen and Prince Philip. Seeing their casual behaviour as I watched this solemn act of worship on television provoked me to write the following letter to *The Times*, which summarizes the concerns which led me to embark on this book:

> In all this talk of a Royal Family more in touch with public opinion, we are in danger of missing the essential nature and purpose of monarchy.
>
> The monarchy is not a democratic institution, still less the creature of popular opinion, but rather a divinely instituted symbol and mystery. At their coronations, our kings and queens are anointed in a ritual which has its origins in Old Testament times and underlines the spiritual nature of their calling. They are thereafter accountable first and foremost to God and not to a fickle populace so easily manipulated and swayed by the mass media. Their role may not be to lead public opinion, though in deep and subtle ways they can both express the mood of the nation and also exert a powerful example, but most certainly they are not there to pander to it.
>
> We need to think much more about the religious basis of monarchy and the exercise of its spiritual function. In the case of our present Queen, it has been expressed in a sacrificial commitment to duty and public service and a sure and steadfast Christian faith fortified and nourished through regular churchgoing. In the case of her eldest son, who I fervently hope will be our next King, it may well take a different form, in keeping with his declared desire to be a defender of faith and his deep sensitivity to spiritual issues.
>
> The Royal Family were clearly engaged in and deeply moved by Thursday morning's service at Westminster Abbey. Many of the courtiers and commoners attending

it, by contrast, were caught by the television cameras chattering, giggling or maintaining a sullen silence through the great hymns of the Christian faith.

They might care to reflect on the message of those familiar words which rang through the Abbey as the Queen and Prince Philip left. God will save the Queen, not public opinion and certainly not the media.[7]

In the Preface to the first edition of this book, which was published in 2002 on the occasion of the Golden Jubilee of the Queen's accession, I wrote that what had really prompted me to write it was my concern that, at a time when it was a subject of considerable public fascination, the monarchy was being analysed and dissected from almost every point of view except the one that seemed to me to stand at its very heart and to be its ultimate *raison d' être*. Weighty books appeared in the 1990s on the constitutional aspects of monarchy, notably Vernon Bogdanor's *The Monarchy and the Constitution* (1995), and on its philanthropic role, notably Frank Proschaska's *Royal Bounty: The Making of a Welfare Monarchy* (1995) and James Morton's *Prince Charles: Breaking the Cycle* (1998). The Royal Family was regularly assessed in terms of its tourist potential and endlessly presented as a soap opera and subject for gossip, yet very few commentators analysed or acknowledged its spiritual dimension. Even those writing about the future of the monarchy from a broadly sympathetic standpoint conceived of it in wholly secular terms. Indeed, the word 'secular' often figured prominently in their prescription of how the monarchy should develop. Bogdanor advocated 'a secularized monarchy ... more in tune with the spirit of the age'.[8] John Taylor, in his somewhat eccentric *British Monarchy, Church Establishment and Civil Liberty* (1996), argued: 'Let the crown be the British institution of secular culture.'[9] The secularization of the monarchy through curtailing all its religious roles and links with churches was a major plank of the reforms proposed in the 1998 Demos pamphlet, *Modernising the Monarchy*, as it was for the authors of *The Windsors: A Dynasty Revealed*

(1994) who argued for a purely civil role for the monarch as defender of the constitution 'rather than a religious one as defender of the faith'.[10]

I noted further that it had been left to a small number of academics, not all of them personally sympathetic to the monarchy and none of them from the disciplines of theology or religious studies, to point to its continuing spiritual dimension and profound popular impact, and to acknowledge the unwillingness of their academic colleagues to recognize this. A seminal article on the coronation in 1953 by two sociologists, Edward Shils and Michael Young, noted its sacred aspects, which amounted for them to nothing less than 'a great act of national communion', and went on to criticize the 'intellectualist bias' that led their fellow academics to shun the subject of monarchy:

> It is avoided because the monarchy has its roots in man's beliefs and sentiments about what he regards as sacred. The decline in the intensity of religious belief, especially in the educated classes, has produced an aversion towards all the sentiments and practices associated with religion. They do not acknowledge the somewhat alarming existence of these sentiments within themselves and refuse to admit that these are at work in others. ... The frequency with which the Coronation was spoken of by ordinary people as an 'inspiration' and as a 'rededication' of the nation, only underscores the egregiousness of the omission.[11]

Snobbish superiority and a secularist outlook, as much as intellectualist bias, have led most academics to continue to ignore and devalue the spiritual dimension of monarchy which is still recognized at a popular level. Commenting on the outpouring of mourning that followed the death of Diana, Princess of Wales, in 1997, the sociologist Ross McKibbin noted:

> The dominant intellectual categories of the twentieth century are secular and rational: we are in a sense taught

not to be able to understand such 'irrational' phenomena
as the reaction to Diana's death, or indeed anything to
do with public attitudes to royalty, and are frequently
embarrassed if asked to do so.[12]

It has taken a social anthropologist, Anne Rowbottom, to show
just how strong a religious element there still is in the continuing
love affair between the British population and royalty. For
her, the ultimate ground of pro-royal sentiment is comparable with a religious force rather than with showbusiness or
celebrity appeal.[13] Another of the few commentators who take
this aspect seriously, the republican-inclined Tom Nairn, has
rightly observed that being pro-monarchy necessarily entails
'believing spirit to be more important than mere matter'.
He identifies monarchy as being crucial to British identity
primarily in a spiritual and ideological way, although for him
it is for this very reason to be derided as 'the invisible bond of
community bestowing a faint halo even upon suet puddings'
and attacked as 'the soul of Europe's last feudal system'.[14] At
least Nairn recognizes the essentially spiritual nature of the
institution that he is committed to destroying.

In fact, I believe there has been a significant shift in attitude
over the past ten years. Books published in the first decade
of the twenty-first century have been noticeably more appre-
ciative of the spiritual dimension of the monarchy than those
that came out in the last decade of the twentieth century.
Several of the biographies of the Queen published to coincide
with the Golden Jubilee of her reign do acknowledge and
discuss this area. In his book *The Queen* (2001), Ben Pimlott
had more to say about the religious aspect of monarchy than
most royal biographers but still clearly found it a somewhat
mystifying and slightly embarrassing subject. He described
the words used at the anointing of the sovereign as 'extraordinary'. Significantly, it was in the context of a discussion of
the reaction to the death of Diana, Princess of Wales, that he
explored the whole notion of sacred monarchy and its magical,
mystical appeal, and offered his definition of 'royal' as 'a

perceived essence that is religious, sacred, familial, dynastic and traditional'.[15] A welcome and refreshing emphasis on the spiritual dimension of monarchy has underlain several of the lectures and pamphlets sponsored by the Temenos Academy which was set up in 1990 by the poet Kathleen Raine, and has Prince Charles as its patron. To mark the Queen's Golden Jubilee, the Academy organized a series of lectures on this theme which were published in 2002 in a booklet entitled *Monarchy*. The liturgical and ceremonial aspects of the coronation service have been given considerable attention in Roy Strong's book *Coronation: A History of Kingship and the British monarchy* (2005), as befitting the author's position as High Bailiff and Searcher of the Sanctuary of Westminster Abbey.

Perhaps the most unexpected and significant acknowledgement of the spiritual heart of monarchy has come from Jeremy Paxman, the presenter of *Newsnight* and *University Challenge* known for his world-weary and insouciant approach to interviewing the great and the good. When the *Sunday Telegraph* revealed that Paxman was writing a book about the Royal Family, a fervent royalist wrote to the newspaper expressing the hope that the only access he be given by Buckingham Palace should be to the corgis' kennels. This reaction was hardly surprising given the dismissal of the monarchy as 'primped, planned and pompous' in Paxman's earlier book, *The English* (1999). By contrast, his book *On Royalty* (2006) ends with a moving apologia for the monarchy and a loyal and affectionate tribute to the Queen's sense of duty and service.

Lurking behind Paxman's highly readable romp through royal scandals and juicy revelations is a serious and important thesis about the monarchy's essentially spiritual character. In an intriguing passage early on, he even turns amateur theologian and ruminates on the doctrines of the Trinity and the Incarnation to explain the institution. Towards the end, he reflects that 'monarchs stand for something beyond themselves, and in that sense are less political creatures than religious ones' and that 'there is certainly an argument for saying that royalty can be properly understood only in religious terms'.[16]

I sense that there are several factors at work which may be changing attitudes towards royalty. The relentless assault of the Murdoch press and other tabloid papers both on royal personalities and on the institution of monarchy seems to have abated somewhat. Perhaps this is a lingering legacy of the circumstances surrounding the death of Diana, Princess of Wales. Media hostility and cynicism have been increasingly directed at politicians, and the Royal Family has been left alone more and pilloried less than it was in the 1980s and 1990s. The Golden Jubilee of 2002 proved not to be the damp squib that many among the chattering classes and scoffing media had predicted, and brought together millions of people from different cultures, faiths and backgrounds in joyful celebration. In contrast to the celebration of the new millennium two years earlier, it had a clear spiritual focus both in national events and in the large number of celebratory church services held throughout the country. The funeral of the Queen Mother in the Jubilee year, the celebration of the Queen's eightieth birthday in 2006 and the wedding of the Duke and Duchess of Cambridge in 2011 brought a return to traditional ritual centred on formal services at Westminster Abbey and St Paul's Cathedral that were watched by millions and seemed to strike a deep chord with many.

These are mostly factors that have to do with particular royal personalities rather than with the institution of monarchy per se. But then monarchy is a very personal form of government. Indeed, personality often helps to shape and chart the spiritual direction of the monarchy in a new and relevant way – but it is not everything. Much of what is written about the monarchy nowadays is entirely personality orientated. As Clifford Longley has observed,

> Once those who believed in the monarchy did so on principle, focusing on the institution more or less

regardless of the incumbent. Nowadays there is a close connection between attitudes to the Crown and whether a person 'likes' the Queen or 'likes' Prince Charles. ... Some would call this the 'touchy-feel' thing; some, the feminisation of British politics. My hunch is that it is to do with the collapse of the metaphysical imagination, and therefore with the marginalisation of religion.[17]

Most commentators, and virtually all the media, continue to think, write and talk about the monarchy almost entirely in terms of personalities. However, their approach has been notably less cynical and more respectful, if not exactly reverential, over recent years. The change of approach has been perhaps most evident in the portrayal of Prince Charles, who although still the butt of some crass attacks and hugely distorted criticism from the likes of the *Daily Mail*, is generally treated with much more respect than in the past. His views on a range of issues are increasingly being taken seriously and not mocked and scoffed at. David Lorimer's fine study of his beliefs and actions in his book *Radical Prince* (2003) helped in this respect and the BBC has given the Prince several opportunities to air his thoughts at some length. A focus on royal personalities in two of the most successful British films of the past decade has actually served to bring out the lonely, sacrificial aspect of monarchy and increase respect both for the institution and its recent incumbents. *The Queen* (2006), starring Helen Mirren as Elizabeth II, and *The King's Speech* (2011), starring Colin Firth as George VI, have shown the two most recent British sovereigns in a highly sympathetic light, emphasizing their fundamental dignity, devotion to duty and vulnerability, and in both cases also subtly hinting at a more spiritual quality in their make-up.

The personal element in monarchy is, of course, emphasized in the song which gives this book its title. The United Kingdom is just about the only country in the world which has as its national anthem a hymn addressed to God and asking his blessing on a particular person rather than a celebration of flag and fatherland or an invocation of some abstract political principle. 'God Save the Queen' underlines two central themes in the British understanding of monarchy over the past 1500 years or more – that its ultimate sanction and reference is divine rather than human, and that it focuses loyalty on a person rather than on an abstract idea. If you buy stamps in France they carry the message '*Liberté, Egalité, Fraternité*'. If you buy stamps in Britain, and I sincerely hope and trust that this will remain the case following the privatization of the Royal Mail, they carry a portrait of Her Majesty the Queen. So does every coin and banknote. The coins proclaim further that the Queen rules by the grace of God (D.G.) and is Defender of the Faith (FID DEF or F.D.). Members of the armed forces and those administering justice swear their oaths of loyalty to a living person who has been consecrated and anointed to represent and reflect God's rule of righteousness, justice and mercy.

Monarchy naturally appeals particularly to those of a conservative, traditionalist and High Church persuasion. The first edition of this book received an enthusiastic response in Roman Catholic and High Anglican quarters and from conservative commentators. I was touched to learn that it had been chosen to be read aloud to the Benedictine monks at Pluscarden Abbey during their mealtimes. It was also encouraging to receive very positive and sympathetic reviews from perhaps less expected sources such as the *Methodist Recorder* and the *Reformer*. The most critical comments tended to come from secularists, as one would expect, and from those sharing my own liberal theological and political persuasions, most notably Theo Hobson who in a perceptive review suggested that the monarch's religious role could be blamed for contributing to the recent devaluation of religion in Britain by associating the gospel with empty traditionalism, and also pointed out that it was arguably the dangerous exaggeration of its spiritual dimension that brought about the downfall of the Stuart monarchy. In his book *Against Establishment* (2003), Hobson makes a more pointed attack on my arguments in favour of a renewed emphasis on a sacramental and spiritual understanding of monarchy, writing: 'Bradley's theology would have gone down well in 1930s Germany.'[18]

I understand why some of the fiercest critics of monarchy should be those who share my own liberal theological and political outlook. I should make it clear that I am not in this book suggesting that monarchy is the only system of government compatible with Christianity. Far from it. I fully accept that many Christians find that their faith leads them to espouse the cause of republicanism and I respect their arguments, even though I do not agree with them. The maxim 'no king, no God' is as erroneous as the Stuart cry 'no bishop, no king'. Many Christians, and others, are rightly uneasy about the privileges, inequalities and trappings of wealth that seem to go with monarchy. There is a strong case for removing the excesses and extravagances that still surround the lives of some members of the royal family. To some extent, this abuse has already been tackled through the pruning of the Civil List and the introduction of economies but there is, I fully concede, more to be done in this area.

I am well aware of the dangers of a kind of idolatry with regard to monarchy. While writing this book I have been very conscious of Shakespeare's dictum:

There's such divinity doth hedge a king,
That treason can but peep to what it would.
(*Hamlet*, act IV, sc.v)

Although I am advocating that divinity should indeed continue to hedge the monarchy, I am not, I hope, guilty of idolatry and specifically of what is sometimes called monarcholatry. We can respect and feel deep loyalty for our monarch without worshipping her – indeed, an important part of the Christian case for monarchy is that it helps us better to worship the God who reigns over all of us. I am certainly not seeking to resurrect the seventeenth-century argument for the divine right of kings, although I do believe that the pendulum has swung too far in the direction of a populist and celebrity understanding of royalty. The monarchy is not a political office like that held by a president or prime minister who has achieved power as the result of a contested popular election. Still less is it a celebrity status created by the fickle mass media and powerful commercial interests. It is rather the shared symbol of the sacred authority that stands above politics, money and sectional interest, a tangible pointer to the ultimate rule of God rather than of man or Mammon.

I ask my fellow liberals, and others of republican inclination, to reflect on why it is that the most open, broadminded and tolerant societies in Europe are almost without exception to be found in countries ruled by a monarch. I am thinking of the Netherlands and of the Scandinavian nations of Sweden, Denmark and Norway, where the monarch has a close relationship with the Church. I also find it very significant that when Spain threw off the shackles of fascist dictatorship, it reverted to a monarchical system of government. Constitutional monarchy provides a particularly stable, harmonious and balanced form of government. We have seen all too clearly in the opening decade of the twenty-first century the damage that can be done by autocratic presidents and corrupt politicians. This should surely make us appreciate all the more the attractions of limited, constitutional monarchy in terms of its tendency to promote and encourage broad consensus, open government and disinterested public service.

I also ask the critics of monarchy to understand and appreciate that its appeal is more to the heart than to the head. It belongs primarily to the region of the imagination and not to that of the intellect. In this respect, I believe that it strikes a very distinct contemporary chord with our postmodern culture where the emotional and experiential are valued as much as the rational, and the importance of symbol, ritual, mystery and magic is being rediscovered and reaffirmed. Let me give three very different illustrations of the continuing fascination with and relevance of the imaginative, metaphysical dimension of monarchy today in the context of contemporary popular culture. The first comes from the cinema. Among the most successful films of the 2000s were the trilogy based on J. R .R. Tolkein's epic fantasy novel *The Lord of the Rings*. The final film, *The Return of the King*, which was released in 2003, was easily the most successful of the three in terms of box-office receipts, Academy awards and critical acclaim. It is essentially the story of the restoration to the ravaged lands of Arnor and Gondor of their rightful king, Aragorn, who rules as the first high king of a vast reunited kingdom, banishing evil and chaos and ushering in the reign of honour, stability and peace. Its overriding theme is the beneficent power and influence of true kingship – when Aragorn takes his rightful crown, the broken sword is mended, the dead tree lives again and joy returns to the kingdom.

A similar message underlies one of the most popular musicals of the last decade, Walt Disney's *The Lion King*, which has been seen by over 55 million people in 15 countries since it opened on Broadway in 1997. It, too, is essentially both a celebration and affirmation of monarchy. Its three leading characters are the good, wise king Mustafa, the evil usurper Scar, and the reluctant heir to the throne Simba, who eventually comes to realize that he must follow his hereditary duty and destiny and assume the crown in order to rescue his land from famine and anarchy. The musical underlines the themes of cosmic order and sacrifice so fundamental to primal notions of sacred kingship. As Mustafa tells Simba, 'Life rises from death. Everything is connected in the great circle of life. As a king you must understand it.' There is also a strong emphasis on the continuity and tradition of hereditary monarchy. Mustafa tells his son, 'Look at the stars. The great kings of the past look down to us from those stars. So whenever you feel alone, just remember that those kings will always be there to guide you.' It is when Simba sees the reflection of his dead father's face in a pool that he realizes his own destiny and responsibility.

My third illustration comes from the world of contemporary psychotherapy. It draws on Jungian psychology and involves the appropriation of royalty, and more specifically kingship, as an archetype. In the words of Kathleen Raine,

> as such, it is not the prerogative of any individual, monarch or commoner, but a universal human attribute, of which the monarch stands as a unifying symbol in relation to a particular nation. So understood, kingship is manhood in its fullest development, and queenship womanhood in its fullest development.[19]

There is a long tradition of poets appropriating kingship and princedom as qualities of being and perfection. Shakespeare wrote in *Macbeth* of 'the king-bearing graces':

> As justice, verity, temperance, stableness,
> Bounty, perseverance, mercy, lowliness,
> Devotion, patience, courage, fortitude.
>
> (Macbeth, act IV, sc.3)

What is particularly striking is the recent emergence of a literature that seeks to address the contemporary crisis of male identity by appealing to the model of the sacred king. It identifies the archetypes of the masculine psyche as being those of king, warrior, magician and lover, with the king combining and embracing the others. The king archetype stands for promoting order, caring for others and taking personal responsibility. Like the other archetypes, it also has its darker, negative shadows in the tyrant, the usurper and the abdicating king who refuses to acknowledge and take on his responsibilities. This last type, epitomized in *The Lion King* by Simba before he sees his father's reflection in the pool, is taken to represent where many men are. They need to connect with the king archetype and access the king within them. Several psychotherapists are presenting kingship, with its primal associations with order as well as with the sacred, as a ruling and restraining element which needs to be affirmed within the male psyche:

In terms of a psychic geography, there is no world without the King. Wherever he is, he makes the world, and the *axis mundi*. He is our means for travelling into the sacred dimension. Without the King, the Warrior within becomes a mercenary, fighting for pay and not for any worthwhile goal. Our Magician becomes a sophist without a King to serve, able to argue any idea convincingly, and believing in none. The Lover without a King becomes a promiscuous philanderer.[20]

In this understanding, accessing the king within is about finding one's identity and facing up to one's responsibilities. There is a parallel movement to affirm the queen as an image and archetype for feminine maturity and generativity. Although the emphasis in both movements is on accessing an archetype within the individual psyche, they also have a more objective side. One of the main handbooks of the 'King Within' school advises men to contemplate and absorb the attributes of actual kings both in history and fiction. It cites examples of different individuals' 'power encounters' with kings, including a daily morning ritual in which one man talks to an imaginary Pharaoh in his bathtub. It also makes much of kingly role models drawn from the Christian tradition:

> What is truly amazing of course is what we can do, once we access and utilize our King energy. The spiritual systems of the world are designed to bring their worshippers in touch with this empowering energy, whether their leaders know it nor not, because the energy has such a virtuous effect on those who access it. The King's virtue is empowering. Hence Jesus of Nazareth, at least in part, makes an excellent paradigm of the King energy in the individuating male psyche. Hence also the enduring appeal of Ignatius Loyola's exercises. They provide their practitioners with one kind of initiation into the mysteries of the King.[21]

If this all seems too redolent to some readers of New Age faddism and psychobabble, then let me remind them that the primal, metaphysical, spiritual values represented by the archetype of monarchy are celebrated in all the great world faiths. The ideal and model of Christian kingship is laid out over the next three chapters of this book. In Judaism, the principle that every man is king and priest in his own home is expressed through the practice of the head of each household presiding over Sabbath prayers and observances and receiving respectful homage from younger members of the family every Friday evening. The ideal of sacred kingship and royal conse-cration pervades the pages of the *Rig Veda*, the foundational classic of Hindu spirituality. In Buddhism, the legend of the *Cakkavatti* king, or wheel-turning monarch, is held out as an ideal for laypeople to follow, just as the Buddha himself is the model for religious ascetics and monks. In the words of Grevel Lindop:

> The legend shows how one with possessions, children, a house, money, and worldly duties may live rightly and benefit the world. It shows that power must grow out of goodness. It demonstrates that inner qualities lead to outer success, and that both must be based on Dhamma – on the sacred laws and traditions of the cosmos – and that we must be ready ourselves to ask for advice from the wise. It shows the part played by the lay person in maintaining the order of the world and suggests that neglect of the poorest and weakest may be the crucial oversight which can lead to the destruction of human society.
>
> Above all it shows the monarch as a symbol of qualities to which all may aspire, and as a secular figure who nonetheless makes the spiritual life possible for himself and others. By living the worldly life in accordance with Dhamma, the wheel-turning monarch becomes a guardian of tradition and the cosmic order for the benefit of all.[22]

Kingship is similarly valued as an archetype and ideal by Muslims. The central theme of the *Shahnameh*, or Book of Kings, the national epic of Persia written in the early eleventh century by Firdowsi, who was influenced by both Shi'ite Islam and Zoroastrianism, is the divine sanction of kingship brought about by *Farr-e-Izadi*, a special grace bestowed upon kings by God. The poet chronicles the early history of Persia through the reigns of 50 kings, drawing on the Sufi notion of *javanmardi*, or spiritual chivalry, a concept which combines courage, magnanimity, gentleness and modesty in the service of God. In her last article before her death from cancer in 2008, the Iranian-born musician and author Shusha Guppy wrote movingly about the tragic descent of her native country from stable monarchy to volatile republic, as a result of the autocratic ways of the last shah and the rise of radical religious fundamentalism, and contrasted its situation with that of the United Kingdom:

> In Britain we are still blessed with a tradition of legitimate kingship, and it seems to me that the Queen and Prince Charles are both endowed with *Farr-e-Izadi*. What could provide greater evidence of the Prince's *javanmardi* than the reports of his work promoting countless good causes? While the Queen draws her inspiration from the more traditional habits of her dynasty, her son is very much a man of our time, somewhat miraculously maintaining the centrality of spiritual values in confronting the issues and needs of this land and century.
>
> The doctors have told me that my cancer is terminal and so I am having to dictate what is certainly my last piece of journalism. I shall end, perhaps unjournalistically, by declaring precisely what I feel: God Save the Queen! And God bless the Prince of Wales.[23]

This common theme throughout the world's great faiths is one of the reasons why I believe that a monarchy understood and expressed in spiritual as well as constitutional and ceremonial terms has a special role to play in a multi-faith society, as a focus of loyalty and for the expression of deeply shared values. Recent statements by the Queen, especially in her Christmas broadcasts, and by the Prince of Wales, suggest that they understand this very well and rightly see it as a natural extension and outworking of their own strong personal commitment to Christian monarchy.

To affirm the value of monarchy and especially of its spiritual and sacramental dimension, as this book does, is to acknowledge the importance of tradition, ritual and history, and also of the transcendent and the metaphysical imagination. It is not, however, to be stuck in the past or to advocate a culture of deference and a social order based on inequality and hierarchy. There is a difference between the principle of loyalty, which is based on steadfastness and respect, and the attitude of subservience, which is demeaning and grovelling, just as there is a difference between tradition, which is dynamic, and conservatism, which is static. The chapters that follow offer a theological apologia for the institution of monarchy and call for a renewed emphasis on its spiritual heart. They advocate certain changes in the way in which the religious character of the Crown is understood and expressed but also a return to basic principles. Christian monarchy has been in a state of constant evolution from its roots in the Old Testament, primal sacred kingship and the example and teachings of Jesus. Yet it has always also had a certain quality of givenness, resulting from its divine origins and ordination. In this book I seek to explore its foundations, trace its history in the British Isles and argue the case for it today. In introducing that case, I can do no better than quote from a fellow minister of the Church of Scotland, Charles Robertson, former minister of Canongate Kirk in Edinburgh and a chaplain to the Queen, who has said in a few paragraphs what is taking me a whole book, while at the same confounding James VI and I's observation that 'a Scottish Presbytery ... agreeth as well with a monarch as God and the Devil'.[24]

The monarchy stands for and enshrines certain principles which enrich and enliven our national life. From the monarch's side, there is the principle of service, of duty faithfully done, of responsibilities steadily fulfilled.

The Queen certainly occupies a high and honoured place in our national life; but, in a sense, she is also a victim to her people, sacrificed, for example, to their continual demands for public appearances and to their expectation that, day after day and year after year, she will competently discharge the many duties of her office. In fulfilling the role as she does, the Queen shows how the Crown embodies the nation's other self – its good self – and serves both as a standard of gracious public behaviour and as an inspiration to all of us to live by the same code of discipline.

From the people's side, there is the principle of respect, of loyalty expressed, of honour given. There is a tendency in our nature that makes us want to pay homage to something higher than ourselves. This faculty of reverence is not surprising, since we are made for God, and therefore made to worship.

But what has this to do with the Crown? More, perhaps, than first meets the eye. For if there is anything sacramental in kingship – and, after all, monarchs are anointed and consecrated to holy office, as well as crowned – earthly monarchy can be seen as an outward and visible sign of the royalty and majesty of God.

Monarchy, and the honour we pay to it, can be seen as instruments to keep alive and make real the reverence and the homage we owe to God. Our sense of a God who rules, a God who defends, a God who judges, could be nourished and strengthened by the consideration we give to the Crown.

None of this prevents monarchs from being ordinary people. They are as likely to have as many deficiencies as the rest of us. But that is all the more reason why we should hold them in our hearts and in our prayers.

God save the Queen![25]

1

Monarchy in the Old Testament

The theme of monarchy looms large in the collection of books which make up the Hebrew Bible and Christian Old Testament. The word 'king' occurs 565 times and 'kingdom' 163 times. Six of the historical books in the Old Testament have the monarchy as their main subject matter, including, of course, the aptly named first and second books of Kings. The psalms and the so-called wisdom books are also full of references to kings. The life of one particular king, David, occupies more space in the Old Testament than that of any other figure, including the great patriarchs Abraham and Moses.

This is not mere ancient history. Much of the ceremonial and ritual associated with the British monarchy today is based on Old Testament practice and precedent. This is particularly true of the coronation service in which the central sacred act is the anointing of the monarch with holy oil. The anthem which has been sung at the most solemn moment of the crowning of every English sovereign since that of Edgar in 973 is taken directly from the account in the first chapter of the first Book of Kings of the coronation of Solomon by Zadok the priest and Nathan the prophet.

More broadly, the Old Testament provides one of the main sources for our understanding of monarchy as having an essentially sacred and spiritual character. There are those who take it as a literal model and who see British monarchs standing in direct descent from King David and having a special covenant relationship with God as rulers of his chosen people. One does not have to be a British Israelite, however, to sense even in our secularized and deritualized age the continuing legacy of Old Testament ideas of kingship. It is there on the face of every

1

coin in our pockets with their abbreviated reminder that the Queen reigns by the grace of God and is Defender of the Faith.

There has been considerable scholarly debate as to whether the general drift of the books that make up the first half of the Old Testament and are often known as the Deuteronomistic history is, in fact, pro- or anti-monarchical. These books, which were almost certainly written either during the last days of Israel's kings or after the fall of Jerusalem in 587 BC and the exile of its people, display a distinct ambiguity about whether monarchy came about as a result of popular pressure or divine will and whether it was basically a good or bad thing for Israel.

The view that the Deuteronomistic history takes a positive view of monarchy was perhaps classically stated by the great German scholar Julius Wellhausen in 1878:

> In the eyes of Israel before the exile the monarchy is the culminating point of the history, and the greatest blessing of Jehovah. It was preceded by a period of unrest and affliction, when every man did what was right in his own eyes, and the enemies of Israel accordingly got everything their own way. Under it the people dwell securely and respected by those round about; guarded by the shelter of civil order, the citizen can sit under his own vine and his fig-tree.[1]

Although most contemporary scholars would read a slightly less enthusiastic endorsement of monarchy into the Deuteronomistic history, it is probably fair to say that a majority see it as basically pro- rather than anti-monarchical in tone. Kingship is presented as both the popularly requested and the divinely appointed answer to the anarchy and disorder prevailing under the judges who ruled the people of Israel for the first 250 years or so after their arrival in the promised land of Canaan. The latter part of the Book of Judges in particular seems to demonstrate the need for kings by emphasizing both the corruption and lawlessness under this form of government.

Its concluding verse notes: 'In those days there was no king in Israel: everyone did what was right in his eyes.'

There are other, earlier indicators of a basically benign and positive view towards monarchy in the opening set of books in the Hebrew Bible known as the Pentateuch. The Hebrew word used in Genesis 1.26 to describe God's intention with regard to the relation between humans and other living creatures and usually translated into English as 'dominion' in fact means 'kingly rule' and suggests the exercise of mercy and justice in responsible stewardship and vice-regency on behalf of God. Its mistranslation, and the unfortunate connotations of domination which have resulted, have led to the wholly erroneous assumption that the Bible gives humans a warrant for exploiting the rest of creation. In fact, the Israelite understanding of kingly rule had a gentle, holistic, nurturing dimension which I have written about elsewhere in terms of its ecological message.[2]

A passage in the Book of Deuteronomy (17.14-20) known as 'the law of kingship' presents the establishment of monarchy in the context of the laws delivered by Moses on the plains of Moab shortly before his death. It highlights the importance of the Torah, the body of written law, in the Old Testament understanding of monarchy, emphasizing the king's responsibility to govern under what was the supreme authority in Israel's political life, and to 'fear the Lord his God ... that his heart may not be lifted up above his brethren'.

The law of kingship closely anticipates the account of the actual establishment of the Israelite monarchy in 1 Samuel, chs 8 to 12. The somewhat contradictory and confused nature of this account has led scholars to suggest that it may represent material from two different traditions, one pro- and the other anti-monarchical. It begins with a demand by the elders of Israel to Samuel for 'a king to govern us like all the nations', which seems to represent a rejection of Yahweh and his divine kingship. This, indeed, is how God himself apparently interprets it when he tells Samuel to spell out to the people the dangers of kingship in terms of the accretion of private wealth and military might leading to the impoverishment and oppression of the nation. These warnings are completely ignored, however, and the people insist 'we will have a king over us, that we may be like all the nations, and that our king may govern us and go out before us and fight our battles' (v. 20). When Samuel reports this to God, he is told, 'Hearken to their voice and make them a king.'

In this account of the origin of monarchy, the initiative seems to lie entirely with the people and to be inspired by a desire to keep up with the Joneses', or more precisely the Canaanites, Moabites and other peoples of the ancient Near East. The Lord is portrayed as acceding to this popular demand with some reluctance. This is certainly consistent with the historical evidence, which suggests that other ancient Near Eastern people had kings long before the Israelites. Yet as the story of the establishment of Israel's monarchy progresses, the initiative seems to lie much more clearly with God, even if there remains a lingering sense that in choosing this form of rule, his people have in some sense signalled their rejection of his all-sufficient protection and salvation.

The subsequent story of the choosing first of Saul and then of David as kings of Israel puts the emphasis firmly on the divine election of kings. There is, indeed, a sense of partnership between Yahweh and his chosen people in the making of kings. The Hebrew verb himlik, which is used to describe the process of making a king, occurs with both God and humans as the subject. Coronations in the Old Testament involve the active participation of priests, prophets and elders as well as acclamation by the people. They are also always described as being carried out 'before the Lord'. The impression given here as elsewhere in the Old Testament is of a three-way covenant between God, the king and the people. This concept of covenant is, in fact, one of the most distinctive and central features of Israelite kingship.

To some extent the institution of monarchy is portrayed in the Old Testament as a consequence of a fallen world. There is an underlying implication that in an ideal world the Israelites would have clung to Yahweh as their king and not needed a human monarch. The sense that Israel's request for a king amounted to a rejection of Yahweh in his role as national defender is never quite lost. It is also significant that the context in which monarchy is established is one of national emergency when enemies, especially the Philistines, are threatening the very survival and integrity of Israel. Yet, although the institution of kingship is adopted in response to the Philistine threat, there is no suggestion that it should be abandoned once that threat has disappeared, as it does thanks largely to the military victories secured by David. Far from it – in peacetime under David and his successor Solomon kingship becomes more centralized and institutionalized, developing extensive ritual and ceremonial, and becoming an accepted and permanent feature of life until the destruction of the two kingdoms of Israel and Judah by the Assyrians and Babylonians.

This change in the view of monarchy from an unfortunate necessity at a time of national emergency to the accepted and natural form of government is paralleled by a theological shift. Whereas kingship initially is presented as a possible challenge to and diversion from the sovereignty of Yahweh, it becomes integrated into Yahweh's rule with the king coming to play a special role in the administration and maintenance of Yahweh's covenant with his people, the worship of the cult and the spiritual as well as the political and military life of the nation. The Deuteronomistic history brings kingship into the sequence of God's mighty acts in history, following on from his gift of land and election of his people. Indeed, it comes to be presented almost as a natural follow-on from these earlier acts. God gives his people a king as he has already given them land and chosen them for his special favour.

The establishment of monarchy in Israel brings with it a new way of looking at God. Several scholars have argued that it was only during the monarchy that Israel began to refer to God as 'king'. Certainly examples of royal language being applied to Yahweh in the pre-monarchical period are few and far between. With Israel's adoption of monarchy, and especially with the building of the temple and royal palace in Jerusalem, images of God as king came into prominence. His kingship was seen as being exercised both from heaven, where he sat enthroned on a footstool made up of cherubim and seraphim, and on earth, where he reigned from his temple on Mount Zion and through the king whom he installed there as his representative.

In one respect kings fit very naturally into the whole history of Israel. The Old Testament makes much of the dominant role played by leaders in Israel's history, from Abraham and Moses, through Joshua and Samuel and on to the kings. At every important point in their history the fate of the people is largely tied up with that of their leader. This is an important motif which points up the charismatic nature of personal leadership and the extent to which a ruler can mould the character of a nation or age, two themes that have informed attitudes to monarchy throughout the ages.

There is a significant message here about the importance of those who are chosen, born or fitted for leadership by character or upbringing not shirking it when it comes their way. This is almost certainly the theme of the 'Jotham fable' in the ninth chapter of the Book of Judges which tells of the trees attempting to anoint a king but being rejected by the olive, the fig and the vine, all of whom decline to reign over them, leaving only the bramble to offer them protection. This parable has often been seen as anti-monarchical but its message is surely that of *The Lion King*, that those who are born or called to positions of leadership should not shirk their responsibilities. Here, indeed, is an early homily on the duties and burdens of kingship.

The establishment of monarchy brought Israel into line with other parts of the ancient Near East. Several of its neighbours seem to have had kings from as early as the third millennium BC. This is of course the context for the coming of monarchy to Israel as it is described in 1 Samuel 8 when, despite Samuel's caveats and warnings, the people persist in demanding a king 'that we also may be like all the nations'. In fact, they are given something rather different. What starts as an imitation of other countries' practice becomes a highly distinctive institution, not least in respect of its spiritual character and relationship to God.

In many ways, Israel took over the view of kingship common throughout the Ancient Near East. This has been well summarized by Henri Frankfort:

> The ancient Near East considered kingship the very basis of civilisation. Only savages could live without a king. Security, peace and justice could not prevail without a ruler to champion them.
>
> Whatever was significant was imbedded in the life of the cosmos, and it was precisely the king's function to maintain the harmony of that integration.
>
> For the truth about their king affected their lives in every, even the most personal aspect, since, through the king, the harmony between human existence and supernatural order was maintained.[3]

Three features characterized kingship as it was understood in the ancient Near East, and, indeed, throughout the ancient world. First, it belonged primarily to heaven. Kingship was vested first and foremost in the gods, and those who ruled on earth did so as mediators of divine rule. Second, as part of their role as mediators of divine order in the perpetual struggle with the forces of chaos, human monarchs had a particular responsibility towards the weak, the widows and the fatherless. Third, the sacral nature of kingship and its derivation from heaven was celebrated in annual enthronement ceremonies in which monarchs were renewed in office. These ceremonies often involved a ritual humiliation and reinstatement, linked to fertility rites and the renewal of the cosmic order.

Elements from these three strands found their way into the Israelites' view of kingship. Even more than their neighbours, the Israelites had an overwhelming sense of the sovereignty of Yahweh and the fact that all human kingship derived from and depended on him. Like their neighbours, they came to endow kings with an almost corporate personality and to see them as the embodiment of their people. The nation as a whole found its focus in the royal house and the personality of the reigning monarch. This meant that the nation's well-being was intimately bound up with the character of the king with the result that disturbance and national disaster could be attributed to his wrongdoing. Because of Israel's special relationship with and attachment to the land, its kings were seen as having particular responsibilities in this area, guaranteeing the continued life of the people on the land and protecting its integrity. More widely, the king was seen as the guarantor under God of order, not just in respect of the rule of justice and law, but in more cosmic terms as the one who promoted harmony and dispensed wisdom. Human and mortal though he was, his earthly reign in some sense mirrored and pointed to the divine reign. In the idealized language often used about kingship, he symbolized and exercised through his rule God's attributes of mercy, justice, faithfulness and righteousness. This is expressed in several of the psalms in the form of prayers addressed to God by the people, as in Psalm 72:

> Give the king thy justice, O God,
> And thy righteousness to the royal son!
> May he judge thy people with righteousness,
> And the poor with justice!

In his important study of the roots of political theology, *The Desire of the Nations,* Oliver O'Donovan has identified three key functions fulfilled by the Israelite monarchs as God's representatives. First, they exercised military leadership, undertaking warfare as an almost sacral performance initiated by Yahweh, in Israelite understanding it being God who won military victories and granted them as a favour to the king. Second, they exercised a judicial function, appointing judges and establishing a uniform system of justice to replace competing tribal jurisdictions and clearly standing as the unique mediators of Yahweh's judgements and upholders of the Torah. Third, and most importantly, the Israelite monarchy offered 'the function of continuity, ensuring an unbroken tradition in the occupation of the territory and the perpetuation of the national identity'.[4]

The Israelites shared their ancient Near Eastern neighbours' sense that kings ruled by divine consent and had a prime obligation to serve the national god. In several countries this led to the king being seen as the nation's high priest and playing a key role in ritual and worship. At an annual ceremony which was part of the New Year festival, the king of Babylon had to 'grasp the hand of Marduk' in the temple of the national god and so affirm his right to rule. Kings of Assyria were priests of Ashur, and the Hittite kings visited religious centres to perform royal rituals in honour of the national gods. In a similar way, the kings of Israel took a leading role in the temple cult and the worship of Yahweh.

In one crucial respect, however, the Israelite king was in a different position from many of his neighbours. In much of the ancient Near East as in other primitive societies, the king was seen in some senses as a divine figure, closely related to the gods if not in fact fully of their number. This understanding of the divine nature of monarchy was perhaps most fully developed in Africa where kings were seen as either possessed by or descended from a god. The king of the Shilluk in Sudan was believed to be possessed by the deified spirit of the first king, Nyikang, the Te Yoruba kings of Nigeria were thought to be descended from the god Odudua, the creator of the earth, and the kings of Buganda (Uganda) were said to be descended from the deified first king, Kintu. In Egypt the Pharoah was regarded as both the son of the god Re and also the incarnation of the god Horus, and after death it was believed that he was assimilated into Osiris. Kings of the Canaanite city states were similarly seen as sons of the god El. Divinization often accompanied the transition from elective to hereditary monarchy. This seems to have been the case with the Hittites

who at first only divinized their kings at death but later came
to endow them with superhuman powers in life too.

The Israelites had a different understanding of the relationship
between monarchy and divinity. Their radical monotheism
which clearly separated Yahweh from his creatures did not
allow for divine kings. Rulers remained essentially human
figures, although they were seen to have a unique relationship
and calling from God which was expressed in the descriptions
'Son of God' and 'anointed one' which were applied exclusively to kings.

The description of the monarch as son of God occurs,
among other places, in Psalm 2.7; Psalm 89.26; and 2 Samuel
7.14. It is widely believed that this phrase was adopted
from Near Eastern neighbours, and perhaps specifically from
Canaanite religion. For the Israelites, however, it did not imply
that the king was a divine being. Rather he became God's son
by adoption. His sonship was effective not from the day of his
birth but from the day of his anointing.

References to the Israelite king as the anointed one (*Messiah*
in Hebrew, *Christos* in Greek) occur, *inter alia*, in Psalm
2.2; Psalm 18.50; Psalm 89.38, 51; Psalm 132.10, 17; and
2 Samuel 20.6 and 22.51. The anointing of monarchs was a
common feature in the ancient Near East. It was practised by
the Syrians as early as the third millennium BC and also by the
Hittites, Egyptians and Canaanites. As with other aspects of
sacral kingship, the Israelites took it over and integrated it into
their distinctive understanding of Yahweh's overarching sovereignty and kingship. Indeed, anointing reinforced the sense
that the initiative in making kings lay with God, as expressed
in Psalm 89.20:

> I have found David, my servant;
>   With my holy oil I have anointed him;
> So that my hand shall ever abide with him,
>   My arm also shall strengthen him.

The act of anointing, which was usually carried out by a

priest, signified the setting apart of the king and signalled his divine election. It was also the moment at which God adopted the monarch as his son and at which his Spirit descended on him. This is clearly represented in 1 Samuel 16.13 when Samuel anointed David with a horn of oil 'and the spirit of the Lord came mightily upon David from that day forward'.

As an act of consecration and setting aside, the anointing of kings was in many ways comparable to the ordination of high priests. There are other striking similarities between kings and priests as they are described in the Hebrew Bible. They seem to wear the same garments. The word *nezer* is used to describe a form of headgear worn by both high priests and kings but is otherwise never mentioned. When David brings the Ark of the Covenant into Jersualem he is described as 'girded with a linen ephod', a special loincloth which was a specifically priestly garment. The extent to which Israelite kings exercised a priestly role is difficult to determine. There is one specific if mysterious order of priesthood mentioned in the Old Testament which seems to belong especially if not exclusively to kings. It apparently originates with Melchezedek, a pre-Israelite Jebusite priest-king of Jerusalem who is described in Genesis 14 bringing gifts of bread and wine to Abraham, and it appears to be applied to the Davidic monarchy in Psalm 110, which is often associated with coronations. There are references in the Old Testament to kings offering sacrifices and blessing people in the sanctuary, both acts reserved to priests, but it is not clear whether these were regarded as normal or exceptional activities. The general view of Old Testament scholars is that while kings assumed a supervisory and initiatory role in temple worship, acting almost as 'supreme governors' of the cult, they did not involve themselves in the daily rituals of sacrifices and offerings.

Israelite kings undoubtedly exuded a sacred aura. This was seen as deriving entirely from the fact of their having been chosen and set apart by God. The divine glory and sovereignty were not compromised or diminished by the majesty of the king. Rather, the latter was a reflection of and a pointer to the former. The monarch's dependence on and obedience to God is a key theme of Old Testament theology, although it, too, is not without its ambiguity and inconsistencies. At some points the Hebrew Bible seems to suggest that the monarch rules at God's pleasure and that disobedience brings his fall, as in the case of Saul. At other times the emphasis seems rather to be on the unconditional and irrevocable nature of God's support for his anointed one, as in the covenant with David.

The concept of covenant is at the heart of the Old Testament understanding of kingship. The king was seen as standing in covenant relationships with both his subjects and God and he also played a critical role in God's overarching covenant relationship with his chosen people. This triple aspect is highlighted in 2 Kings 11.17 when, following the crowning of Joash, the high priest Jehoiada 'made a covenant between the Lord and the king and the people, that they should be the Lord's people; and also between the king and the people'. The king did not stand over or above the covenant. Like his subjects he was expected to obey the law and to be totally loyal to Yahweh. Indeed, he was expected to lead the people in loyalty to Yahweh. The prime responsibility of kings, as portrayed by the Deuteronomist, was not to win battles, provide economic stability or even maintain justice and peace. Rather, it was spiritual – to maintain and oversee the covenant with Yahweh through worship, faithful obedience and trust in the Lord.

As well as presenting this complex and sometimes ambiguous theology of covenant and kingship, the Old Testament also paints delightfully personal pictures of the characters and achievements of individual kings. It is here, as much as in the more abstract and theoretical discourses, that the spiritual dimension of Israelite kingship is highlighted. As for the authors of *1066 and All That*, so for the Deuteronomist there were good kings and bad, indeed rather more of the latter than of the former. Despite the apostasy and disobedience of many individuals, however, there is a persistent vein of idealism running through the Old Testament which views monarchy as an essentially worthy and intrinsically spiritual enterprise.

Before looking briefly at the personalities of the Israelite kings who have so stamped their mark on our understanding of monarchy, and especially of its sacred dimension, it is worth mentioning the figure of Samuel who is given a prominent role in the story of the institution of kingship in the Old Testament. He acts as an intermediary between Yahweh and his people, first delivering to them the Lord's initial warnings about kingship and then, when they persist in asking for a monarch, selecting the first two kings under divine guidance. In many ways he stands between the old and new systems of government. The last of the great judges, he makes his own sons judges, and yet he is also the first king-maker and presides over the coronations of both Saul and David. These latter roles were to be taken up in the Christian era by monks and priests. In seeking out and identifying both Saul and David, Samuel acts as prophet and seer as well as agent of Yahweh. He similarly acts as God's mouthpiece when he tells the people the rights and duties of kingship and informs Saul that he has disobeyed God by sparing Agag, king of Amalek. He stands as the prototype of the disinterested churchman/prophet who plays a crucial role under God in the whole process of king-making (and king-breaking).

The man chosen by Samuel to be Israel's first king is a distinctly ambiguous figure who does not get the institution of monarchy off to a very good start. Saul is first introduced in terms of his good looks and manly physique, 'a handsome young man' (1 Samuel 9.2) who is taller than any other Israelite. This emphasis is important. Throughout ancient societies and beyond. the physical appearance and strength of the monarch is significant. Saul is pointed out by God to Samuel as the one who will be 'prince over my people Israel. He shall save my people from the hands of the Philistines' (9.16). This clearly sets the context for the establishment of monarchy as that of national emergency. Saul is presented initially as a military leader, the one who will deliver Israel from her enemies. It is precisely in these terms that Samuel addresses and describes the new king after anointing him with a vial of oil.

While Saul is portrayed first and foremost as a military leader, leading successful campaigns against the Philistines and the Amalekites, his kingship is also represented in a more spiritual dimension. After being anointed, and 'the spirit of God having come mightily upon him', Saul meets up with a band of prophets among whom he prophesies, giving rise to the much-asked question, 'Is Saul among the prophets?' (10.12). Saul is, in fact, the only one of the Israelite kings who is specifically portrayed as engaging in prophecy and taking on the mantle of the prophet as a function of his kingship.

A careful balance is kept in the story of Saul's elevation to the kingship between the themes of election by God and popular acclamation. There is no doubt that the initiative throughout lies with God. It is he, through Samuel, who chooses Saul and causes his spirit to descend on him through anointing. Saul is presented by Samuel to all the tribes of Israel at Mizpah as the one chosen by the Lord, whereupon all the people spontaneously shout 'Long live the king', the acclamation that has sounded out at the proclamation and coronation of every British monarch. Later at a second gathering at Gilgal, also convened by Samuel, 'the people made Saul king before the Lord' in a ceremony of which we are told only that it involved the sacrifice of peace offerings before the Lord.

Despite this promising start, the subsequent story of Saul's reign focuses largely on his disobedience of and rejection by God. The matters on which he transgresses seem rather technical – offering sacrifices preparatory to his battle with the Philistines in Samuel's absence and so usurping the function of the prophet, sparing the king of the Amalakites, and using his enemies' best sheep and oxen for a burnt offering rather than destroying them as the Lord had commanded. They are, however, enough to make God clearly reject Saul as king and to regret that he had ever made him ruler of Israel. The message seems to be that Saul has listened to the people rather than to God – he admits to Samuel that he transgressed the commandment of the Lord because he feared the people and obeyed their voice. Samuel obeys God's command and anoints David with oil, whereupon the spirit of the Lord departs from Saul and an evil spirit torments him. The rest of his reign and his life is a sorry tale of madness and paranoia, turning to a medium when the Lord fails to answer him either through dreams or prophets, and determining to kill David. It ends with him committing suicide when facing the Philistines on Mount Gilboa.

Saul's rule provides a disappointing start to the Israelite experience of monarchy. Yet for all God's repentance that he chose Saul, there is no suggestion that it was a mistake to have given Israel a king at all. Although at the beginning of his reign there is a sense that in calling for a king, the Israelites were signalling rejection of God, at the end there is no hint that because they have had a bad king, the whole institution is therefore condemned and that Israel should revert to rule by judges or some other form of government.

The second king, David, is introduced in a very similar way to Saul, as a bold and courageous military man who will deliver Israel from the Philistines. Like Saul he is picked out by Samuel, acting on the direct instructions of God, and is presented in striking physical terms – 'he was ruddy, and had beautiful eyes and was handsome'. He too is anointed by Samuel and from that moment 'the Spirit of the Lord comes mightily upon David and departs from Saul', even though it is some considerable time before he succeeds as king. In this intermediate period, when he is first and foremost a fugitive from Saul, his character is built up in a highly sympathetic way, not least in terms of his capacity to pardon and indeed to soothe the man determined to kill him. This, almost as much as his military prowess, seems to confirm his fitness for royal office. We are introduced here to a new, more complex paradigm of the king as gentle-giant killer, healer and poet.

David's kingship, like Saul's, is a matter of popular choice as well as divine election. The tribes of Israel come to him at Hebron, saying, 'Behold, we are your bone and flesh. In times past, when Saul was king over us, it was you that led out and brought us into Israel' (2 Samuel 5.1-2). This sense of David as deliverer of the nation is reinforced by the people repeating the Lord's words to David: 'You shall be shepherd of my people Israel, and you shall be prince over Israel.' Here a new and highly suggestive image of kingship is introduced – that of the king as shepherd. This image has already featured in the story of David. When Samuel first went to Bethlehem to identify the king that the Lord told him he would find among Jesse's sons, David, as the youngest, was away looking after the sheep. He would have been overlooked had not Samuel insisted on him being brought and had the Lord not told Samuel that David was indeed the one to be anointed. For Christians there is of course a pre-echo here of Jesus the Good Shepherd, but even without this connection the image of the monarch as shepherd exercising pastoral care over his flock has a powerful resonance.

David's initial encounter with the tribes of Israel at Hebron is followed by a coronation ceremony at which he makes a covenant with all the elders of the people before the Lord and they anoint him king. It is significant that David uniquely seems to have a double anointing, first by Samuel after he has been chosen by God to succeed Saul, and then by the elders when he actually becomes king. Again, the elements of divine election and popular choice are both present, with the former having priority.

David is in many ways the pivotal figure in the history of Israel as it is recorded in the Hebrew Bible. Forty chapters are devoted to his 40-year rule, which probably began around 1000 BC. By contrast, the ensuing 400 years between his death and the end of the two kingdoms are dealt with in just 46 chapters. As presented in the Old Testament, his reign marks a significant turning point in the history of Israel from an epic tale of patriarchs, wandering tribes and wilderness to a more domestic and settled story centred around the royal dynasty established on the throne in Jerusalem.

David is portrayed in several different lights – as the

heroic military commander and fighting man who sees off the Philistines, Moabites and Syrians; in the gentler guise of the musician who soothes Saul's madness by playing the lyre and the poet who composes psalms; and as the religious leader who calls his people to prayer, initiates and presides over cultic worship, gives the sacred Ark of the Covenant a permanent and fixed dwelling place, and personally plans and designs the first temple. He is clearly identified as the man who puts kingship on a firm footing after its rocky start with Saul. With his reign the authority of the king becomes paramount, clearly superseding that of the local tribal elders – 'so David reigned over all Israel, and David administered justice and equity to all his people' (2 Samuel 8.15).

David also crucially centralizes and concentrates in his own hands both secular and religious power. He appoints high priests like Abiathar and Zadok and resident court prophets like Nathan and Gad as well as judges and administrators. A key element in this process of centralization is his establishment of Jerusalem as both the political and the religious capital of Israel. In David's determination to locate the temple, and so in Israelite understanding God's resting place on earth, at the heart of his own capital we see an early expression of close relations between church and state with the monarchy acting to bring the two together. This is not interpreted in terms of personal power building and vainglory. Rather, David's determination that the God of Israel shall come to dwell in the city of his anointed is a sign of his obedience and faithfulness to Yahweh.

David is also portrayed as a man of piety and prayer who takes on an almost priestly role. Several prayers are put on to his lips, including the affirmation recorded in 1 Chronicles 29.10-19 which has been taken up in a number of eucharistic liturgies: 'Thine Lord, is the greatness, and the power, and the glory, and the victory, and the majesty; for all that is in the heavens and in the earth is thine.' He is also credited with being the author of another much-used eucharistic sentence: 'All things come from thee, and of thy own have we given thee.' He is, indeed, the first in a long line of praying kings, a species particularly found in the two books of Chronicles where it is kings rather than prophets who pray.

The picture given of David is not without its blemishes. He is revealed to be an adulterer and a murderer. When his mistress, Bathsheba, becomes pregnant, he orders her husband, Uriah, who is one of his own soldiers, to the front line and makes sure that he is killed. David then marries Bathsheba. The prophet Nathan denounces the king's sin and David genuinely repents, leading God to forgive him. This image of the king as penitent sinner is important in showing that monarchs can have their own moral failings like other human beings, that they can be censured for them, and that for them as for others sincere repentance brings God's forgiveness.

At the heart of David's kingship and the establishment of the dynasty that was to bear his name is his covenant relationship with God. This is explored in the all-important seventh chapter of 2 Samuel which brackets David's promise to build a permanent temple for God to replace the temporary tent, or tabernacle, in which the Ark of the Covenant has rested with the Lord's promise to establish his dynasty for ever. Like the earlier passage describing the origins of Israelite kingship, it is shot through with ambiguity. As transmitted through Nathan the prophet, the Lord seems uneasy about having a permanent temple as his dwelling place on earth and to prefer the provisional, moving *locus* of the tent. Yet at the same time he promises David that his house and kingdom will be established for ever. This unconditional covenant clearly establishes the Israelite monarchy as hereditary. From David onwards, the kings of Israel are not elected by the people or chosen by a prophet, but come to the throne by virtue of having being born to the house of David. This is made very clear in verses 12-16:

> When your days are fulfilled and you lie down with your fathers, I will raise up your offspring after you, who shall come forth from your body, and I will establish his

kingdom. He shall build a house for my name, and I will establish the throne of his kingdom for ever. I will be his father, and he shall be my son. When he commits iniquity, I will chasten him with the rod of men, with the stripes of the sons of men; but I will not take my steadfast love from him, as I took it from Saul, whom I put away from before you. And your house and your kingdom shall be made sure for ever before me; your throne shall be established for ever.

This is a remarkable promise which has rightly been compared to the covenant made with Moses. The reference to Saul shows that he had been an aberration. The real monarchy starts with David and is invested with God's confidence and unconditional promise of its continuance through the direct line of succession for ever. Although there is still a lingering sense of lost innocence, and a hint that the desert experience is more authentic and closer to the spirit of God than monarchical establishment, there is also a clear emphasis on the great spiritual beauty and potential in the institution of monarchy. This is expressed in highly idealized terms in the poem known as 'the last words of David', identified as 'the anointed of the God of Jacob, the sweet psalmist of Israel':

The Spirit of the Lord speaks by me,
his word is upon my tongue.

The God of Israel has spoken,
the rock of Israel has said to me:
When one rules justly over men,
ruling in the fear of God,

He dawns on them like the morning light,
like the sun shining forth upon a cloudless morning,
like rain that makes grass to sprout from the earth.

Yea, does not my house stand so with God?

For he has made with me an everlasting covenant,
ordered in all things and secure.
For will he not cause to prosper
all my help and my desire?

(2 Samuel 23.2-5)

Unlike his predecessors, Israel's third king, Solomon, comes to the throne not because he is recognized and anointed by a prophet but because he is David's son and so the legitimate heir to his kingdom and his covenant with God. Significantly his reign starts, according to 2 Chronicles 1, with an act of worship when, like his father, he leads his people in adoration of God before the altar and personally offers a thousand burnt offerings.

The dominant theme in the Deuteronomist's portrayal of Solomon's reign is introduced in the story of the dream in which God appears to the new king and asks what he would like to be given. Solomon requests 'wisdom and knowledge to go out and come in before this people'. Because he has answered in this way and not asked for possessions, wealth, honour, or the life of his enemies, God tells him that he will have all these things as well, 'such as none of the kings had who were before you, and none after you shall have the like' (2 Chronicles 1.12). So begins the most splendid reign of any king in the Old Testament. In respect of his power and prestige, Solomon is described as being even more favoured by God than David – 'the Lord gave Solomon great repute in the sight of all Israel, and bestowed upon him such royal majesty as had not been on any king before him in Israel'. Indeed, he comes to be the very epitome of majesty, arrayed in all his glory with the full panoply and pomp of court ceremonial and wealth almost beyond measure.

Yet if Solomon comes to symbolize royalty in its most glittering and ostentatious aspects, he comes even more to stand for wisdom and discernment, those qualities which he had originally asked of God. His name, which literally translates from Hebrew as 'his peace', was, of course, to become a byword for wisdom and judgement, inspiring the apocryphal book *The Wisdom of Solomon*, purportedly written by him but in fact most probably the work of an Alexandrian Jew living in the first century BC. Addressed to kings, it counsels rulers to love justice, and to cultivate the sagacity, virtue and wisdom that comes from God, and reminds them that 'a multitude of wise men is the salvation of the world and a wise king is the sheet-anchor of his people' (6.24). In his own lifetime, Solomon was acknowledged as the supreme representative of God's peace on earth, the fount of order and stability as well as wisdom. It is this reputation which leads the Queen of Sheba to visit him and she is not disappointed. Finding that there is nothing that he cannot explain to her, she showers him with gifts of spices, gold and precious stones.

With Solomon, the Deuteronomist presents the paradigm of the wise king, that figure who is so familiar in other ancient traditions and in so many fairy stories and tales from folklore. There are earlier references to this particular attribute of monarchy, as when the woman of Tekoa observes, after meeting David, 'the king is like an angel of God in discerning good and evil' (2 Samuel 14.17); and later ones, like the observation in Proverbs, 'when a king sits on his throne to judge, he winnows out all evil with his eyes' (Proverbs 20.8). It is Solomon, however, who is portrayed *par excellence* as the wise king, perhaps supremely when he resolves the dispute between two harlots over the child they both claim as their own. The whole country hears of his judgement in this dispute and stands in awe of the king 'because they perceived that the wisdom of God was in him' (1 Kings 3.28). Significantly, it is God's wisdom which is seen as dwelling in Solomon. The image of wisdom as a peculiarly royal attribute established by Solomon has persisted down to our own times. One of the earliest surviving inscriptions about a British king describes Cadfan of Gwynedd, who died around 625, as 'the wisest and most renowned of men'. Summing up the character of our present Queen, the Duke of Devonshire has written, 'her accumulated wisdom is extraordinary', and a children's picture book about British monarchs describes her (quite rightly) as 'wise, dignified and hard-working'.[5]

Wisdom is not the only quality which the story of Solomon associates with monarchy. He also conforms to the model developed by his father of the king as a priestly figure and man of prayer. Solomon builds the temple in Jerusalem and so fulfils David's project of giving the Lord a dwelling place on earth. The prayer that he recites at its dedication, which is recorded in 1 Kings 8.23-53, is a remarkable *tour de force* combining petitionary and intercessory prayer of a high poetic order with profound theological musings, as in his question: 'Will God indeed dwell on the earth? Behold, heaven and the highest heaven cannot contain thee; how much less this house which I have built.' Significantly, after this great prayer Solomon assumes a priestly role, blessing the assembly of Israel, offering a sacrifice to the Lord of 22,000 oxen and 120,000 sheep and consecrating the temple court.

In building, dedicating and blessing the temple, Solomon confirms and consolidates the link established by his father between the monarchy and the public worship of God. Here is a further step towards civic religion, the close association between church and state and especially between established church and monarchy. It is no coincidence that it is the description of Solomon's coronation, the fullest such account in the Bible, that has formed the basis for the crowning of all English monarchs in Westminster Abbey:

> So Zadok the priest, Nathan the prophet and Benaiah the son of Jehoiada, and the Cherethites and the Pelethites, went down and caused Solomon to ride on King David's mule, and brought him to Gihon. There Zadok the priest took the horn of oil from the tent, and anointed Solomon. Then they blew the trumpet; and all the people said, 'Long live King Solomon!' And all the people went up after him, playing on pipes, and rejoicing with great joy, so that the earth was split by their noise.
>
> (I Kings 1.38-40)[6]

Even Solomon, however, is not portrayed as a wholly good king. His initial humility, which leads God to shower blessings on him, gives way to complacency and oppressive rule. His heart is turned by idolatry and he incurs divine displeasure. The rending of his kingdom into two halves is portrayed as a divine retribution for his sins in a way which shows that there is an element of conditionality in God's support for the Davidic monarchy:

> If you will walk before me, as David your father walked, with integrity of heart and uprightness, doing according to all that I have commanded you, and keeping my statutes and my ordinances, then I will establish your royal throne over Israel for ever, as I promised David your father … But if you turn aside from following me, you and your children, and do not keep my commandments and my statutes which I have set before you, but go and serve other gods and worship them, then I will cut off Israel from the land which I have given them; and the house which I have consecrated for my name I will cast out of my sight.
>
> (1 Kings 9.4-7)

Once again there seems here to be a note of ambiguity and even of contradiction. The unconditional covenant with David turns out to have conditions and to be dependent on faithful obedience to God. This is confirmed by the ultimate fate of the two kingdoms which results from the splitting of Israel owing to Solomon's idolatry. Most of their subsequent rulers are roundly chastised for doing evil in the sight of the Lord and failing to live up to the standards of David. The northern kingdom of Israel is portrayed as descending into idolatry and Baal worship, largely as a result of the apostasy of its first king, Jeroboam who worships a golden calf, and it is this that leads directly to its destruction and the exile of its people in 722. The southern kingdom of Judah fares slightly better. Of its 20 kings, 12 are condemned but eight are commended for

doing what was right in the sight of the Lord. Yet ultimately it
too faces destruction in 597 at the hands of the Babylonians,
who are portrayed as the instruments of divine vengeance
against a nation that has been led by its rulers into apostasy
and away from covenant obedience to Yahweh.

Two kings of Judah singled out for commendation by
the Deuteronomist add to the attributes of Old Testament
monarchy. Hezekiah, who ruled from around 716 to 687,
destroyed the idols which his father Ahaz had worshipped, and
reopened and repaired the temple. At a time of national crisis
and emergency, he put his trust in the Lord and prayed rather
than relying on military alliances or seeking to pay tribute
to potential aggressors. Like David, his kingship is expressed
in terms of leading his people in worship, calling on them to
consecrate themselves to the Lord and bringing sacrifices and
thank offerings to his house. Even more than David, indeed,
he is portrayed as a man of prayer and penitence, going to the
temple covered in sackcloth and being cured of sickness by the
strength of his prayer. He is also described as having a good
relationship with the prophet Isaiah, a significant achievement
at a time of increasing tension between prophets and kings
when the former are emerging as having greater spiritual
authority.

The other pre-eminently good king is Josiah, who ruled
Judah from around 640 to 609. He too led the kingdom back
to God after the apostasy of his father, Amon. During the
rebuilding of the temple which he instituted, his high priest
Hilkiah found the book of the law, the scroll on which were
written the commandments which God had given to Moses.
Josiah realized that these had been neglected and departed
from and he determined to get the people of Judah to recommit
themselves to keep the Lord's commandments. A covenant
renewal ceremony was held, a new national celebration of
the passover instituted and the cult purified and centralized.
Josiah restored the Davidic model of the monarch as covenant
administrator and reformer of worship. It is quite likely that
the Deuteronomistic history was written in or shortly after

his reign, and that this accounts for its emphasis on the king's role in leading his people in covenant obedience and loyalty to Yahweh.

Despite its various vicissitudes, kingship was clearly regarded as the accepted and natural form of government until the destruction of the two kingdoms of Israel and the exile of its people. There is no evidence that during nearly 400 years of monarchy any segment of society in either the north or the south objected to it on religious, social or political grounds. Prophets opposed individual kings but never seriously challenged the institution itself. In the words of a recent scholarly study:

> The monarchy remained the sole system of government in Israel until foreign powers destroyed it. Although the people participated actively in politics from time to time, the monarchy, as a political system, never became a target of criticism, let alone the dynastic position.[7]

It is not just the historical books of the Old Testament that have interesting and important things to say about monarchy and its spiritual dimension. So too do the wisdom books, the prophets and the Psalms. The first of these sources, as one might expect, emphasizes the theme of kings as exemplars of wisdom, judgement and righteousness. This is noticeably the case in the Book of Proverbs which is, indeed, attributed to Solomon, whose name is also associated with Ecclesiastes and the Song of Songs. It presents a highly idealized picture of kings as upholding God's justice on earth and displays a simple faith in their goodness – 'It is abomination to kings to do evil, for the throne is established by righteousness. Righteous lips are the delight of the king' (16.12-13). At times, indeed, Proverbs reads like a panegyric to monarchy which is often bracketed with divine rule, as in the command: 'My son, fear the Lord and the king' (24.21-22). Comparisons between the king and God extend to the observation that the royal mind, like that of Yahweh, is mysterious and unfathomable: 'As the heavens for height, and the earth for depth, so the mind of kings is unsearchable' (25.3). While there is still a clear understanding that the king is under God, and under an obligation to act according to his rules of justice and mercy, there is also a strong suggestion that the king (or at least the good king) epitomizes the principles of divine rule and stands as a pointer to God. A recent study of the portrayal of kingship in wisdom literature emphasizes the close link which it makes between human and divine authority:

> The king has God-given power to effect good, power which can, if used wrongly, corrupt himself and others. He is the ultimate human authority and yet his power is divinely legitimated. He is in fact upholding the divine order and his role is God-given. He is therefore part of the manifestation of God to humanity, standing at the crossroads of the human and the divine.[8]

The prophets are more ambivalent about the benefits of human monarchy. In their utterances, the language of kingship is predominantly directed to God. Isaiah in particular is fond of calling God the king of Jacob, the king of Israel or simply 'your king'. He also envisages the Lord seated on a throne surrounded by seraphim, as in the majestic description of Yahweh's enthronement in Isaiah 6.1-8. This motif is also found in Ezekiel. This emphasis on Yahweh's supreme kingship in some ways recalls the anti-monarchical argument advanced when the Israelites first called for a king. Yet although the prophets focus very much on the kingship of God, they do not advocate the abandonment of human monarchy. Indeed, they portray a close partnership between prophets and kings on the model of the relationship between Nathan and David. Prophets continue to anoint kings, as Elijah does in the case of both Hazael, king of Syria, and Jehu, king of Israel, and also counsel, rebuke and give promises to monarchs from a position of independence.

The psalms provide some of the most fascinating and

complex images of kingship in the entire Hebrew Bible. Many have apparent royal associations. Of the 150 psalms in the Old Testament, 73 in the original Hebrew version and 84 in the Greek Septuagint have the heading *le dawid*, clearly suggesting a royal link, either with David directly, his dynasty or the royal office. It is quite possible that David instituted the whole tradition of singing psalms – certainly he set up guilds of singers and musicians – and that he wrote some himself. There has been a considerable debate among Old Testament scholars about just how many of the psalms are 'royal psalms' pertaining to kings of the Davidic dynasty and probably written to be sung at specific ceremonies associated with monarchy. At the very least nine almost certainly fall into this category – Psalms 2, 101 and 110 seem to belong to enthronement ceremonies, 21 and 72 probably relate to a royal anniversary, coronation or birthday, 18 and 20 describe the king in a situation of war and national danger, 45 is appropriate for a royal wedding and 132 for the anniversary of a royal palace.

There is also debate as to how far the psalms speak of monarchy in idealstic rather than realistic terms. Perhaps more than any other part of the Hebrew Bible, they idealize the sacred role of the king. The dominant image presented is of the righteous king who is pleasing to God and who brings fertility to his land and people. Several psalms are very similar to royal texts from Egypt and Mesopotamia which celebrate the divine aura of royal office. They pick up many of the themes already noted in the historical books – the king as God's son, servant, covenant partner and anointed one, and his role in representing the land and the people before the Lord. Psalm 110.4 has the Lord telling David 'You are a priest for ever after the order of Melchizedek' and other psalms present the king in a priestly role, as God's chief cultic minister, leading his people in worship, prayer and, in the case of Psalm 42.5, sacred dance. The portrayal of David leading 'the dancing procession up to the house of God' was picked up in the film *David, the King*, and is made much of by the authors of *The King Within* who link it to the image of Jesus as the Lord of the Dance and to the Indian god Shiva. For them, 'the dance here is a metaphor for the chaotic, actively shifting universe along with the emergence of the created order, which the archetypal King engenders'.[9]

The psalms make much of the kingship of God. The motif *Yhwh malak* ('Yahweh is king') runs through several and is sometimes found as an opening chorus. There is considerable debate about whether those psalms which speak of the enthronement of kings refer to human monarchs or to Yahweh. Certainly the enthronement of Yahweh seems to be the dominant theme in those like Psalms 93 and 99 which begin with the phrase 'The Lord reigns'. It is these and other psalms which have inspired classic hymns about the majesty and kingship of God such as 'O worship the king, all glorious above', 'Praise to the Lord, the Almighty, the King of creation', 'How shall I sing that majesty which angels do admire', 'The Lord is king, lift up thy voice', 'Rejoice, the Lord is king', 'King of glory, king of peace' and 'Let all the world in every corner sing "My God and King" '. There is a move in some quarters to alter the language of such hymns to give them a less regal flavour. In several modern hymnals used in the United States hymns, for example, 'Lead on, O King eternal' has been changed to 'Lead on, O cloud of Yahweh'. This process of removing references to God's kingship and majesty seems to me to be wholly misconceived. Of course, we also need hymns which speak of the vulnerability, self-giving and suffering of God and Jesus Christ, but this does not mean that we should stop singing about divine majesty. The celebration of God's kingship, as proclaimed in the psalms, is central to Christian doctrine and it would be sad indeed if the classic hymns which express this theme were to be edged out of contemporary liturgy because of a misconceived aversion to the institution of human monarchy and an imperfect understanding of the notion of divine kingship.

Several scholars have suggested that the enthronement psalms which celebrate Yahweh's kingship were sung in

the context of annual ceremonies, similar to those found in
other Near Eastern cultures, where human kings renewed
their power and claim to rule. They point to the apparent
participation of kings in the great annual festivals of Israelite
religion, notably the autumn festival of the booths, or taber-
nacles, which seems also to have been an enthronement
festival. It has been suggested that these occasions incorporated the enactment of an annual ritual in which the
king symbolically fought against evil forces and died in
atonement for his people's sins, later rising to life and glory.
Other scholars are unhappy with the application of this
Near Eastern ritual to the Israelite situation. It is certainly
beyond doubt that the enthronement psalms speak of God's
kingship, especially as it is exercised in conflict with the
forces of chaos and disorder. What is not so clear is whether
this is also applied by analogy or extension to the Lord's
anointed, the Davidic king. It is, perhaps, significant that the
same Hebrew word for king, *melek*, is used both of God
and human monarchs. If the enthronement psalms were,
indeed, sung at ceremonies marking both the enthronement
of an Israelite king and the annual confirmation or renewal
of his rule, it is easy to see how the proclamation of God's
overarching kingship was linked to the ritual celebration
of human kingship. John Eaton suggests that these psalms
involve a series of liturgical episodes which show the king
being chosen, anointed and granted grace to serve the cause
of God's kingdom:

> The Lord, creator and king of all, invites his chosen one
> to sit beside him on Mount Zion, a 'priest for ever' and
> victor over evil. Through him God sends out justice, care
> and health to nature and society. It is God's laws that he
> must uphold. He witnesses to the world and preaches of
> God's sovereignty and faithfulness. To God he turns with
> all the burdens of his people and prays with peculiar
> intimacy and acceptance – 'My father, my God and rock
> of my salvation' etc.[10]

It has also been suggested that during these enthronement festivals Israelite monarchs may have gone through a ritual process of humiliation and reinstatement, and that this was the context for psalms of lament like Psalms 18 and 22. Psalm 89 may also fall into this category. It starts as a song of praise to the steadfast love of God, goes on to celebrate the Lord's everlasting covenant with David and his line, and then becomes a lament that God has cast off and rejected his anointed one – 'Thou hast removed the sceptre from his hand, and cast his throne to the ground.' The king feels mocked and scorned, 'bearing in my bosom the insults of the people'.

The parallels between this last image and the suffering servant passage in Isaiah have led some scholars to suggest that the Israelite king may even have had an atoning role, bearing the sins of his people and suffering in some represent-ative way for them. In this interpretation Psalm 22, quoted by Jesus on the cross, and Psalm 69 have been taken to be royal cultic passion psalms which refer to the ritual humiliation of the king and his representative role to suffer on behalf of a suffering nation. Whether they can in fact bear such an inter-pretation is debatable. These and other psalms do, however, seem to point to a ritual drama in which the nations of the earth, representing the forces of darkness and death, unite in an effort to destroy Yahweh's chosen people by slaying the Davidic king. At first, the king is allowed to suffer defeat and is nearly engulfed in the waters of the underworld, but at the last moment, after a plea of loyalty to the Davidic Covenant and an acknowledgement of his ultimate dependence on Yahweh, he is delivered and restored. The prosperity of the nation, for which the king is directly responsible, is thereby assured for another year.

Another controversial issue is the extent to which the treatment of kingship in the psalms is eschatological. Do they speak about actual living kings or point forward to a final messiah who will save Israel? There is considerable debate about the precise meaning of the term *messiah* as it is used in the psalms. As the fortunes of Israel and its rulers declined, culminating in the catastrophe of the Babylonian exile, the messianic hope became increasingly eschatological and looked beyond the actual historical institutions of Israel for its fulfilment. During and after the exile the Jews pinned their hopes on the future emergence of a saving king from the seed of David. This may be what lies behind Psalm 72 with its vision of a king who will live 'while the sun endures, and as long as the moon, throughout all generations', reign with justice and righteousness, and establish an everlasting kingdom such that all other kings will fall down before him and all nations will call him blessed.

Whether or not the psalms found in the Old Testament bear this kind of eschatological interpretation, it does seem to be valid for later texts like the so-called Psalms of Solomon which are thought to have been written between 61 and 57 BC and look forward to the coming of a new 'son of David' who will be raised up by God to deliver Jerusalem and bring about a new world order of justice and righteousness. Later prophets, writing after the exile of the Israelites to Babylon, also seem to look forward to a restoration of the monarchy and the emergence of a new Davidic king or Messiah who will reign again from Jerusalem and restore and reunite Israel. In the increasingly apocalyptic literature from the second century BC this restored kingship is linked to the predestined inauguration of a final age.

Whether or not there is a messianic and eschatological element in its treatment of kingship, there can surely be no doubting the Old Testament's emphasis on the sacred and spiritual nature of monarchy. It clearly establishes that the institution derives from God, with whom the human monarch stands in a close and special relationship. Described both as God's son and as his anointed one, the Israelite king assumed a priestly and a representative role which involved leading his people in the worship of God, embodying the nation in a corporate persona and defending the land. Within the pages of the Hebrew scriptures we are given pictures of the wise king, the praying king, the psalm-singing king, the temple-building king, and the king who mediates and promotes God's covenant with his people. Overall, the clear impression given is of monarchy as a sacred institution, with kings having a close and intimate involvement with the nation's public worship and a high and solemn calling as both the principal channel for, and the human model of, God's rule of righteousness and justice.

2

Monarchy in the New Testament

If kings figure prominently in the Old Testament, it is the word 'kingdom' which occupies an important place in the New Testament. More specifically, the kingdom of God is a central theme in the Gospels, frequently proclaimed by Jesus and explored in his parables. At first sight this emphasis on God's kingdom rather than on human kings seems to hark back to the theocracy of Israel's pre-monarchic days. As understood in the New Testament, the kingdom symbolizes the rule and sovereignty of God, whether here and now or in some future eschatological state, and appears to have little to do with human monarchy and its spiritual dimension.

It is certainly true that not many individual kings figure directly in the New Testament narrative. The one who does so most prominently, Herod the Great, the 'baddie' of the Nativity story, hardly gives much encouragement for a positive Christian view of monarchy. Yet the theme of kingship is an important one in the New Testament. The Israelite view of monarchy is taken up and carried on, and both David and Solomon are invoked in a way that is much more than casual. Jesus is portrayed by all four Gospel writers as a king, in terms of his birth, his life, his passion, his death and his resurrection. The titles which are applied to him by his disciples, by others who meet him, and by his enemies in mockery – Messiah/ Christ, Son of God, Son of Man, King of the Jews and King of Israel – all clearly denote royal status. Indeed, it is hardly too much to say that Jesus' kingship is the most striking and incontrovertible feature of his portrayal in the New Testament.

This in itself has clear implications for the spiritual character of temporal monarchy in Christian societies. There are also more direct pointers within the New Testament and early Christian tradition to the sacred role, authority and responsibility of Christian monarchs.

The kingdom theme in the New Testament has proved an even more problematic and controversial subject than that of monarchy in the Old Testament. In the words of the American scholar Norman Perrin, 'In the whole realm of New Testament hermeneutics there is no more intractable problem than that of the interpretation of the symbol "Kingdom of God" in the message of Jesus.'[1] The kingdom has been variously interpreted as existing in the here and now (realized), located in the future, or somehow both already breaking in yet not wholly present. It has been given both earthly and heavenly locations, and huge numbers of books have been written arguing that it should primarily be understood politically, spiritually, eschatologically, apocalyptically, ethically, historically or in none of these categories. There is some agreement that the phrase 'kingdom of God', sometimes 'kingdom of heaven', so often used by Jesus, expresses the idea of divine sovereignty and asserts God's claim to rule all. If so, then does Jesus' announcement that the 'the kingdom of God is at hand' suggest the imminent arrival of a theocratic state and take away both the focus on and the argument for human monarchy found in the Old Testament?

It is certainly the case that a key element in Jesus' teaching seems to be the dethroning of earthly powers and potentates and the proclamation that there is no king but God. Yet he himself is referred to as a king and described in royal language so persistently and emphatically as to suggest that this aspect of his earthly life is extremely important. Jesus seems to inaugurate the kingdom as well as to announce its imminent coming. Does his own clearly highlighted royal role and status in fact provide a new model for future human kings to follow and indeed a new justification for the spiritual institution of monarchy, especially in the 'in-between times' between his announcement or inauguration of the kingdom of God and its full realization on earth?

It may, in fact, be the case that in the minds of those writing the books that make up the New Testament the concept of 'the kingdom of God' had more to do with earthly monarchs and less to do with the eschatological or heavenly realms favoured in later Christian interpretation. Much modern New Testament scholarship has focused on the Jewishness of Jesus and suggested that he was seen very much in terms of a Davidic king who would rule temporally as well as spiritually from Jerusalem. George Wesley Buchanan has argued that 'kingdom of heaven' was used as a code word to mean the promised land of Israel back under Jewish control and that 'the titles attributed to Jesus were those appropriate for a king and the kingdom he was trying to obtain was the kind of kingdom all other kings rule'.[2] Bernhard Lang has advanced the theory that the Lord's Prayer was first framed by the circle around John the Baptist and later taken up by Jesus. He believes that its original context was highly political and that the phrase 'Your kingdom come' might be better rendered 'Restore the independent Jewish kingdom!'

> Misconstruing the original sense, Christians have often thought of God's kingdom as a universal empire that will be established after the end of human history as we know it, a commonwealth directly and miraculously ruled by God or Christ, a kingdom not of this world. This is clearly not what John the Baptist and his circle were expecting and praying for. For them, the kingdom of God was a rather small, this-worldly state in the Near East, ruled by an ordinary human person.[3]

These and other modern interpretations of the kingdom motif in the New Testament, which give more significance to the idea of human monarchy, have not gone unchallenged by other scholars who want to view it in a more universalist, ethical and metaphorical light. There is, in fact, no need to polarize or contrast these two aspects of the kingdom which, as it is presented in the New Testament, has both a national and universal dimension, just as it is conceived of as being both individual and corporate, political and spiritual, realised and apocalyptic.

Perhaps even more striking than the emphasis on the kingdom theme throughout the New Testament is the portrayal of Jesus in royal terms both in the Gospels and in later Christian tradition. All four of the Gospel writers use royal titles and monarchical allusions in their descriptions of Jesus. He is, indeed, defined as the Messiah or anointed king, the Greek word for which, *Christos*, was to give his followers the name of Christians by which they have universally been known. From his birth in David's city to David's line, and his baptism where he is identified by God as his beloved Son, to his trial and crucifixion for being 'King of the Jews', the royal theme runs as the most distinct thread through his life and death.

Central to the Gospel writers' portrayal of Jesus' royal identity is their assertion that he is born of the house and family of David. The importance of the hereditary principle in determining Jesus' identity as the direct heir of David is underlined in what are among the most overlooked parts of the Gospel narratives, namely the detailed genealogical tables provided by both Matthew and Luke. They form the basis for the familiar words of the Angel Gabriel to the shepherds at Bethlehem which are sung every Christmas: 'To you in David's town this day is born of David's line.' The two Gospel writers treat the genealogy of Jesus in rather different ways. Luke introduces the subject after covering both the birth and baptism of Jesus and at the point where his ministry is beginning. His genealogy traces Jesus' descent back to God, via David, Abraham and Noah. Matthew begins his Gospel with what he calls 'the book of the genealogy of Jesus Christ, the son of David, the son of Abraham'. For him the Davidic descent is of particular importance. The first section of his three-part genealogy starts with Abraham and comes to a triumphant end with 'David the king'. The second section of the genealogy takes the line through the kings of Israel and Judah, ending with Josiah and his sons at the time of the Babylonian exile, and the third part provides a family tree through the period of exile down to Joseph, 'the husband of Mary, of whom Jesus was born, who is called Christ'. Jesus' direct descent from David continues to be a major theme in the first chapter of Matthew's Gospel. The angel of the Lord who appears to Joseph in a dream to tell him that his wife Mary is about to bear a son greets him as 'Joseph, son of David'.

This theme of Jesus' hereditary succession through the royal line of David is beautifully portrayed in the Jesse windows found in a number of churches. There is a particularly fine example in St Dyfnog's Church, Llanrhaeadr, North Wales. Completed in 1533, it depicts Jesse sleeping with the branches of the family tree which end in Jesus emerging from his upper torso. Pride of place is given to David who is depicted rather like a medieval troubadour playing his harp and wearing a red coat with gold buttons. Also depicted prominently are Solomon holding a model of the temple in his hand, and Rehoboam, Asa, Josaphat, Joram and Ozias. While monarchs predominate in the family tree, emphasizing Jesus' royal descent and kingship, there are also the prophets Isaiah, Obadiah, Zecharaiah and Joel, and Zadok the priest, symbolizing the two other main attributes of Jesus. The triple depiction of Jesus as prophet, priest and king has been another popular theme for stained-glass artists – a good example is the magnificent window at the east end of Brechin Cathedral designed by Henry Holiday in 1902.

There are several other allusions to Jesus' royal status in the Nativity accounts in the Gospels. His Davidic descent forms an important motif in Luke's account of the angel of the Lord's appearance to the shepherds to tell them of their Saviour's birth. The shepherds are located very deliberately in Bethlehem, the city of David who was himself a shepherd before he became a king. It has been suggested that for Luke they underlined the Davidic connection, and may even have symbolized royalty. It is significant that the angel tells the shepherds that Jesus has been born 'in the City of David' and attaches the name Messiah/Christ, or anointed one, to him. This is often related to prophecies in Micah 5 which speak of one coming forth from Bethlehem who will be the ruler of Israel and 'shall stand and feed his flock in the strength of the Lord'. Like David, Jesus is a king who comes from humble origins, being born among the shepherds of Bethlehem rather than in Jersualem.

Luke's account of Bethlehem shepherds being the first to honour Jesus is paralleled by Matthew's story of the wise men who come from the East. Here the royal note is struck again – the wise men are described as coming to Jerusalem to ask: 'Where is he who has been born king of the Jews? For we have seen his star in the East, and have come to worship him.' This introduces a new phrase to describe Jesus' royal status which is to feature most prominently in the passion narratives when it is put on to the lips of his mockers and accusers. The phrase 'king of the Jews' seems to have been used largely by non-Jews and perhaps first by Hasmonean high priests, descended from leaders of the Maccabean revolt, who established an independent state in Palestine and called themselves 'kings of the Jews'. It had clear political connotations, and directly challenged Herod who saw himself as King of the Jews, but it almost certainly had other, more spiritual resonances as well.

The gifts which the *magi* – variously seen as astronomers, magicians or wise men – brought to the infant Jesus also emphasized his royal status. Notably, of course, the gold symbolized his kingship, with the frankincense pointing to his divine being and fitness to be worshipped, and the myrrh with its 'bitter perfume' prefiguring his suffering. There are echoes here of the accounts in 1 Kings and 2 Chronicles of the Queen of Sheba coming to Solomon bearing gold, spices and precious stones, and of Isaiah's prophecy that

A multitude of camels shall cover you,
    the young camels of Midian and Ephah;

all those from Sheba shall come.
They shall bring gold and frankincense.

(Isaiah 60.6)

The visit of the *magi* to the baby Jesus seems also to fulfil the hope expressed in Psalm 72, traditionally relating to Solomon but often taken as referring to a future Messiah:

May the kings of Tarshish and of the isles render him tribute,
May the kings of Sheba and Seba bring gifts!
May all kings fall down before him, all nations serve him!

(Psalm 72.10-11)

It was in the light of these prophetic passages from the Old Testament that Matthew's *magi* came to be elevated to the rank of kings in popular Christian mythology and iconography. This happened very early in the Church's history. Tertullian reported that by the end of the second century 'the East considers the *magi* almost as kings' and this identification was certainly taken for granted in the west by around AD 500. The sixth-century Armenian Infancy Gospel identified and named three specific kings: Melkon (or Melchior as he came to be known in Europe), king of the Persians; Gaspar, king of the Hindus; and Balthazar, king of the Arabs. It described them as arriving from Persia with 12,000 soldiers on horseback. By the eighth century the story of the three kings bringing their gifts to the baby Jesus was well established throughout Europe. In the twelfth century three embalmed bodies in a perfect state of preservation found buried under a church near Milan were declared to be those of the kings. They were transferred to Cologne Cathedral where they became the object of veneration and pilgrimage.

The fact that Matthew's gift-bearing visitors came almost universally to be seen as kings produced a new paradigm of Christian monarchy and a model of the king as worshipper, leading his people in the adoration of Christ, whose majesty he recognized in a particularly acute way owing to his own royal position. In their homage to Jesus, the three kings came to represent the peoples of the world and also to show the proper attitude for earthly monarchs to adopt towards their heavenly king.

These themes are reflected in a little-known event in the Royal Family's annual cycle of religious observances which has been going on for at least 500 years. On the feast of the Epiphany (6 January) every year, the sovereign attends a service of sung Eucharist in the Chapel Royal in St James's Palace at which offerings of gold, frankincense and myrrh are carried to the altar. Until the reign of George III the sovereign always made the offerings in person, but they are now usually carried to the altar on silver gilt salvers by two gentlemen ushers led by the Serjeant of the Vestry and escorted by three Yeomen of the Guard. Until 1859 the gold was offered in the form of a small roll of gold leaf. This was changed, at the suggestion of Prince Albert, into a dish of 25 new sovereigns. The frankincense and myrrh, which are provided by the Royal Apothecary, are obtained directly from the Holy Land. After the service, the incense is sent to a church which uses it and the myrrh is sent to the Anglican Benedictine community at Nashdom Abbey to be mixed with the incense prepared there.

The significance of the royal gifts brought to Jesus by royal gift-bearers is well captured in Edward Caswall's translation of the early Latin hymn by Prudentius, 'Bethlehem of noblest cities':

> Fairer than the sun at morning
> was the star that told his birth;
> to the lands their God announcing,
> seen in fleshly form on earth.
>
> By its lambent beauty guided
> see the eastern kings appear;
> see them bend, their gifts to offer,

gifts of incense, gold and myrrh.

Solemn things of mystic meaning:
incense doth the God disclose,
gold a royal child proclaimeth,
myrrh a future tomb foreshows.

Other hymns speak of kings acknowledging the majesty of
Jesus in a more radical way, by resigning their own crowns
and surrendering utterly to his sole reign. This is the theme of
James Montgomery's 'Palms of glory, raiment bright':

Kings for harps their crowns resign,
crying, as they strike the chords,
'Take the kingdom, it is thine,
King of kings, and Lord of lords.'

Yet this verse is not saying what it might appear to when taken
out of context. It applies not to earthly kings but to those in
heaven who, along with other members of the communion of
saints, are girded with 'crowns that never fade away'. There is
a clear and explicit contrast in the Christian tradition between
the permanence of the reign of God and the temporary and
provisional nature of all human kingdoms. It is well brought
out in lines from two other very familiar hymns, 'So be it, Lord,
thy throne shall never like earth's proud empires pass away',
and 'Crowns and thrones may perish, kingdoms rise and wane,
but the Church of Jesus constant will remain'. Yet there is no
imperative on earthly rulers to surrender their crowns. The
three kings travel far to see Jesus, offer him gifts and kneel at
his feet. They do not, however, resign their crowns and give
up ruling their people after having seen him. Their calling is
rather to lead the way in worship and adoration.

While we are on the subject of hymns, it is interesting to
notice how many use royal language about Jesus. From the
early centuries of the Church come such phrases as 'King of
kings, yet born of Mary' (from 'Let All Mortal Flesh Keep

Silence'), 'Eternal monarch, King most high' and 'Thou art the
King of Israel, Thou David's royal Son' (from 'All Glory, Laud
and Honour'). Eighteenth- and nineteenth-century hymns
incite us to 'Hail the heaven-born Prince of Peace', 'Bring forth
the royal diadem, to crown him Lord of all' and 'Crown him
with many crowns, the lamb upon his throne'. Contemporary
worship songs urge us to 'Make way, make way for Christ the
king' and to 'worship his majesty'. Several hymns pick up the
theme of the *kenosis*, or self-emptying of Jesus, explored in
Philippians 2.5-8, and speak of him divesting himself of his
royalty and kingly attributes. Perhaps the best known is Emily
Elliot's 'Thou didst leave thy crown, and thy kingly throne
when thou camest to earth for me' which acknowledges his
'royal degree' and speaks of Jesus regaining his crown in
heaven. In similar vein, Caroline Noel's 'At the name of Jesus'
speaks of one who is 'humbled for a season' and then raised
'to the throne of Godhead'. It ends with the injunctions 'in
your hearts enthrone him', 'crown him as your captain' and
'confess him King of glory now'.

In applying metaphors of kingship to Jesus, these hymns
are closely following the Gospels where royal language is used
about Jesus throughout his life. It is applied particularly at
significant moments of revelation and identification, as after
his baptism by John when the voice of God is heard from
heaven saying, 'This is my beloved Son, with whom I am well
pleased', a phrase which echoes the Lord's words to the king
he has set on his holy hill, in Psalm 2.7: 'You are my son,
today I have begotten you.' The recognition of Jesus as God's
son which is signalled by these words seems to parallel what
was understood as happening at the anointing of Israelite
kings, the crucial difference being that in Jesus' case it signified
recognition of an existing (indeed, pre-existing) state rather
than adoption as the Son of God at the moment of anointing.

At several subsequent points in his life as it is recorded in
the Gospels, Jesus is accorded kingly status by those whom
he meets and who follow him. Nathanael, spotted by Jesus
under a fig tree in Galilee, hails him as 'the King of Israel'

(John 1.49). Two of his most faithful disciples, James and John, ask respectively to sit on his right and left hand in glory (Mark 10.37). His royal status is especially highlighted in the descriptions of his entry into Jerusalem on a donkey prior to his passion. Both Matthew and John quote from the prophecy in Zechariah 9.9, although neither gives its full form:

> Rejoice greatly, O daughter of Zion!
>   Shout aloud, O daughter of Jerusalem!
> Lo, your king comes to you;
>   triumphant and victorious is he,
> humble and riding upon an ass.

Matthew describes the crowd hailing Jesus as 'the Son of David' as they cast their palms before him, Luke has them chanting 'Blessed is the King who comes in the name of the Lord', and John has them hailing 'the King of Israel'.

It is significant that Jesus never denies any of these claims nor seeks to repudiate the royal titles which he is given. Indeed, at times he seems to hint at his own royal status, as when he tells the scribes and the Pharisees: 'The queen of the South will arise at the judgment with this generation and condemn it; for she came from the ends of the earth to hear the wisdom of Solomon, and behold, something greater than Solomon is here' (Matthew 12.42).

Jesus' entry into Jerusalem on the first Palm Sunday offers important pointers both to popular expectations of his kingship and his own understanding of his royal status. All the actions of the crowd, as they are described by the Gospel writers, bear witness to his majesty. The spreading of clothes on the road along which he is to pass recalls the behaviour of the Israelites following the anointing of Jehu as king – 'Then in haste every man of them took his garment and put it under him on the bare steps, and they blew the trumpet and proclaimed "Jehu is king"' (2 Kings 9.13). Similarly, the strewing of palm branches has a precedent in the reception of Simon Maccabeus, the conquering hero of the Jews, into Jerusalem 'with praise and palm branches' following one of his military triumphs (1 Maccabees 13.51). These actions, and the shouts of 'Hosanna' and other acclamations clearly suggest that the crowd who gathered to welcome Jesus into Jerusalem saw him as the Messiah who was coming in triumph into his royal city from which he would rule in majesty. This is also, of course, what that part of the prophecy from Zechariah which is not quoted by the Gospel writers also suggests when it speaks of the king coming 'triumphant and victorious'.

Jesus himself, however, seems to have a very different sense of his kingship. This is signalled principally by his choice of an ass on which to make his entry into the city. He deliberately opts for an animal associated with humility, humiliation even, rather than a proud charger or stallion more fitting for a king on a triumphal progress. Here is the other element in Zechariah's prophecy which is quoted by the Gospel writers with its possible reference to the public humiliation of the Israelite king during the autumn festival. As portrayed in the Gospels, Jesus' ride into Jerusalem, far from being a triumphal progress, is a journey towards death, its ambivalence so well captured in Henry Milman's couplet: 'Ride on, ride on in majesty! In lowly pomp ride on to die.'

This entire episode may be read as profoundly anti-monarchical in tone and having a similar message to those passages in Samuel which suggest that monarchy is what the people want and what God emphatically does not want. The crowd are willing Jesus to be a king, rather as they are portrayed as doing in John's Gospel at the end of the feeding of the 5,000 when he perceives 'that they were about to come and take him by force to make him king' (John 6.15). He, however, wants none of it. Yet this is a somewhat over-simplistic and in some ways positively misleading interpretation. There is a distinct ambivalence as to what this first Palm Sunday has to say about Jesus' kingship. At one level, it does seem to involve Jesus' self-presentation to the people of Israel as a Davidic king. In the words of Oliver O'Donovan:

By the manner of his entry into royal city Jesus set himself self-consciously in the role of the coming king expected in Zecheriah 9:9. According to St Mark and St Matthew this gesture was understood as a reference to the long-suspended Davidic throne. As David's dynasty was the form in which earthly political authority had been given most decisively to Israel, so, when God acted through his anointed to assume authority to himself, David's house was represented in the act. By this narrative we are forbidden to dismiss Israel's political expectations as an irrelevance to Jesus' Gospel.[4]

Yet if Jesus through his entry into Jerusalem lays claim to the legacy of Davidic expectation, the first Palm Sunday experience also shows that he is not bringing a restored kingship to Israel on the basis of a popular movement and popular election. His authority rests on the arrival of God's rule rather than coming from the people's search for a successor to David. Jesus as king derives his authority from above and not from below, but the fact remains that he is clearly a king. Indeed, his identification by the crowds as king could be taken to indicate their faith in the coming of God's kingdom. To quote O'Donovan again:

> To recognise God's rule was to see him as the figure who satisfied the hopes and expectations which had been vested in the reappearance of traditional monarchical leadership. In that sense the coming of the Kingdom was proved by the acknowledgment of Jesus as king.[5]

The entry into Jerusalem demonstrates the redefinition of kingship. Jesus does not reject the people's hailing of him as a king but he does reject their expectation of what a king does. Those who welcome him with palms expect a king who will challenge the power of Rome. Instead they get a king who bursts into tears at the sight of Jerusalem. They expect a powerful military commander: they get a prophet proclaiming the reign of righteousness and peace. They expect a conquering hero full of pomp and show: they get a man of sorrows, acquainted with grief and suffering. This is not, of course, a wholly new concept of kingship. It harks back to the Israelite ideal in many respects. With Jesus, the ideal becomes the reality.

Jesus' kingship is nowhere made more of by the Gospel writers than in the passion narratives where the application of royal language reaches its zenith, albeit often employed in a derogatory and mocking way. This is perhaps particularly marked in Mark's account of the passion, as has been highlighted by Frank Matera:

> Chapter 15 (of Mark) moves inexorably to the death of Jesus and the centurion's confession through a series of incidents which continually point to the kingship of Jesus. First, Jesus is accused as a King (15.2), rejected as a King (15.9, 12) and mocked as a King (15.18). Second, Jesus is crucified as King (15.26) and mocked as King of Israel (15.32). Third, Jesus cries out as a forsaken Messiah king (15.34), is mocked as a Messiah King for whom Elijah will not come, and is confessed as the King he truly is, God's royal Son (15.39). Finally, in 15.44, a highly redactional verse, Mark makes the burial scene a royal burial by reminding the reader of the opening scene (15.2) and the centurion's confession (15.39). In every instance then, Mark unfolds the royal theme as he presses to his story's climax.[6]

While the royal motif is particularly striking in Mark's treatment of the passion, it is also there in the other Gospels. It is especially evident in the mocking of Jesus by the soldiers who robe him, crown him, and according to Matthew's account, also hand him a mock sceptre in the form of a reed. The chief priests also mock him when he is on the cross as 'the Christ, the King of Israel' and he is mocked again as a false Messiah after crying out to God in the opening words of Psalm 22. This psalm, as we have seen, may possibly have been associated with the ritual humiliation of the king acted out at the annual enthronement festival in Israel. Its use in this context raises the question of how far the Gospel writers were aware of this connection and sought to portray Jesus as the mocked and rejected king with a redemptive and representative role in bearing and atoning for the sins of his people through his suffering. This theme is perhaps also suggested in Jesus' own words that 'the Son of Man must suffer'. For Matera, the kingship theme which is so central in Mark's Gospel has three key dimensions:

1 Kingship is inseparable from rejection and suffering. Mark consistently refuses to make a public proclamation of Jesus as King of Israel until the passion has begun.
2 Kingship possesses a glorious aspect which will be revealed when the only Son returns in his capacity as the Son of Man. But this kingship cannot be disclosed until Jesus has completed his suffering and death.
3 Kingship finds its supreme title in 'Son of God' but no one can make this proclamation until the temple curtain has been torn. This event, the result of Jesus' death, allows the Markan community and all believers to confess Jesus as God's son.[7]

This sense of a kingship that is only revealed through suffering and not fully expressed until death is well conveyed in some of the great passiontide hymns. 'The royal banners forward go', J. M. Neale's translation of Venantius Fortunatus' sixth-century Latin hymn, pictures Jesus as the 'universal Lord' who 'reigns and triumphs from the tree ... with royal purple robes'. This image of Jesus actually reigning from the cross of crucifixion is more commonly expressed through the symbol of the crown of thorns, variously interpreted in terms of its tragic irony ('O kingly head surrounded, with mocking crown of thorns'), its pointer to the true nature of God and to the vesture that those who follow him must adopt ('Look upon the crown of God, see what he is wearing' from Athelstan Ridley's translation of a thirteenth-century Latin hymn entitled 'The Crown of Thorns') and its contrast with the crown of glory worn by the risen and ascended Christ ('The head that once was crowned with thorns is crowned with victory now, /a royal diadem adorns the mighty victor's brow'). There is also a powerful association of kingship and suffering in the comparison 'His dying crimson, like a robe' in Isaac Watts' great hymn which begins with another royal reference, 'When I survey the wondrous cross on which the prince of glory died'.

Another more historical and less theological dimension to Jesus' kingship as it is described in the Gospel accounts of his passion and crucifixion turns on the meaning of the phrase 'King of the Jews'. It was first used, as we have noted, by the *magi*, but was later taken up by Jesus' accusers and inscribed as a title on his cross. It is widely accepted that Jesus was, indeed, crucified for being, or claiming to be, the king of the Jews, a political offence in the eyes of the Romans because it constituted a challenge to the rule of Herod, the Roman-appointed puppet king, and a religious offence in the eyes of Jews who did not recognize him as the true Messiah and saw him as a false prophet claiming to be the Son of God. In all the Gospels Pilate asks Jesus repeatedly whether he is indeed the king of the Jews and receives a non-committal answer along the lines of 'You have said so'. We are left with a sense that in Pilate's mind at least Jesus is, indeed, the king of the Jews – he asks the Jews 'Shall I crucify your King?' and it is he, according to John's Gospel, who writes the inscription to put on the cross: 'Jesus of Nazareth, the King of the Jews'. When the chief priests ask him to change the description to 'This man said, I am the King of the Jews', he refuses.

Historically, then, it seems that Jesus of Nazareth was put to death for being, or claiming to be, the King of the Jews. But what was his own attitude to this title? Did Jesus see himself as a king, and if so of what kind? Although he never volunteered the title when speaking about himself, he never contradicted it when it was used by others and he did use the term 'Son of Man' of himself. Whether this had messianic and royal connotations is a matter of much debate, but it certainly seems to have been associated in inter-testamental times with the person of the Davidic heir, as in Daniel 7.14 where the Son of Man is described as having 'sovereignty and glory and kingly power'. Other phrases apparently used by Jesus may conceivably suggest that he saw himself in royal terms. His statement, recorded in Matthew 11.19, that 'wisdom is justified by her deeds' seems to refer to himself and could suggest an identification with the wisdom tradition and so with Solomon and the figure of the wise king. His self-identification as 'the good shepherd' in John 10.14 may also conceivably have royal connotations, specifically with Davidic monarchy, which, as we have seen, was particularly associated with shepherd imagery.

Jesus comes closest to defining his own sense of his kingship in his exchange with Pilate, which is recorded in most detail in chapter 18 of John's Gospel. In response to Pilate's repeated question as to whether he is King of the Jews, Jesus simply says, 'My kingship is not of this world.' This remark can be taken at various levels. Does it simply mean that Jesus has no interest in trying to establish an earthly kingdom to rival Caesar's? That such a project is in his mind is, of course, what worries Pilate and the Roman authorities, and what the Jews suggest Jesus is about when they tell Pilate, 'if you release this man, you are not Caesar's friend; everyone who makes himself a king sets himself against Caesar' (John 19.12) and protest their own loyalty with the words, 'We have no king but Caesar' (John 19.15), thereby apparently repudiating Yahweh's kingship over Israel of which they are supposed to be the faithful representatives. Yet Jesus' reply to Pilate does not seem principally intended to assure him that he has no ambitions in terms of worldly power and is not seeking to be a direct threat to Caesar. His statement that his kingdom is not of this world suggests rather that it has a more radical quality, either being essentially spiritual and rooted in heaven rather than earth, or counter-cultural and opposed to the values of the world. This latter interpretation certainly fits with the

whole *contra mundum* theme of John's Gospel. When Pilate
goes on to say 'So you are a king?' Jesus answers, 'You say that
I am a king. For this I was born, and for this I have come into
the world, to bear witness to the truth.' This elusive statement
seems as far as he is prepared to go. He makes no answer to
Pilate's follow-up question, 'What is the truth?' Is this because
Pilate will not be able to understand a kingdom that is not
established by human endeavour but by God, or that there
is simply no point in seeking to communicate with someone
who is not of the truth? Are we given here a new paradigm of
kingship in terms of bearing witness to the truth, and specifically the truth sent from above, or is it simply an instance of
John's rather exclusivist theology and belief that only true
believers can recognize the king?

Overall, John's Gospel provides a particularly fascinating
treatment of Jesus' kingship. This is the subject of an interesting study by Wayne Meeks who sees a close interplay
in John's portrayal of Jesus between the roles of king and
prophet. His starting point is the verses that come at the end
of the account of the feeding of the 5,000:

> When the people saw the sign which he had done, they
> said, 'This is indeed the prophet who is to come into the
> world!' Perceiving then that they were about to come
> and take him by force to make him king, Jesus withdrew
> again to the mountain by himself.
>
> (John 6.14-15)

This passage emphasizes the popular desire to make Jesus a
king that we have already identified in the accounts of his
entry into Jerusalem. For Meeks, it also links Jesus' kingship
with his prophetic role. This link is confirmed in the conversation with Pilate recorded in John 18 where Meeks sees Jesus
radically redefining his kingship in terms of the mission of the
prophet whose role is to bear witness to the truth.[8]

The kingship of Jesus is an undeniably complex and
ambiguous theme. It is shot through with paradox – that

the servant is the master – and it undoubtedly involves a redefinition of monarchy, or at least an actualization of some of the ideals expressed on the subject in the Old Testament. O'Donovan points out that Jesus takes on two distinct monarchic roles:

> There is the mediator of God's rule, the role focussed centrally upon the Davidic monarch ... and there is the representative individual, who in lonely faithfulness carries the tradition of the people, its fate and its promise, in his own destiny.[9]

Jesus is portrayed in the New Testament as the servant-king, the priest-king and the prophet-king who bears witness to the truth. At one level, his kingship is expressed in terms of his birth in Bethlehem as the direct heir of David, his recognition as God's beloved son and his popular acclamation as the Messiah. At another level, it is expressed and in some sense even obtained through his acts of obedience, humility and suffering. His crown is made of thorns and his throne is the Cross. Yet he is nonetheless a king for all that, both during his earthly life and in his risen and ascended state seated on the right hand of his father in heaven.

Our egalitarian, republican-inclined, politically correct culture does not have much time for Jesus the king. Rather, in the words of Francis Lauderdale,

> We want the man who loved
> the poor and oppressed,
> who hated the rich man and the king
> and the scribe and the priest.[10]

Several modern theologians regard the notion of a royal or kingly Christ as a perversion of the true meaning of the Gospels. Gail Ramshaw maintains that 'Christ is not a king who was crucified in a golden robe and a bejeweled diadem. ... Rather kingship itself was crucified.'[11] The distinguished

hymn writer, Brian Wren, castigates the authors of contemporary worship songs for their use of royal language about
both God and Christ. He concedes that it is biblical but
regards its continuing use today as an archaic hangover from
a hierarchical and deferential age which is totally incompatible
with modern democratic spirit and, more seriously, positively
idolatrous – 'the regal Christ sitting in triumph with God the
Almighty King is an idol, not the one, loving and living God'.[12]

Our understanding of Jesus Christ should surely embrace
both the marginal Galilean prophet/healer and the king who
rules with his father in glory. That Jesus is both the man of
sorrows acquainted with grief and the Christ triumphant,
ever reigning, is the glorious paradox that stands at the heart
of the Christian mystery of incarnation. That paradox is well
expressed in Graham Kendrick's two outstanding modern
hymns, 'Meekness and Majesty' and 'The Servant King'.
Previous generations may have leaned too far in depicting and
imagining Jesus Christ as a worldly emperor clad in purple
robes and have over-emphasized his regal power and triumph.
We need to be careful not to lean too much the other way and
over-emphasize his marginality at the expense of his majesty.

It is good that the festival of Christ the King, instituted by
Pope Pius XI in 1925, is now celebrated by a growing number
of churches of different denominations on the last Sunday of
the Christian year. The collects for this Sunday, prepared by
the International Commission on English in the Liturgy and
commended by the Joint Liturgical Group for all churches
using the Revised Common Lectionary, speak eloquently
of Christ's kingship in its different aspects. That for Year A
speaks of Jesus' 'sovereignty over every age and nation' and
asks God that 'we may be the subjects of his dominion and
receive the inheritance of your kingdom'. The Year B prayer
asks that 'we may imitate the sacrificial love of Christ our
King and, as a royal and priestly people, serve you humbly in
our brothers and sisters'. The prayer for Year C points to the
Saviour who was rejected and acknowledges that 'the mystery
of his kingship illumines our lives'.[13]

How does Christ's kingship relate to the human institution of monarchy? Does it render human kings redundant,
or indeed idolatrous? At first sight this may indeed seem to
be the case. Jesus is presented in the New Testament as an
all-sufficient Lord and Saviour, just as he is presented as the
sufficient and perfect sacrifice and oblation for the sins of the
world. If we are to enthrone him in our hearts, can there be
room for the claims of any other ruler when, as the Book of
Revelation so powerfully insists, there is only one throne and
'sovereignty over all the world has passed to Our Lord and
his Christ' (Revelation 11.13)? Has he not completely fulfilled
the messianic promise and served as the final priest-king, the
last in Melchizedek's line, inaugurating God's kingdom and
so bringing all human kingdoms to an end? Are not all his
followers in some senses both kings and priests, as suggested
by Peter's words to the Gentile Christians scattered throughout
the Roman provinces of Asia Minor in the latter half of the
first century: 'You are a chosen race, a royal priesthood, a
holy nation, God's own people' (1 Peter 2.9)? It is certainly
true that all Christians participate in some way in both the
attributes and work of Jesus as priest and king. Yet just as the
church continues to set aside priests and ministers to represent
Christ to his people, so it is fitting that there are also Christian
monarchs who rule according to Jesus' example and serve as
pointers to his kingship. This is not just a consequence of the
fact that we live in a fallen world and in the in-between times
when the kingdom of God and its values have still to be fully
realized. It is also, more positively, a reflection of our creation
in imagine Dei and of the mirroring of the courts of heaven in
the life of the world.

There is another way in which Jesus might seem to have
spelled the end for human monarchy. Much of his teaching
amounts to a sustained attack on human hierarchies and
authorities. The Magnificat sets the tone by casting him as
the one who 'hath put down the mighty from their seat and
hath exalted the humble and meek'. Jesus preaches that 'the
last shall be first and the first last'. His preference, eloquently

stated in the Beatitudes and expressed practically throughout his ministry, is clearly for the poor and dispossessed rather than for the rich and powerful. He is portrayed by both the Gospel writers and Paul as a counter-king to Caesar who was the centre of a considerable cult in the first-century Mediterranean world. Yet although he challenges human presuppositions about authority and hierarchy, Jesus is not an advocate of popular democracy. The kingdom of God that he preaches is not an institution run on the basis of taking votes to discern the majority view on issues of ethics, church practice or belief but rather a new order based on faith, justice and radical obedience.

Although he is clearly deeply uneasy about worldly power and the way in which it is often exercised, Jesus never explicitly attacks the institution of human kingship. His remark 'Render to Caesar that which is Caesar's and to God that which belongs to God' (Matthew 22.21) and his question to Peter about from whom the kings of the earth take toll and tribute (Matthew 17.25) in fact suggest that he sees human rulers as having a legitimate role and a legitimate claim to the allegiance of their subjects. Paul and the authors of the pastoral epistles have a much more explicit sense of the Christian ordination of human authority and of the duty of subjects towards their rulers.

> Let every person be subject to the governing authorities. For there is no authority except from God, and those that exist have been instituted by God. Therefore he who resists the authorities resists what God has appointed, and those who resist will incur judgment. For rulers are not a terror to good conduct, but to bad.
>
> (Romans 13.1-3)

> Submit yourselves for the Lord's sake to every authority instituted among men: whether to the king, as the supreme authority, or to governors, who are sent by him to punish those who do wrong and to commend those

who do right ... Show proper respect to everyone: Love
the brotherhood of believers, fear God, honour the king.

(1 Peter 2.13, 17)

These texts have been cited in justification for much tyranny
and oppression down the years and they cannot be used on
their own to make the case for monarchy being sanctioned,
let alone sanctified in the New Testament. They do, however,
point to the Christian understanding that in the aftermath of
Christ's triumph secular authority and order still have their
place and that the structures of the old age should continue
to exercise their sway in the new. There is, indeed, a place for
'Christian kings, princes and governors', to quote the words of
the Book of Common Prayer.

The New Testament takes the model of human kingship
presented in the Old Testament and transforms it, or perhaps
more accurately realizes it, in the person of Jesus. In the new
age that his coming inaugurates, and in which we live until
he comes again to gather all things up, human kingship is
to be exercised in imitation of him. Christian monarchy is
to be patterned on his own royal attributes of righteousness,
justice, mercy, wisdom, peace and humility as well as on the
principle of hereditary succession. The Christian king, taking
Jesus as his example, is to be actuated by a sense of duty and
a spirit of self-sacrifice, to be the suffering servant and always
to remember the words of Mark 10.43: 'Whosoever will be
great among you shall be your minister.' He is to lead his
people in worship and adoration of the Triune God, just as the
three kings do in the Nativity paintings and carols. Christian
monarchs stand like all Christians as subjects of the kingdom
of God, and as witnesses to the kingship of the risen and
ascended Jesus, 'the faithful-witness, the first-born of the dead,
and the ruler of the kings on earth' (Revelation 1.5).

3

Sacred kingship in Celtic, Anglo-Saxon and Medieval Britain

Biblical principles and practices found in the Old and New Testaments have not been the only influence on the British understanding of the spiritual character of monarchy. Older pre-Christian ideas of sacral kingship which came into the British Isles through the Celts and Anglo-Saxons were grafted into the new faith of Christianity as it became established from the sixth century. Their legacy remained strong throughout the Middle Ages and, even now, traces of them continue to inform royal pageantry and rituals.

The understanding of kings as having a particularly intense spiritual aura and sacred function is common to virtually all primitive societies. James Frazer, the pioneer anthropologist, began his classic study of magic and religion, *The Golden Bough*, with a lengthy analysis of this subject, noting that

> kings were revered, in many cases not just as priests, that is as intercessors between man and god, but as themselves gods, able to bestow upon their subjects and worshippers those blessings which are commonly supposed to be beyond the reach of mortals, and are sought, if at all, only by prayer and sacrifice offered to superhuman and invisible beings.[1]

Frazer saw the origin of sacred kingship lying in the importance of magic in primitive societies and the emergence of particular individuals seen to possess special supernatural powers. 'In many parts of the world,' he noted,

> the king is the lineal successor of the old magician or medicine-man. When once a special class of sorcerers has been segregated from the community and entrusted by it with the discharge of duties on which the public safety and welfare are believed to depend, these men gradually rise to wealth and power, till their leaders blossom out into sacred kings.[2]

Perhaps the term *shaman* best describes the figure in primitive societies whose role lies at the root of sacred kingship. Associated particularly with hunter-gatherer tribes in the Arctic regions but also found elsewhere, shamans were not just involved in conjuring tricks like shape-shifting but acted as seers and prophets, and were widely revered for their qualities of discernment and their closeness to the supernatural world. There was a strongly sacrificial element to shamanic power which was exercised on the principle of the wounded healer and through the maintenance of a posture of self-giving and sacrifice. The secrets of shamanic union with the other world were passed down from generation to generation, producing a caste which combined the attributes of warrior, philosopher, healer and priest.

The earliest monarchs were almost certainly chosen from these shamanistic families and functioned very much as priest-kings who came to power through a combination of election and hereditary descent. The crowns that they wore may have been based on the shaman's headdress which itself probably derived from the torque or noose worn around the neck to symbolize the sacrificial posture. It has striking parallels with the Christian image of the crown of thorns as a symbol of suffering and sacrifice which yet also signifies royalty and divinity.

Central to primal notions of the sacred character of kingship was the understanding of the king as the one who took on the forces of chaos, often represented by dragons and monsters, and embodied the principle of order in both the cosmic and everyday world. In mythology the king was located at the *axis mundi*, or centre of the world, a place often associated with a sacred tree, from which he ruled both the natural and social order. He was seen as the steward of the gods with whom he stood in a special relationship, maintaining the sacred harmonic balance variously described in different religious traditions as karma, ma'at, dharma, tao or torah.

These aspects of sacred monarchy were clearly apparent in Celtic societies where the king was seen as possessing special powers of healing and divination, and as upholding the moral and spiritual order of his people. In Ireland the *rí* or *righ* (equivalent to the Latin *rex*, Indic *raj* and Gallic *roi*) held his *fír*, or truth, a mystical entity from which radiated harmony and good fortune. A rule characterized by *firinne flatha* – truth of a sovereign – brought fertility to the land and prosperity to the people, while its opposite, *go flatha* – falsehood of a sovereign – brought about natural disasters. If the king pronounced an untruth, the centre literally ceased to hold and there would be physical as well as moral collapse. A sixth-century legend about the kings of Connaught describes the wall of the royal palace at Tara starting to collapse when the usurper Lughaidh mac Con gave a false judgement. When the true king Corma mac Airt gave a wise and true judgement, however, the wall steadied itself of its own accord.

The fullest description of the role of the *fír*, or truth, of the king in upholding the whole order of creation is almost certainly that contained in *The Testament of Morand* which probably dates from the late seventh century and is the oldest treatise on kingship in the Irish language:

> It is through the truth of the ruler that plagues, a great army, or lightenings are averted from people. It is through the truth of the ruler that he judges great kingdoms, great riches. It is through the truth of the ruler that he consummates peace, ease, joy, repose,

comfort. It is through the truth of the ruler that he drives back great armies as far as the borders of their allies. It is through the truth of the ruler that every heir establishes himself in his fair inheritance. It is through the truth of the ruler that the manna of the great acorn-yield of a great wood is tasted. It is through the truth of the ruler that the milk of a great herd of cattle is enriched. It is through the truth of the ruler that there is every abundance of high, lofty grain. It is through the truth of the ruler that greatness of fish swim in the streams. It is through the truth of the ruler that fair offspring are well begotten.[3]

Kingship seems to have survived longer in Ireland than in other Celtic societies like Gaul where by the century or so before Jesus' birth it had been undermined by the power of the nobility. There was a hierarchy of Irish kings with local rulers each presiding over a *tuath* of a few thousand people owing fealty to superior kings and ultimately, in the later development of the institution of monarchy, to the high king of Ireland ruling from the sacred hill of Tara. Early Irish sacral kingship was in many respects similar to that found in the ancient Near East. The king was the special interme-diary between humans and gods and stood in relation to his kingdom as the gods stood in relation to the cosmos. He had a specific responsibility for the re-creation of the land, and this was sometimes expressed in terms of sacrificial ritual. Irish kings developed a particularly close relationship with their priest-advisers, the so-called druids, who played a key role in choosing monarchs and presiding over their inauguration. As druids took over the old shamanistic tasks of prophesying and passing judgements, kings tended rather to practise reserve and cultivate silence, preserving their sacred aura and distance and just occasionally making solemn pronouncements. In keeping with their sacred cosmological role of maintaining order and harmony, their movements were strictly circumscribed. There were particularly strict rules about where a king should go before sunrise or after sunset, reflecting the importance of sun worship in primal Irish religion.

Rituals surrounding the choosing of Irish kings gave an important role to supernatural forces. The druids sacrificed a white bull as a preliminary to forecasting a new king. One man was required to consume his fill of the meat of the sacrificed animal and to drink soup made from its blood. As he slept after the meal, four druids sang over him a charm of truth, and the identity of the next king was then revealed to him in a vision or dream. Several stories tell of the involvement of animals and birds in the choosing of a king, and another common motif is a sexual union with a goddess representing sovereignty. Legends surrounding the fifth-century king Niall of the Nine Hostages describe how when out hunting he and his four brothers went to a well guarded by an ugly hag. The brothers all refused the woman's demand for a kiss and as a result got no water to quench their severe thirst. Niall, however, threw himself on the woman and gave her a kiss, whereupon she changed into the shape of a beautiful maiden, revealed herself to be 'sovereignty' and hailed him as King of Tara. The word used for the inauguration of a king, *feis*, meant 'spending the night' and carried connotations of sexual intercourse with Meadbah, goddess of Tara, who also gave her name to the ritual drink Meduva preferred to a new king at his inauguration.

With the coming of Christianity into Ireland from the fifth century, the understanding of monarchy as having a sacred and spiritual dimension did not die. Indeed, in many ways it was reinforced by the gradual incorporation of insights and practices from the Old and New Testaments. For a long time pre-Christian inauguration rituals symbolizing the marriage of the king to his country coexisted with Christian consecration ceremonies centred on the sacred site of Tara. Christianity did bring one fundamental change in the way kings were viewed. Increasingly, it was the Church rather than the monarch that was seen as the principal intercessor between people and God. Kings lost part, although not all of their priestly role to bishops and clergy. However, they gained a new role as protectors of the Church and the Christian faith.

Kings were among the first converts to Christianity in the British Isles. In part this was because they were targeted by the early missionaries who realized that in tribal and hierarchical societies the way to reach people was through their rulers. Missionary work in a particular area could not succeed without the support of the king. With him on their side, missionaries could set up churches and monasteries and begin systematic evangelism of the people. For their part, kings were often impressed by the claims and powers of Christian priests who promised them a kingdom beyond this world and who became loyal and trusted advisers, fulfilling the counselling role previously occupied by druids and playing a key role in choosing the next ruler. The old Irish *Book of Ui Maine* tells of Diarmait wandering in the wilderness after being exiled by his father and meeting Ciaran. The saint, busy building a church, recognizes Diarmait as the one God wants to be king and says to him: 'Plant the post with me and suffer my hand to be above your hand, and your hand and your rule shall be over the men of Ireland before this hour comes again.'[4] The prophecy is fulfilled when the men of Ireland make Diarmait king. The story echoes the Old Testament theme of God's identification of the king through the figure of the prophet/saint and the subsequent popular acknowledgement of the divinely appointed one.

The extent to which Christianity created a new paradigm of sacred monarchy in the British Isles is well illustrated in the life and activities of Columba, the sixth-century Irish monk who is best known for founding the monastery on Iona. Both during his early years as a monk in Ireland, and his time as abbot of Iona, king-making was one of Columba's major preoccupations. He was in many ways instrumental in forging the close bonds between king and priest, and more broadly between crown and church, which were to be so important in defining the Christian character of monarchy in Britain. Columba himself came from royal stock, from the Conal sept of the Uí Néill family who supplied many of Ireland's high kings, and had he not taken monastic vows and clerical orders might well have become a king. As a monk, he maintained his contact and fascination with royalty, taking a keen interest in dynastic disputes in his native Ireland and forging links with rulers to aid his missionary and pastoral efforts in Scotland. He also ruled his own extensive family of monasteries centred on Iona much as an Irish king would rule his *tuath*, showing a mixture of fatherly benevolence and autocratic authority.

In an age when there was much political anarchy and violence as well as spiritual and cultural darkness, Columba looked to the new institution of monarchy as it was developing in Ireland to provide order, stability and community in place of the arbitrary rule of warlords and chieftains. He was happy to throw the support of the church behind kings who would exercise power under the law and in accordance with Christian principles of justice, humility and mercy. He also realized the benefits to the Church of having royal patronage and protection. His decision to leave Ireland and settle in the new Irish colony of Dál Riata on the west coast of Scotland may even have been encouraged by his Uí Néill relatives in order to promote an alliance with the rulers of this potentially powerful new kingdom. He built up extremely close relations with the king of Dál Riata, Conall mac Congall. Some sources suggest that Columba made Conall's stronghold at Dunadd on the Kintyre peninsula his first port of call after sailing across from Ireland and that the king subsequently gave him the island of Iona for his monastic foundation. The close relationship forged between Columba and Conall proved mutually beneficial to their successors. It ensured royal patronage and protection for the Church centred on Iona while greatly enhancing the prestige and legitimacy of the new Irish kingdom in Scotland. For the next 200 years or more the fortunes of the Columban monastic family and the royal house of Dál Riata were inextricably intertwined.

Thanks to Columba, sixth-century Dál Riata may well have been the first region in mainland Britain to experience

Christian kingship. It may also conceivably have been the site of the first-ever Christian coronation service in either Britain or Europe (see p. 94). Several of the earliest lives of Columba cast him in the role of king-maker. The one surviving fragment of the earliest life of the saint, written by Cummíne, the seventh abbot of Iona, in the 630s or 640s, tells of Columba promising the kingship to Conall's cousin, Aedán mac Gabhráin, and his descendants, on condition that they are loyal to his successors as abbots of Iona and his royal kinsmen in Ireland. In his slightly later life, Adamnan, the ninth abbot of Iona, devotes a chapter to this episode, describing an angel of the Lord visiting Columba and commanding him to ordain Aedán as king, which, after some initial reluctance, he does. Adamnan later describes the saint discussing with Aedán who will succeed him. The king mentions his three oldest sons, but the saint prophesies that each of them will be slaughtered in battle and asks Aedán if he has any other younger sons, prophesying that 'the one whom the Lord has chosen will run directly to my arms'. Aedán's younger sons are duly called and one of them, Eochaid Buide, rushes up and leans on Columba's bosom whereupon the saint kisses and blesses him and says: 'This one will survive to be king after you, and his sons will be kings after him.' This story, with its close echoes of the choosing of David to replace Saul, is clearly designed to present Columba in the guise of Samuel and to suggest that his king-making activities are in the tradition of the Old Testament.[5]

Columba's close interest in the fortunes of kings and princes was not only confined to his adopted Scottish homeland of Dál Riata. He continued to maintain close contact with his royal relations back in Ireland and, if Adamnan is to be believed, also prophesied about the outcome of their battles and dynastic disputes. He forged close relations with Roderc, king of the Strathclyde Britons, and made a long journey across the Scottish Highlands to see Brude, king of the Picts, possibly to secure safe passage for some of his monks who wished to go to Orkney. Royal patronage was extremely important not just

prowess in securing victory over his enemies. He is described as going into one battle carrying the image of the holy and perpetual Virgin Mary on his shoulders with the result that the pagan Saxons turned and fled. During another battle, identified as that which took place at Mount Badon around 516, he apparently bore a cross on his shoulders for three days and nights. Arthur was not the first ruler to enlist the power of Christianity against his enemies and to display its symbol as a battle standard. According to the historian Eusebius, the Roman emperor Constantine converted to Christianity after having a vision on the eve of a great battle against his rival Maxentius at Milvian Bridge on the River Tiber near Rome in 312. The emperor ordered his troops to paint the sign of the cross on their shields. His subsequent victory confirmed him in the new faith and led him to transform the status of Christianity from persecuted minority cult to the favoured and established religion of the Roman Empire.

Welsh medieval sources describe Arthur as the High King of Britain with a substantial base in the South West, a considerable Court and close links with the Welsh saints. They also weave a magic spell around him, suggesting that he had a cloak of invisibility and other supernatural attributes. The *Historia Regum Britanniae*, written by the twelfth-century chronicler Geoffrey of Monmouth, added further details to the increasingly elaborate tale of the king hailed as the personification of the British nation. According to him, Arthur was born at Tintagel in Cornwall, established his court at Caerleon-on-Usk (other contenders for Camelot are Winchester and Cadbury Castle in Somerset), achieved victories over the Scots and Picts as well as the Angles and Saxons, ruled from York as well as from the South West, conquered Ireland and Iceland, and planned to conquer the whole of Europe. Betrayed by treachery, he was mortally wounded while putting down a rebellion and carried off to the Isle of Avalon. Although a failure in political terms, this last Celtic king before the Anglo-Saxon takeover of Britain vowed to return to rescue his native land from its foreign thraldom. So was born the potent myth of the once and future king with its echoes of the Christian belief in the second coming of Jesus.

Geoffrey of Monmouth's account of King Arthur is also notable for taking the figure of Myrddin, a legendary Welsh seer and wild man of the woods, and turning him into Merlin, the druidic prophet and shaman at the royal court. Along with the dragons, prophecies and miraculous happenings introduced in Geoffrey's account, Merlin adds a touch of pagan wizardry to the story of Arthur. In later medieval reworkings, the Arthurian legends were made ever more fantastic and fanciful, being linked with the mysterious quest for the Holy Grail and wanderings to the other-world.

Retold and further embellished by Thomas Malory and more recent writers like T. H. White and Rosemary Sutcliff, the legends about King Arthur provide a fascinating blend of primal and Christian perspectives on the sacred dimension of monarchy. Both strains are evident in one of the most common versions of the story of how Arthur became high king of Britain. In it, Merlin, who had groomed Arthur for this role from birth but kept him out of the limelight, visits Dubricius, Archbishop of the Britons, in London. In Rosemary Sutcliff's words:

> Merlin held by an older faith than the Archbishop's and followed the patterns laid down by other gods. But Dubricius was a wise man, wise enough to allow for other wisdoms and other patterns beside his own. And he listened to what Merlin had to say; and he called a great gathering of knights and nobles and lesser kings for Christmas Day, promising that Jesus Christ who was born upon that day would show them by some miracle who was the rightful High King.[6]

The miracle duly occurs when during Mass on Christmas morning a block of marble appears in the churchyard. Embedded in it is a sword and written in letters of gold around the block is the message that whoever pulls the sword from

We're told this very special tree
grew from the staff of thorn,
brought by a man called Joseph
from the land where Christ was born.

It now is our tradition
to send a sprig of thorn
to greet Her Gracious Majesty
on the day that Christ was born.

This ceremony, which may have originated in pre-Reformation times but fell into abeyance and was revived in 1929 by a vicar of Glastonbury whose sister-in-law was a lady-in-waiting to Queen Mary, preserves a link between Arthurian legend and the modern British monarchy. Other current activities centred on Glastonbury also keep the Arthurian tradition of spiritual monarchy very much alive. The ecumenical Quest Community, based in the town, has a particular interest in 'the mystical, Arthurian and Christian heritage of Wessex from which the English royal line sprang' and emphasizes in its prayers and literature the continuing spiritual power of the symbolism of royalty. One of its founder members, Anne Stallybrass, has written of how 'the figures of Prince and Princess especially live in the soul of every child as spiritual realities, bearers of excellence, virtue, integrity, the power of righting wrong and the power of protection'.[8]

Like the Celts, the Anglo-Saxons also brought into Britain ideas of sacred kingship which were subsequently integrated into a Christian understanding of the spiritual dimension of monarchy. In Anglo-Saxon mythology, kings were descended from Wotan, or Odin, the high god of the Teutonic pantheon. As with the Celts, when Christianity came to the Anglo-Saxon kingdoms of England, kings were among the first to espouse the new faith. Aethelbert of Kent was possibly the earliest royal convert, soon after the arrival of Augustine's mission from Rome in 597. He was already well aware of the new faith through his wife Bertha, a Christian princess from the

Frankish royal house. Aethelbert's subsequent support for the Church led to the establishment of the first English bishoprics at Canterbury and Rochester. The King of Essex followed his example, supporting the establishment of a see in London in 604. By the mid-seventh century most of the Anglo-Saxon kings in England had been converted and in 655 Penda of Mercia, the last great pagan king, was killed in battle by Oswy, brother and successor of Oswald as King of Northumbria. The last kingdom to remain under pagan rule was the Isle of Wight which finally came under a Christian king around 686.

Not all the Anglo-Saxons kings came quickly to Christianity. It was often only after much deliberation with their counsellors. In several cases, as perhaps with Aethlebert, it was their queens who were converted first and who then brought their pagan husbands into the Christian fold, although the reverse could also happen – according to Bede, Raedwald, King of East Anglia, who died in 627, was seduced by his wife from Christianity back to the old pagan gods. The reasons why monarchs converted varied considerably. Some were undoubtedly impressed by the lifestyle and teaching of the missionaries and by their qualities of loyalty and discernment. The promise of salvation and a continuing kingdom in heaven as well as on earth was another potent factor. Like Constantine and Arthur, several Anglo-Saxon kings took to Christianity partly because it offered them the assistance of divine power against their enemies. Oswald erected a Cross before the contest with Cadwallon in 634 which brought him the kingdom of Northumbria. The site of the battle was subsequently named Heavenfield and associated with miraculous happenings. The power of the Cross was enlisted against the Anglo-Saxons as well as on their behalf. When Pictish forces led by King Angus confronted a much larger army of Angles and Saxons at Athelstaneford in 832, his prayers for deliverance were apparently rewarded by the appearance in the sky of the outline of a white diagonal cross. The Picts' subsequent victory was attributed to the divine power behind this vision, which is sometimes taken as the origin legend for the Scottish

Constantine had done when he called the Council of Nicaea in 325 and asserting the monarch's role as supreme governor of the church within his realms and his responsibility to arbitrate on doctrinal and procedural disputes.

Both Celtic and Anglo-Saxon Christianity emphasized the ties of loyalty and kinship and made a clear link between earthly and heavenly monarchy. Christ was seen as the King of the Archangels and the High King of Heaven, as in the eighth-century Irish poem known to us now as the hymn 'Be Thou My Vision'. In his book on Anglo-Saxon Christianity Paul Cavill points to the natural convergence of heroic and Christian concepts of loyalty and lordship.

> It was relatively easy for those brought up with an ethic of loyalty to a human lord to understand and translate that loyalty into a spiritual principle. Loyalty to one's lord becomes loyalty to the Lord. Early missionaries went straight for the kings, knowing that if they could convert the kings, then the men would follow. Loyalty to a secular lord, if he is a Christian, must mean that the one owing allegiance is also a Christian of some sort. Thus Christian teaching slips easily into a Germanic mould.[9]

While Christianity enhanced the power and prestige of kings by providing a religious aura and supernatural sanction, it also brought new obligations and responsibilities. Both changes had a profound impact, as the authors of a recent history of the British monarchy point out:

> Christianity transformed the very nature of kingship in England. It magnified the powers of kings and gave them more extensive rights, as well as emphasizing their obligations and duties in a Christian society. The emergence of Christian kingship was indubitably the most profound and revolutionary change that kingship underwent in the early medieval West ... From the kings' point of view, it meant more than shrugging off one

loyalty and set of rituals and adopting others: it transformed their attitudes to themselves and to their role on earth. Henceforth, they could look forward to joining the company of other kings under the aegis of the Heavenly King of Kings; they had His protection and favour and, in war, every expectation that He would give them the victory over their enemies and assure them of prosperity and fame in peacetime ... From the Church's point of view, royal protection and patronage were the keys to Christian advance and consolidation.[10]

One individual in particular came to epitomize the new ideal of Christian kingship both through his own writings and activities and through the cult that grew up around him. The Saxon king Alfred lived from around 849 to 899. The youngest son of King Ethelwulf of Wessex, he showed himself as a boy to be a devoted scholar of literature and lover of poetry. Following his mother's early death he accompanied his father on a pilgrimage to Rome where Pope Leo IV administered the rite of confirmation, an act magnified by Alfred's biographer Asser into a consecration to future kingship. His five older brothers were all killed by invading Danes during their brief reigns, and Alfred succeeded to the throne of Wessex around 871 with the threat of annihilation hanging over the kingdom. Thanks partly to his innovative use of naval power, he managed to beat back the Danes and secure their withdrawal from Wessex. In a relatively rare example of a ruler turning to Christianity in defeat rather than in victory, the vanquished Danish leader, Guthrum, forsook paganism and Alfred stood sponsor at his baptism, giving him the name Athelstan.

Having secured the safety of his kingdom, Alfred devoted the latter part of his reign to administrative and ecclesiastical reforms, and to encouraging learning and faith. He promulgated the first systematic set of laws in England, drawing heavily on Old Testament law codes, and seeking to promote the principles of justice and equity. He inaugurated a great movement of reform in the Church, personally translating

own intrinsic benefits. 'Study Wisdom,' he wrote, 'and, when you have learned it, condemn it not, for I tell you that by its means you may without fail attain to power, yea, even though not desiring it.'[14]

Solomon was not the only ancient Israelite king from whom Alfred drew inspiration and to whom he was compared. David, like him, had been anointed as a child above his brothers and lived as a fugitive in hiding before consolidating his crown through military prowess, and was another model. It has been suggested that the figure depicted in the centre of the Alfred jewel, the small golden pendant apparently made for him, which was found in Somerset in 1689 and is now in the Ashmolean Museum, Oxford, may be that of David, holding in his hands the rod of judgement and staff of comfort mentioned in Psalm 23, although there is another theory that it represents Christ as the personification of wisdom. Like David, Alfred saw himself as leading his people in worship and standing at the head of the Church just as he was at the head of law and government. The bishops who gathered around him as advisers and scholars or fulfilled episcopal duties in their sees were his spiritual servants and vassals. His writings express clearly the Anglo-Saxon fusion of notions of earthly and heavenly lordship. He believed that his own authority came from God who was his lord, and extended over his subjects to whom he was lord. For Alfred lordship was a sacred bond instituted by God himself for the purposes of human government. He even altered Jesus' second commandment from 'love your neighbour as yourself' to 'love your lord as you would love Christ himself'. The lord in his turn should show friendship and generosity to all of those who gave him their allegiance. In the words of his biographer, Richard Abels, Alfred believed in 'a doctrine of divine rewards and punishments rooted in a vision of a hierarchical Christian world-order in which God is the Lord to whom kings owe obedience and through whom they derive their authority over their followers'.

This was not a cynical use of religion to manipulate his subjects into obedience, but an intrinsic element in Alfred's world-view. He believed, as did other kings in ninth-century England and Francia, that God had entrusted him with the spiritual as well as the physical welfare of his people. If the Christian faith fell into ruin in his kingdom, if the clergy were too ignorant to understand the Latin words they butchered in their offices and liturgies, if the ancient monasteries and collegiate churches lay deserted out of indifference, he was answerable before God, as Josiah had been. Alfred's ultimate responsibility was the pastoral care of his people.[15]

A key role in both the unifying and Christianizing of Britain was played by Alfred's grandson Athelstan, King of Wessex from 924 to 939. At a meeting at Eamont Bridge, near Penrith in Cumbria in 927, his supremacy was acknowledged by the kings of the Scots, the Welsh, the Strathclyde Britons and the Northumbrians, who also agreed to suppress idolatrous practices in their territories. This gathering, the first occasion when the rulers of the Celtic realms in the British mainland paid homage to an English king, has been taken as marking the establishment of Christianity as the accepted and official religion of the new United Kingdom. Holding together Anglo-Saxon Wessex, Mercia and Northumbria, the Britons of Strathclyde, Wales and Cornwall, the Scots and the Anglo-Scandinavians, Athelstan could reasonably claim to be, as coins issued during his reign proclaimed, '*rex totius Britanniae*'. A passionate collector of religious relics, he took his responsibilities as a Christian ruler seriously, describing himself as 'supervisor of the Christian household' of his extensive realms. Like the Roman emperor Constantine, he actively promoted Christianity and promulgated laws to make Sunday trading illegal.

The religious compact at Eamont Bridge seems to have been made specifically to counter the reintroduction of pagan practices into parts of Britain taken over by the Vikings. Although they continued to dominate much of Northern and Eastern England during the tenth century they did not substantially destroy the pattern of Christian kingship established by the Celts and Anglo-Saxons. Indeed, several Viking monarchs became exemplary Christian kings in the Alfredian mould. One such was Canute, whose famous encounter with the waves was, according to one tradition, an exercise in Christian humility in which the king rebuked the flattery of his nobles by demonstrating that not even he could halt the movement of the tide.

By the end of the first millennium the institution of Christian kingship was firmly established throughout the British Isles. Monarchs were the principal patrons and protectors of the Church. The great majority of the monasteries and minsters which provided pastoral care and worship before the establishment of parish churches were royal foundations, built on land provided by kings and supported by their endowments. Establishing religious houses remained a favourite royal activity, following in the tradition of Alfred who had set up a monastery at Athelney, his base in Somerset, and Athelstan, who founded Malmesbury Abbey where he was subsequently buried. Edgar, King of the Anglo-Saxons from 959 to 975, and his wife were particularly assiduous planters of religious houses where monks and nuns engaged in a ceaseless round of penitential prayer. The tradition was continued by later Anglo-Norman monarchs and in eleventh-century Scotland by the Hungarian-born Queen Margaret, who brought in monks from the new Continental religious orders and supported the ailing religious community on Iona.

As well as bringing major new responsibilities in providing for and defending the Church, Christian kingship also emphasized the monarch's role as the fount of justice, order and peace. This latter aspect is well brought out in a charter drawn up in 1063 by Edward the Confessor:

I, Edward, through the contribution of divine providence,

by which all things are governed, appointed king and defender of the English bounds, invoke God with unsleeping mind not only that I may be famed for my royal protection, but also that, invested with God's aid, I may prevail in thought and deed against God's enemies and earn the right to advance my kingdom in the quietness of peace ... it is our duty courageously to oppose the wicked and take good men as models, by enriching the churches of God, relieving those oppressed by wicked judges, and by judging equitably between the powerful and humble: all things which are pleasing to God.[16]

Christian kingship brought new titles as well as new responsibilities for Britain's rulers. Perhaps the first to be appropriated was that of ruling through the grace of God, or *Deo Gratia*, the idea that is still expressed on every coin of the realm through the abbreviation DG. The late eighth-century Anglo-Saxon king Offa described himself as 'by the divine controlling grace king of the Mercians'. From the mid-tenth century several English kings also began styling themselves Christ's vicar or deputy. Edgar described himself in this way when founding a new monastery at Winchester in 966. He is pictured in the monastery's charter book flanked by St Peter and the Virgin Mary and offering the new foundation to Christ. Some years later King Ethelred II, known as the Unready, stated that 'the king must be regarded not only as the head of the church but also as a vicar of Christ among Christian folk'.[17]

The Christian king's role as Vicar of Christ was understood at various levels. Like the later title, Defender of the Faith, it could be taken as a reminder of the monarch's responsibility to promote the Christian faith and defend its cause, a view which reached its apogee during the Crusades when Richard I led a great army to Palestine to stop the holy places of Christianity falling into Muslim hands. It also affirmed a priestly, quasi-episcopal view of monarchy in the tradition of Melchizedek. This aspect, which was reinforced by the growing practice of anointing kings at their coronation described in the next chapter, is clearly to the fore in an anonymous clerical tract probably written in the twelfth century:

> Kings and Priests have a common unction of holy oil. A common spirit of sanctification, a common quality of benediction, the name and power of God and Christ in common. ... Both Kings and Priests are deified and sanctified by the grace of unction and by the consecration of their benediction. ... If therefore the King and the Priest are both, by grace, God's and Christ's of the Lord, whatever they do by virtue of this grace is not done by man but by a God and a Christ of the Lord. And when the King gives a bishopric or a Priest a kingdom, it is not a man who gives them but a God and a Christ of the Lord.[18]

It is significant that this tract refers specifically to the royal appointment of bishops and priests. Several historians have suggested that it may have been drawn up to counter moves on the part of the papacy to prohibit the royal investiture of bishops. In claiming that they acted as vicars of Christ, England's Norman kings were making clear that they were not the Pope's vassals. The high doctrine of Christian kingship associated with the title Vicar of Christ was developed in direct challenge to the attempt by the papacy to assert more control over the emerging national churches in Europe. Episcopal investiture was the main battleground over which the competing claims of king and Pope were fought. The Norman kings' practice of directly investing English bishops with ring and crozier as well as nominating and consecrating them under royal writ provoked fierce controversy with Rome. A compromise was reached in 1107 by Henry I and Anselm whereby bishops received their ring and staff at their consecration, having already done homage to the king. This was not the end of hostilities between the English crown and Rome however, and both Henry II and John found themselves excommunicated. In 1213 John was forced to concede defeat and acknowledge the subordination of the English Church to the Pope.

Behind this struggle lay the realization by medieval monarchs that the Church was one of the most important institutions in their realm and a desire to ensure that its leaders were also chief ministers of the Crown. The close relationship between king and archbishop established by Anglo-Saxon kings was continued and, indeed, strengthened after the Norman Conquest with William the Conqueror bringing Lanfranc as his Court chaplain from Normandy and then installing him in the see of Canterbury. Not that there was any doubt who was master between archbishop and king, as was shown by the murder of Thomas à Becket in 1170 apparently on the orders of Henry II in one of the most disgraceful episodes in the history of the British monarchy's dealings with the Church.

The idea that kings were superior to bishops was also asserted at a less brutal and more theological level. The anonymous twelfth-century tract quoted above noted that both kings and bishops 'are in spirit *Christus et Deus*: and in their offices they act as antitypes and images of Christ and God; the priest of the Priest, the king of the King'. However, it went on to point out, 'the priest acts as the antitype of the inferior office and nature, that is, His humanity: the king, as that of the superior office and nature, that is, His divinity'.[19] This tract, in fact, asserted that monarchs uniquely imitated Christ in having two natures and being both human and divine:

> The king is a twinned being, human and divine, just like the God-man, although the king is two-natured by grace only and within time, and not by nature and within eternity. The terrestrial king is not, but becomes a twin personality through his anointment and consecration.[20]

This extremely high view of kingship, in which the monarch was seen not just as Christ's vicar but as his *mimetes*, literally imitator or impersonator, was probably rare and is found in its most developed form in this particular text. Much more common was the view that as a bishop bore the image of Christ, so a king bore the image of God. This notion clearly pervades the treatise on kingship written by the great medieval scholastic theologian Thomas Aquinas around 1260. Principally intended to inculcate among rulers the virtues of peace and concern for the well-being of their subjects and to remind them that they are answerable to God and should look to him rather than to men for their rewards, Aquinas' tract described the king as 'the minister of God in governing the people' and went on to spell out the high nature of his calling:

> The greatness of kingly virtue appears in this, that he bears a special likeness to God, since he does in his kingdom what God does in the world ... Let the king recognize that such is the office which he undertakes, namely, that he is to be in the kingdom what the soul is in the body, and what God is in the world. If he reflects seriously upon this, a zeal for justice will be enkindled in him when he contemplates that he has been appointed to this position in place of God, to exercise judgment in his kingdom; further, he will acquire the gentleness of clemency and mildness when he considers as his own members those individuals who are subject to his rule.[21]

If Aquinas' view remains broadly consonant with the biblical models of kingship, the medieval notion of the king's two natures seems to go well beyond them. The miraculous powers associated with certain monarchs might similarly seem a hangover from the world of primal sacred kingship, although they belong to the general cult of saints and relics which developed in the Middle Ages. Oswald of Northumbria was perhaps the first English king to possess apparently miraculous powers after his death. Among several subsequent monarchs credited with similar posthumous powers, the most interesting is surely Edward the Martyr, hacked to death on the orders of his wicked stepmother in 978. His body was removed from its original burial place at Wareham in Dorset in 980 after miracles apparently took place as a result of his intercession and reinterred at Shaftesbury Abbey. Bones unearthed in an archaeological dig there in 1931 were later offered to both the Anglican and Roman Catholic churches but were declined for reinternment as relics. However, the Russian Orthodox Church in exile accepted them and enshrined the remains in 1984 in their chapel at Brookwood Cemetery in Surrey. A High Court ruling ordered the bones to be deposited in the Midland Bank in Woking but in 1988 they were returned to the Orthodox Church in Brookwood where they remain to this day.

Perhaps the most striking example of the survival and, indeed, revival of the shamanistic aspects of sacral kingship was the development of the practice of touching for the king's evil, which became widespread in medieval England and France. The notion that monarchs possess miraculous healing powers does not have much scriptural warrant. There is a story in 2 Kings 5 about a Syrian army commander suffering from leprosy being sent to the King of Israel for a cure, although in the event, it is through the agency of the prophet Elisha rather than through the king that he is cured. The belief in royal healing powers could, of course, be related to the idea of the king's two natures and Christ-like character, although it may well have been a reflection of a more primal sense of the religious aura and magical power of monarchy. The disease for which the royal touch was regarded as particularly efficacious, known popularly as scrofula and in medical terminology as tuberculous adenitis, was an inflammation of the lymph nodes which often had the effect of making the victim's face putrid. The first English king who is clearly recorded as touching for scrofula was Henry II. Henry I may well also have done so and two chroniclers of his reign, William of Malmesbury and Ailred of Rievaulx, suggested that the practice had originated with Edward the Confessor, a tradition taken up by Shakespeare in *Macbeth* where Malcolm, fleeing from the hatred of the Scottish tyrant and taking refuge in Edward's Court, is impressed both by his miracles and by the wider aura of sacred monarchy:

> How he solicits heaven,
> himself best knows; but strangely visited people,
> all sworn and ulcerous, pitiful to the eye,
> the mere despair of surgery, he cures,
> hanging a golden stamp about their necks,
> put on with holy prayers; and 'tis spoken,
> to the succeeding royalty he leaves
> the healing benediction. With this strange virtue,
> he hath a heavenly gift of prophecy;
> and sundry blessings hang about his throne,
> that speak full of grace.
>
> (*Macbeth*, act IV, sc. iii)

The golden stamps referred to in this passage were specially minted coins, known as 'touch pieces', hung by the king around the necks of those suffering from scrofula. Other coins, known as angels, were distributed as alms. As well as touching those afflicted by the disease, monarchs also often made the sign of the cross and sometimes washed affected parts with water. There was more than one theory as to the source of the royal healing powers. One view held that they arose out of Edward the Confessor's personal sanctity and were conveyed to his successors through their being consecrated with his relics. A more common belief was that they derived from the monarch's anointing. A letter by an ecclesiastic attached to Henry II's court, which describes the king's healing powers as extending to 'that plague affecting the groin', states that 'to attend upon the king is something sacred, for the king himself is holy; he is the Anointed of the Lord'.[22]

A second, related custom which developed in the Middle Ages was the distribution by English kings of cramp rings, which by virtue of their royal consecration were held to have the power to restore strength to epileptics and relieve muscular spasms. The rings were made out of gold and silver coins placed on the altar of the royal chapel by the king in the course of his Good Friday devotions. The origins of this practice, which seems to have been initiated by Edward II and lasted until the reign of Henry V, were said to lie in healing techniques found in the books of Solomon and brought to Britain by Joseph of Arimathea.

Marc Bloch, author of the classic study on the practice of touching for the king's evil, has written that 'the conception of sacred royalty imbued with the miraculous runs all through the Middle Ages'.[23] It did not, in fact, die out with the Reformation. Although the Tudor monarchs were not enthusiastic about the practice, the Stuarts revived it with a vengeance. Charles II touched 23,000 people in the four years following the restoration of the monarchy in 1660, and James II 4422 between March and December 1685. The last reigning British monarch to perform the ritual was Queen Anne in April 1714. The Book of Common Prayer included a service for the healing of the sick by the monarch from 1633 to 1715. The Jacobite pretenders kept the practice going and Prince Charles Edward Stuart held a healing ceremony in Edinburgh in 1745. There are still lingering echoes of the association of royalty with miraculous healing powers. Philip Ziegler noted that as Queen Elizabeth II walked through crowds during the celebrations of her Jubilee celebrations in 1977, 'their hands stretched out to her as if she were a medieval monarch whose touch would cure'.[24] Diana, Princess of Wales, exhibited an approach to the sick and the suffering which in many ways recalled the old royal healing touch.

Another religious ceremony which seems to have begun around the same time as touching for the king's evil still remains an important annual event in the royal calendar. King John is the first English monarch recorded as having distributed alms to his people in the context of a service on Maundy Thursday, in his case at Knaresborough in Yorkshire in 1210. The practice was continued by successive monarchs, with Henry IV ordering that the number of recipients of

Maundy money, clothes and shoes should correspond with the monarch's age. During the Royal Maundy Service the monarch personally washed the feet of the poor in imitation of Jesus' actions at the last supper. Elizabeth I delegated this task to the yeomen of the royal laundry but the Stuart kings revived it and the last monarch personally to wash the feet of the poor was James II. Thereafter the task of washing the Maundy recipients' feet was undertaken by the almoner, an official drawn from the ranks of the royal chaplains whose role originally included gathering food from the royal table and visiting the sick, orphans, widows and prisoners. The foot-washing was abandoned in 1754. The monarch's personal participation in the distribution of alms, by now restricted to specially minted silver coins, also lapsed until it was reinstated by George V in 1932. Elizabeth II has made the significant innovation of holding the Royal Maundy Service in different cathedrals around the country rather than just in London. The recipients of Maundy money are pensioners of modest income, most of whom are selected on the basis of their service to church and community. The annual service remains an important symbolic expression of the monarchy's Christian inspiration and both the Lord High Almoner (currently the Bishop of Manchester) and the sub-almoner, traditionally the sub-dean of the Chapel Royal, wear linen aprons as a reminder of the foot-washing ritual inspired by Jesus' own example which was once a central part of the service – as, perhaps, it might be again.

The Maundy Service was one of many activities that came under the care of the Chapel Royal, as the ecclesiastical arm of the royal household came to be known. The history of this fascinating institution, which survives to this day in the form of a group of clergy and choristers who regularly sing divine service in St James's Palace and the Queen's Chapel, Marlborough Gate, and also take part in other royal and state services, is well told in David Baldwin's *The Chapel Royal Ancient and Modern* (1990). It underwent considerable expansion during the Middle Ages and by Henry V's reign had a strength of 27, of whom at least half were in priests' orders and the rest made up of choristers and clerks. The entire Chapel Royal travelled with the king and the English army to France where they celebrated Mass on the night before the Battle of Agincourt in 1415. The famous Agincourt Song, beginning '*Deo gracias, Anglia*', was almost certainly composed by a member of the Chapel Royal, possibly in thanksgiving for the victory at the battle and to be sung at Henry's triumphant homecoming.

Standing at the very heart of the royal household, the Chapel Royal epitomized the inextricable link between the institutions of church and monarchy which had grown up together in medieval Britain. It also reflected the ambiguity in the spiritual dimension of medieval kingship. Part of its role was undoubtedly to support and strengthen the ruler and add to his religious aura. Its central function, however, was the daily worship of Almighty God before whom kings bowed down as much as commoners. Every royal residence and hunting lodge had its chapel where prayers were said and the Eucharist celebrated.

The Middle Ages saw the flowering of the cult of Christian monarchy in all its branches – splendid and servant-like, pious and chivalrous, full of knightly virtue, gung-ho triumphalism and supernatural magic. At times it might seem over the top, as when Richard II used the titles 'highness' and 'majesty' and had himself depicted in the Walton Triptych in the presence of the saints and the Virgin Mary. Yet if medieval monarchy developed a magnificence that echoed the splendour of Solomon's Court and its more worldly trappings, it also espoused the theme of the servant-king and acknowledged its utter dependence upon God's grace. Both of these elements were reflected in the civic triumphs staged in the later Middle Ages for the entrance of monarchs into the cities of their realms. Gordon Kipling's fascinating study, *Enter The King*, shows the extent to which these events were built around the liturgical themes of Advent and Epiphany with the king being portrayed as the type of Christ with *Majestas Domini* and the queen as the *Virgo Mediatrix* and bearer of heavenly glory. If the ceremonial entries of medieval monarchs into their capital cities were deliberately modelled on Jesus' entry into Jerusalem, then they also often served as a reminder of the journey to be undertaken by all souls, including royal ones, towards death and the throne of heaven. The intensely spiritual dimension to monarchy in the Middle Ages produced humility as well as triumphalism, as reflected in this prayer by one of the last and perhaps most saintly of the medieval kings of England, Henry VI:

> O Lord Jesus Christ, who hast created and redeemed me, and hast brought me hither where I am: thou knowest what thou wouldst do with me; do with me according to thy will, with mercy. Amen.[25]

4

The coronation service

It is the coronation service more than any other institution or event that underlines the essentially spiritual and sacred nature of British monarchy. Packed with religious symbolism and imagery, it exudes mystery and magic, binds together church and state through the person of the monarch and clearly proclaims the derivation of all power and authority from God and the Christian basis on which government is exercised, justice administered and the state defended. Here, if anywhere, we find the divinity which, as Shakespeare so rightly observed, hedges around the English throne. This has been as true in relatively recent times as in the heyday of Divine Right theory in the seventeenth century. On the day of the coronation of Queen Elizabeth II in 1953 the Archbishop of Canterbury solemnly announced that England had been brought closer to the kingdom of heaven. More recently Clifford Longley has written:

> The Coronation of our Queen was an act of God performed by human hands, and the assembly held its breath at the mystery and wonder of it. It was one of the central acts of statehood, the moment whereby all temporal authority in the realm flowing from the king was legitimised and sanctified. This is the doctrine of Christian kingship.[1]

At their coronations kings and queens are not simply crowned and enthroned but consecrated, set apart and anointed, dedicated to God and invested with sacerdotal garb and symbolic insignia. Often following after the accession of a new monarch by a year or more, coronations are primarily religious services rather than constitutional ceremonies. In several early accounts they are described as benedictions or ordinations, and from the tenth century onward as consecrations, with the king being described after his anointing as *rex ordinatus*. The French used the term 'sacring'. The actual crowning and enthronement is just one of five distinct elements in the coronation service, the others being recognition by the assembled congregation of their sovereign, administration of the coronation oath, anointing with holy oil and investiture with the royal regalia.

The United Kingdom coronation service has been subtly adapted over the centuries but has retained the same basic format used in England for over a thousand years. It is closely modelled on the inauguration ceremonies for the kings of Israel as described in the Old Testament. Its most solemn moment, the anointing of the new monarch with holy oil, is directly compared to the anointing of Solomon and accompanied by the singing of the verses from 1 Kings 1: 'Zadok the priest and Nathan the prophet anointed Solomon king; and all the people rejoiced and said: God save the king, Long live the king, May the king live for ever. Amen. Hallelujah.' Since 1727 these words have been sung to G. F. Handel's thrilling setting written for the coronation of George II. Coronation sermons have frequently contained references to Solomon, and also to David and Josiah. The sermon preached at Charles II's Scottish coronation at Scone in 1651 also mentioned Saul, Joash, Ahaziah, Asa, Hezekiah, and even the wicked queen Athaliah to whom Charles' mother was compared.

The strong Old Testament influence is also evident in the centrality of the covenant theme in British coronations. Through the solemn oaths sworn near the beginning of the service and the act of homage towards the end, God, monarch and people are bound together in a three-way covenant. Not surprisingly, the psalms have long played a prominent part in coronation services. Settings by Handel of the opening verses of Psalm 21, 'The king shall rejoice', and verses from Psalm 89,

'Let thy hand be strengthened' were sung as the opening and closing anthems at the coronations of George II and George III. Elizabeth II's coronation began with the opening verses of Psalm 122, 'I was glad when they said unto me, we will go to the house of the Lord', set to the majestic tune written by Hubert Parry for the coronation of Edward VII in 1902.

The development of coronation services based on the Old Testament model played a key role in the transition from primal sacred kingship to Christian monarchy. Crownings and enthronements were a central feature of pre-Christian kingship and they often involved rituals indicating the divinity of the new monarch. With the coming of Christianity, kings were no longer seen as gods. Through being anointed at their coronations, however, they were set apart and given quasi-priestly status. Much reference was made to Melchizedek as the model priest-king in early Christian coronation orders and even as late as 1308 he was explicitly cited as the model for the king of England. The priestly, and even episcopal attributes of the monarch remained a significant theme in the coronation service but the emphasis shifted from the Melchizedekian model of the priest-king to the notion of the monarch as one who rules by the grace and through the authority of God. While preserving the concept of popular choice, symbolized by the act of recognition at the beginning of the service, the Christian coronation emphasized the monarch's crowning by God rather than by people. As such it easily accommodated and, indeed, facilitated the transition from popular election to hereditary succession which occurred in both Celtic and Anglo-Saxon monarchy. In Christian coronations, the focus was not on choosing a king, or even crowning and enthroning him, but rather on invoking the divine blessing, setting him apart and reminding him of the derivation of his power from God and of his responsibilities to rule wisely, justly and merci-fully. Christian consecration took over from constitutional investiture as the main function of the coronation ceremony which came to be seen as a religious service for which the monarch prepared with spiritual reflection and prayer and which generally took place in the context of a celebration of Holy Communion.

It is not clear when the first Christian consecration or inauguration of a monarch took place. Gildas, a Welsh monk writing in the sixth century, speaks about the unction or anointing of British kings ruling after the withdrawal of the Romans. Adamnan tells of Columba being three times visited by an angel commanding him to ordain Aedán to the kingship of Dál Riata according to the rubrics laid down in a glass book. If he is to be believed, the ordination which Columba duly performed on Iona in 574, by laying his hand on Aedán's head and blessing him, is the first clearly recorded Christian coronation of a king not only in the British Isles but anywhere in Europe. This is certainly how it has been interpreted. A purple passage in *The Times*' special supplement on the coronation of 1937 noted that 'our first remote glimpse of the consecration of a king on British soil is by a ray of dim religious light falling upon the sacred isle of Iona'.[2] A recent monograph argues, however, that 'the consecration of Aedán in the *Vita Columbae* must now be regarded as propaganda and not as history'.[3] According to its author, Michael Enright, Adamnan, writing at the end of the seventh century, invented the story of Aedán's ordination by Columba in order to bolster the concept of Christian kingship in general and more specifically to support the claim of the abbots of Iona in his own time to consecrate the kings of Dál Riata.

Anachronistic as it may be, Adamnan's reference suggests that by the late seventh century abbots of Iona may have been consecrating the kings of Dál Riata, using Columba's supposed ordination of Aedán as a precedent. If this is the case, then it is still a very early example of Christian coronations being carried out in the British Isles. The ceremony probably took place on the summit of the rocky crag of Dunadd in mid-Argyll, the site of pre-Christian inauguration rites, where the king placed his foot in a specially carved indentation in the rock to signal his marriage to the land and the continuity of his succession. A modern artist's impression of a Christian coronation at

Dunadd in Ewan Campbell's book, *Saints and Sea Kings: The First Kingdom of the Scots*, shows the abbot of Iona with his crook consecrating the king on the rocky promontory, with nobles and monks looking on. This may well be how successive kings of Dál Riata were inaugurated in the centuries following Columba. The ceremony almost certainly blended Christian and pre-Christian elements, with a priest presiding but the king still placing his foot in the rock-cut footprint. This particular feature of pre-Christian ritual was preserved throughout the Middle Ages in the ceremony of inauguration for the Lord of the Isles which took place at Finlaggan on Islay and was conducted by the Bishop of Argyll and the Isles in the context of the celebration of Mass. The incoming lord, clad in a white habit to symbolize innocence and integrity, received a white rod and sword while standing in a footprint carved into the stone to signify that he would walk in the footsteps of his predecessors.

The coming of Christian consecrations did not mean the ending of other symbolic practices associated with royal inaugurations in pre-Christian times. Many monarchs continued to be crowned sitting on stones, chosen both for their symbolic strength and stability and because their enduring nature enabled succeeding generations to enthrone monarchs on the same seat. The coronation stone at Kingston upon Thames did duty for the crowning of Christian Anglo-Saxon kings, as it had for their pagan predecessors, as that on the rock of Cashel did for the kings of Munster. The Stone of Scone was almost certainly used for all Scottish coronations from that of Kenneth Mac Ailpín in the mid-ninth century until its removal by Edward I in 1296. Although the church assumed responsibility for coronations, with its priests taking the druids' role of crowning the king and presenting him with the symbols of white rod and sword, the ceremonies long continued in their old pre-Christian outdoor sites, often on a rocky outcrop like Dunadd or Cashel. It was only after the Norman conquest that coronations were moved into church buildings, but even then they continued to retain some of the symbolism and ritual of pre-Christian sacred kingship.

While pre-Christian practices of enthronement and investiture with weapons and regalia were incorporated into the new Christian coronation services, other new elements distinguished them from what had gone before. The replacement of the traditional warrior's helmet by a *corona* or crown was an important symbolic step in the Christianization of royal inauguration rituals. From the time of Constantine, the soldier's torque, similar to those worn around the neck, was replaced by a crown or diadem for the coronation of emperors. Murals and mosaics depict emperors being crowned by a heavenly hand, perhaps echoing depictions in early Christian art of martyrs being crowned from heaven. The crown preserved the association with sacrifice found in the shamanistic torque but also introduced Christian notions of martyrdom and consecration and drew on imagery found in both the Old and New Testaments. Some scholars suggest that it derives from the rays of glory which played around the head of Moses on his descent from Mount Sinai. The action of Pope Leo III in placing a crown on the head of Charlemagne on 25 December 800 clearly signalled the Church's takeover of the imperial inauguration process.

More important than the substitution of crown for helmet in Christianizing royal inauguration rituals was the introduction of the Old Testament practice of anointing the new monarch. If Adamnan's account of Columba's ordination of Aedán in 574 is fictitious, the first Christian king in Europe to have been anointed may have been Wamba of Spain in 672. Historians are generally agreed that full-scale Christian inauguration rites for monarchs involving ecclesiastical blessing and anointing in the context of a proper liturgical service were probably developed in the eighth century by the Merovingians, drawing on earlier Byzantine practices in the Eastern Roman Empire. Some maintain that the first well-attested anointing of a European monarch did not take place until 751 when the Frankish king Pippin was crowned and anointed in a ceremony which Enright suggests might well have been influenced by Adamnan's account of Columba's ordination of Aedán. Orders of services which have survived from the archives of Egbert, Archbishop of York from 734 to 766, include what is described as 'Mass for Kings on the day of their Benediction', suggesting that the four kings who acceded to the throne of Northumbria during his time as archbishop may have been anointed by him. However, there is no direct record of their coronations and the earliest clearly documented royal anointing in England is that of Ecgfith, the son of Offa, who was anointed King of Mercia by visiting papal legates in 787. Seven years later Atri of Munster became the first Irish king known to have been anointed.

The practice of anointing kings was largely confined to England, Ireland, France and Sicily. It does not seem to have been taken up in Scotland until 1331 when David II was crowned and anointed, apparently in response to a request from Robert the Bruce and according to the terms of a Bull from Pope John XXI. Scottish monarchs continued to be anointed through the period of the Reformation, by bishops in the case of James VI and Charles I and by Presbyterian ministers in the case of Anne of Denmark, James VI's consort. However, there was no anointing for Charles II at Scone in 1651, in what was the last coronation to be carried out in Scotland and the only one of a reigning monarch to be celebrated according to Presbyterian practice.

The first English coronation of which both a clear record and a full order survive was that of Edgar in 973, twelve years after he had become king of England. The long delay may be explained by the desire of the Church to wait until he was 31, the age at which priesting took place. Certainly his coronation, which was held on Whit Sunday, the traditional day for ordinations to the priesthood, laid considerable emphasis on the theme of consecration and the sacerdotal aspects of kingship. Bedecked with the roses of martyrdom and the lilies of chastity and clad in priestly robes, Edgar was anointed and crowned by Dunstan, Archbishop of Canterbury, in Bath Abbey. His wife Aelfthryth was anointed as queen at the same ceremony. Despite its pagan setting, the tenor of the coronation service was strongly Christian with the king being entrusted with the protection and supervision of the church and graced with the titles *rex dei gratia* and *vicarus dei*. In 1973 Queen Elizabeth II and the Duke of Edinburgh visited Bath Abbey to give thanks for 1,000 years of English monarchy.

The order drawn up by Dunstan, which seems to have borrowed from Carolingian and Frankish rites as well as from indigenous Celtic and Anglo-Saxon practices, contained many of the key elements found in all subsequent English coronations. The oaths which the king was required to swear were similar to those in the orders used by Archbishop Egbert of York more than 200 years earlier, when the king swore that 'the Church of God and all Christian people keep true peace at every time', that 'he forbids all robberies and all iniquities unto all degrees' and that 'he commands righteousness and mercy in all judgments'. Dunstan's *Ordo* also included anointing, enthronement, crowning with gold helmet and investiture of the monarch with a short sceptre and a long rod. At the close of the service all those present hailed the king with words taken directly from the Old Testament, '*Vivat rex*', and the nobles bound themselves to their new ruler with a kiss. Dunstan's *Ordo* clearly established clerical control over royal inauguration rites in England, and specifically the key role of the Archbishop of Canterbury in presiding over the ceremony.

A particularly full record survives of a second coronation over which Dunstan presided: that of Ethelred II at Kingston upon Thames in 979. At his baptism, which had also been at the hands of Dunstan, the infant Ethelred had caused some consternation by urinating into the font and it was perhaps partly in atonement for this act of sacrilege that the coronation service began with the king prostrating himself before the altar while the *Te Deum* was sung. The service was full of Old Testament references. The opening prayer of consecration, at which the crown was held over the king's head, invoked the coronation of David and asked that Ethelred might have 'the faithfulness of Abraham, the meekness of Moses, the courage of Joshua, the humility of David and the wisdom of Solomon'.[4] The prayer of anointing began, 'O Christ, anoint this king with the power with which thou hast anointed priests, kings, prophets and martyrs.'[5] Following promises by the king to preserve the Church and govern with justice and equity, his investiture with a sword, sceptre and staff, and the consecration of the queen, Dunstan preached on the duties of a consecrated king, describing him as the shepherd over his people and reminding him that while ruling justly would earn him 'worship in this world' as well as God's mercy, any departure from his duties would lead to punishment at Doomsday.

The Norman Conquest brought a more settled succession with the hereditary principle replacing election and choice by nobles. This confirmed the function of the coronation not as a king-making ceremony but as a religious service in which the monarch whose accession was already secure was consecrated and given divine blessing. Orders used for the coronation of Norman kings broadly followed Dunstan's Anglo-Saxon *Ordo*. The coronation of William I on Christmas Day 1066 was the first to take place in the newly built Westminster Abbey, which became the venue for the coronation of virtually all subsequent English monarchs. William was actually crowned by Aldred, Archbishop of York, but after some wrangling in the twelfth century the principle was established that only the Archbishop of Canterbury was entitled to crown the king and queen.

Since 1307 every English sovereign, with the exception of Mary I and Mary II, has been crowned while seated on the special coronation chair made on the orders of Edward I to house the Stone of Scone which he brought from Scotland in 1296 and dedicated to Edward the Confessor. Before its spiriting away by the 'Hammer of the Scots', the stone had played a key role in the coronation of Scottish kings. A potent symbol of Scottish identity, it was stolen from Westminster Abbey in 1950 by Scottish nationalists, recovered and finally returned to Scotland in 1996, with the understanding that it will be brought back to London for future coronations. This relatively insignificant piece of red sandstone, weighing about 400lb, cracked through the middle and decorated only by a very simple cross, carries a huge weight of religious symbolism, and its legendary history illustrates well the sacred aura surrounding the British monarchy. Even Oliver Cromwell had himself installed as Lord Protector seated on the coronation throne and the Stone of Scone.

Legend has it that the Stone of Scone, or Stone of Destiny as it is sometimes called, started life as the pillow on which Jacob slept when he had his dream of the ladder leading up to heaven as recounted in Genesis 28.12-17. The biblical story recounts that after rising early in the morning, Jacob took the stone that he had put under his head and set it up for a pillar, having poured oil on top of it. He called the place where God had delivered his promise to the descendants of Abraham Bethel. Many years later God told Jacob to return to Bethel where he renamed him Israel and said, 'a nation and a company of nations shall come from you, and kings shall spring from you' (Genesis 35.11). Again Jacob set up a pillar of stone in the place where God had spoken to him and poured oil on it. Some stories identify this with the pillar beside which Abimelech was crowned King of Israel and Josiah made his covenant with the Lord to keep his commandments and statutes.

The next chapter in the legendary history of the coronation stone provides an origin legend for the Scots and forges a link between Old Testament kingship, the pharaohs of Egypt and the kings of Ireland. There are various versions of the story. One recounts that around 580BC, when the Babylonians under King Nebuchadnezar were invading Israel, the prophet Jeremiah and King Zedekiah's daughter, Tea, the last survivor of the Davidic line, smuggled the sacred stone out of Israel so that it would not fall into the hands of the Babylonian invaders. They went first to Egypt as guests of the Pharaoh and then via Spain to Ireland where Tea married Eochaid, king of Ireland, and took the name Scota. According to another version, the stone remained in Egypt for some time where it became the property of the country's rulers before being taken to Spain by Scota, Pharaoh's daughter, and subsequently to Ireland by one of her descendants, Simon Brek. This links up with the wider origin legend for the Celtic peoples of the British Isles as the descendants of the lost tribe of Dan and also with stories of the appearance in early sixth-century Ireland of an elderly prophet who made laws based on the Ten Commandments by which the nations of Ireland were said to be governed for the next 1000 years.

In its 'Irish period', the stone acquired the name *Lia Fail*, or Stone of Destiny, and is said to have been sited at Tara, the holy hill on which Ireland's high kings were crowned. A piece of it was apparently broken off and taken to the Irish colony of Dál Riata in Argyllshire, possibly even by Columba who, according to some stories, used it as his pillow or his altar. After residing at Iona for a time, and possibly being used at Dunadd for the crowning of Dál Riatan kings, it was taken to Dunstaffnage Castle near Oban, the seat and burial place of later Dál Riatan kings. Around 840 it was moved to Scone in Perthshire, the capital of the new united kingdom of Picts and Scots established by Kenneth Mac Ailpín. Kings of Scotland were thereafter enthroned sitting on the stone at Scone, the last to do so before Edward's removal of the stone to London being John Balliol in 1292. Edward seized the stone as part of his bid to annex the Scottish crown to that of England, reckoning that its possession made him the legal king of Scotland and that any subsequently elected Scottish king would be a usurper and not properly crowned. Although they no longer had the stone to sit on, nearly all subsequent kings of Scotland continued to be crowned at Scone.

It is in fact highly dubious whether the stone which currently resides in Edinburgh Castle is the one which Mac Ailpín brought to Scone, let alone whether it originally came from the Holy Land. The sandstone of which it is made is of a type that is relatively common in the areas around both Scone and Dunstaffnage but unknown in the vicinity of Tara or in the

Middle East. This is an area, however, where hard facts are less important than legend and myth. The Stone of Destiny symbolizes the sacred character and history of monarchy in the British Isles and illustrates the considerable efforts which have been made to connect it with Old Testament kingship and biblical narratives. For British Israelites, it is an important part of the evidence showing a direct descent of the British royal house from the throne of David. Symbolically and spiritually, the stone links the crowns of Ireland, Scotland and England. In the words of Arthur Stanley, Dean of Westminster from 1863 to 1881,

> It carries back our thoughts to races and customs now almost extinct, a link which unites the throne of England to the traditions of Tara and Iona, and connects the charm of our complex civilization with the forces of our mother earth – the sticks and stones of savage nature.[6]

The coronation service has changed relatively little over the past 1000 years. A beautifully illuminated service book, the *Liber Regalis*, drawn up for the coronation of Richard II in 1377 and preserved in the library of Westminster Abbey, has been used as the basis for all subsequent coronations. The major modifications have been in respect of the Coronation Oath, changed to reflect the monarch's position as Supreme Governor of the Church of England after the Reformation and the requirement for the sovereign to defend the Protestant religion following the Glorious Revolution of 1689. There have also been small changes in the anointing ritual. The *Liber Regalis* laid down that there should be two ampullae, as the anointing vessels are known, one containing pure oil and the other a holy chrism made of olive oil and balm. Tudor monarchs received a double anointing but since Stuart times a mixture of oil and balm in a single ampulla has been used. Early English coronation orders seem simply to have provided for the monarch to be anointed on the crown of the head, but later a fivefold anointing ritual was used involving the hands, breast, shoulder, elbows and head. The boy king Edward VI was actually laid on the altar so that Archbishop Cranmer could anoint his back. Later anointing was reduced to the hands, breast and crown of the head.

Most of the Stuart monarchs enjoyed a double coronation, with three being crowned separately in Scotland and England. Charles James, the only son of Mary Queen of Scots, and the first British sovereign to bear more than one Christian name, was crowned James VI of Scotland at Stirling in 1590, and James I of England in London in 1603. Charles I was crowned at Westminster Abbey in 1626, and at Holyrood Abbey, Edinburgh, in 1633 in the only Scottish coronation to have used the rites of the Church of England. The order was reversed in the case of Charles II, who was crowned at Scone Abbey on New Year's Day 1651 in a Presbyterian service and at Westminster Abbey on St George's Day 1661. James II effectively also had two coronations, being crowned and anointed in a private Roman Catholic service in his chapel at Whitehall the day before his coronation at Westminster Abbey at which the celebration of communion was omitted. All subsequent British sovereigns have been crowned in Westminster Abbey in the context of a service of Holy Communion according to the rites of the Church of England.

Not all monarchs have taken their coronations as seriously as they should. Dunstan, abbot of Glastonbury, was appalled by the behaviour of King Eadwy immediately after his anointing in 955. He noted that 'the lustful man suddenly jumped up and left the happy banquet and the fitting company of his nobles for the caresses of loose women'. Dunstan and another cleric were sent to drag the king back to the ceremony. When they entered his apartments, they found the royal crown carelessly thrown down on the floor and the king wallowing between two ladies 'in evil fashion, as if in a vile sty'. He was reluctant to leave, but Dunstan, 'after first rebuking the folly of the women, drew him by the hand from his licentious reclining by the women, replaced the crown, and brought him with him to the royal assembly, though dragged from the women by force'.[7] King John apparently laughed throughout his coronation and refused to take communion. Richard II fell asleep halfway through the ceremony, although as he was only 10 years old his exhaustion is understandable. George IV caused offence by nodding and winking to his mistress, Lady Conyngham, throughout his coronation.

Several coronations have been marred by disasters and mishaps which were not the fault of the monarch. During the crowning of William I the Norman cavalry outside Westminster Abbey mistook the shout of acclamation inside for a riot and proceeded to massacre a group of Saxons who had the misfortune to be in the vicinity. The oil used to anoint Elizabeth I was rancid and had a foul smell, and during James II's coronation the royal standard flying over the Tower of London tore in two and the crown would not stay firmly on the King's head. Victoria's coronation was a muddled affair in which the officiating clergy demonstrated particular ineptness. The Archbishop of Canterbury made a mess of delivering the orb to the Queen and shoved the ring on to the wrong finger, causing considerable delay and much pain. When the Queen withdrew to St Edward's Chapel after the anthem she was upset to find the altar covered with sandwiches and bottles of wine. George VI also suffered from episcopal incompetence and clumsiness at his coronation in 1937:

I had two bishops, Durham and Bath and Wells, one on either side to support me, and to hold the form of service for me to follow. When this great moment came, neither Bishop could find the words, so the Archbishop held his book down for me to read, but horror of horrors, his thumb covered the words of the oath. ... The supreme moment came when the Archbishop placed St Edward's crown on my head. I had taken every precaution as I thought to see that the crown was put on the right way round, but the Dean and the Archbishop had been juggling with it so much, that

I never did know whether it was right or wrong. ...
As I turned after leaving the Coronation Chair I was
brought up all standing, owing to one of the Bishops
treading on my robe. I had to tell him to get off it
pretty sharply as I nearly fell down.[8]

In general, however, British coronations have been dignified
and spectacular affairs seen by both those taking part and
observers as significant and moving occasions which have
enhanced both the spiritual significance of the monarchy and
the religious life of the nation. Monarchs have often prepared
spiritually as well as physically and emotionally for their
coronation days and this moving prayer written by Elizabeth
I testifies to a commonly felt sense of the spiritual nature of
the occasion:

O Lord Almighty and everlasting God, I give Thee most
hearty thanks that Thou hast been so merciful unto me as
to spare me to behold this joyful day. And I acknowledge
that Thou hast dealt wonderfully and mercifully with
me, as Thou didst with thy true and faithful servant
Daniel, Thy prophet, whom thou deliverest out the den
from the cruelty of the greedy and roaring lions. Even
so was I overwhelmed, and only by Thee delivered. To
Thee, therefore, only, thanks, honour and praise, for ever.
Amen.[9]

Those who have witnessed coronations have often been struck
by their spiritual power as well as their colour and spectacle.
After attending the English coronation of Charles II in 1661,
Samuel Pepys wrote,

Now after all this, I can say that, besides the pleasure of
the sight of these glorious things, I may now shut my eyes
against any other objects, or for the future trouble myself
to see things of state and show, as being sure never to see
the like again in this world.[10]

The evangelical Lord Ashley, later the Earl of Shaftesbury, had no time for those who scoffed at Victoria's coronation:

> An idle pageant, forsooth! As idle as the Coronation of King Solomon, or the dedication of his Temple. The service itself refutes the notion; so solemn, so deeply religious, so humbling, and yet so sublime! Every word of it is invaluable; throughout the Church is everything, secular greatness nothing. She declares, in the name and by the authority of God, and almost enforces, as a condition preliminary to the benediction, all that can make Princes wise to temporal and eternal glory.[11]

Similar sentiments have characterized newspaper coverage of twentieth-century coronations. *The Times* leader on the day of George VI's coronation in 1937 sounded a distinctly religious note:

> Nothing is heard nowadays of the 'divine right'; and not since the last of the Stewarts, Queen Anne, has any sovereign of England been credited with the magical 'touch' for the cure of the 'King's Evil'. Yet, seeing the king thus exalted at this most solemn moment above common humanity, the mind's eye may catch, beyond all the pomp, another vision. It is a vision to hush the enthusiasm, but only in order to deepen the feeling of loyalty and turn good will into prayer. The king is on his way to be enthroned, indeed, and acclaimed. The trumpets will sound and the people will cry out 'God save King George!'. But he is on his way also to be consecrated – to be dedicated. Once that is done, he is no longer an ordinary man. He is a man dedicated.

The leader went on to discuss the pagan idea of the king being sacrificed:

> In the modern world, the king is dedicated to a harder

sacrifice. Day in and day out, for his people he must live. ... The more closely the burden of kingship is looked at, the more impossible does it seem that any man should bear it unless he were sustained and fortified and inspired by the spiritual power conferred on him in Westminster Abbey today.[12]

For its leader on coronation day 1953 *The Times* returned to the primal image of the monarch as incarnation of her people:

Today's sublime ceremonial is in form, and in common view, a dedication of the state to God's service through the prayers and benedictions of the Church. That is a noble conception, and of itself makes every man and woman in the land a partaker in the mystery of the Queen's anointing. But also the Queen stands for the soul as well as the body of the Commonwealth. In her is incarnate on her Coronation day the whole of society, of which the state is no more than a political manifestation. She represents the life of her people ... as men and women, and not in their limited capacity as Lords and Commons and electors. It is the glory of the social monarchy that it sets the human above the institutional.[13]

If this language seems somewhat hyperbolic and overblown now, it is nothing to the claims made by Edward Shils and Michael Young in a celebrated article in the *Sociological Review* in 1953. For them, 'the coronation was the ceremonial occasion for the affirmation of the moral values by which the society lives. It was an act of national communion.'[14] Their argument was based in part on their observation of the coronation's impact upon 'ordinary' people. They noted that it was frequently spoken of as an 'inspiration' and a 're-dedication of the nation'. The ceremony had 'touched the sense of the sacred' in people, heightening a sense of solidarity in both families and communities. They pointed to examples of reconciliation between long-feuding neighbours and family members brought about by the shared experience of watching the coronation, and noted that the crowds lining the streets of London on coronation day were not idle curiosity seekers but 'looking for contact with something which is connected with the sacred'.

Shils and Young argued that Queen Elizabeth II's coronation had enabled people to affirm moral values, notably 'generosity, charity, loyalty, justice in the distribution of opportunities and rewards, reasonable respect for authority, the dignity of the individual and his right to freedom'.[15] The sacred properties and charisma of the crown strengthened the moral consensus prevailing in Britain.

> The monarchy is the one pervasive institution, standing above all others, which plays a part in a vital way comparable to the function of the medieval church ... the function of integrating diverse elements into a whole by protecting and defining their autonomy.[16]

What is remarkable about these statements is that they came not from churchmen or monarchists but from two left-leaning academic sociologists. Shils was Professor of Sociology at the University of Chicago and Young a former research secretary of the Labour Party. Both men were particularly struck by the morally cohesive effect produced by the actual form of the coronation ceremony:

> The Coronation Service itself is a series of ritual affirmations of the moral values necessary to a well-governed and good society. The key to the Coronation Service is the Queen's promise to abide by the moral standards of society.[17]

In addition to the oath which they singled out as being especially important in this regard, the act of anointing and the investiture with the bracelets of sincerity and wisdom, the orb and the sword were also identified as being not just symbolic but transformative in bringing Queen and people 'into a great nation-wide communion'.[18] 'The Coronation,' they concluded, 'provided at one time and for practically the entire society such an intensive contact with the sacred that we believe we are justified in interpreting it as we have done in this essay, as a great act of national communion.'[19]

Perhaps surprisingly, Shils and Young did not make a great deal of the fact that the 1953 coronation was the first to be televised, and therefore shared in by the nation in a way not possible with any previous ceremony. At a time when ownership of television sets was still relatively limited, this heightened the sense of national communion as those with sets invited friends and neighbours to watch the ceremony with them. There had, in fact, been a considerable debate within royal, ecclesiastical and government circles as to whether the coronation should be televised, and in the event neither the anointing nor the communion of the monarch was filmed or shown. Some feared that television would turn the coronation into a piece of entertainment, but, given the reverential way in which the event was handled by the BBC, the overall effect of allowing the cameras into Westminster Abbey was almost certainly to deepen the popular sense of the mystery and religious dimension of monarchy and to produce, in Grace Davie's words, 'a ceremony which brought together the Church of England, the monarchy and the nation in an impressive act of sacralisation witnessed by a television audience numbered in millions'.[20]

Because what actually happened in Westminster Abbey on 2 June 1953 was of so much significance and because it is outside the memory and experience of many readers of this book (as it is for the author), I am devoting the rest of this chapter to an account of the service which, as has already been noted, broadly followed the form of all coronations in England over the past 1000 years.

Queen Elizabeth II entered Westminster Abbey by the west door and processed up the aisle wearing a crimson robe, traditionally worn in remembrance of Christ's sacrifice and to signify the monarch's own willingness to live sacrificially. Since the coronation of Charles I, the entrance into the Abbey has been accompanied by the singing of the opening verses of Psalm 122. Having reached the theatre, as the special raised platform erected for coronations is known, the Queen knelt before the high altar on which were placed the Bible, paten, chalice and royal regalia with which she was to be invested.

The first stage of the coronation service, the recognition, is a survival from the days of elective monarchy when at least part of the function of a coronation was to confirm the choice of monarch. In 1953 it took the form of the Archbishop of Canterbury formally presenting the Queen to the people, represented by those gathered in the Abbey. As she turned to face those standing at each corner of the theatre, the Archbishop asked if they were willing to do her homage and service. The order of service then states: 'The people signify their willingness and joy by loud and repeated acclamations, all with one voice crying out "God save Queen Elizabeth". Then the trumpets shall sound.'[21]

Elizabeth then returned to her chair to take the coronation oath. This was in three parts: the first a solemn promise to govern the peoples of the United Kingdom of Great Britain and Northern Ireland and other direct dependencies and nations of the Commonwealth 'according to their laws and customs', the second an undertaking to 'cause law and justice, in mercy, to be executed in all your judgements', and the third a commitment to maintain 'the laws of God and the true profession of the Gospel, maintain the Protestant Reformed Religion established by law and maintain and preserve inviolably the settlement of the Church of England, and the doctrine, worship, discipline and government thereof, as by law established in England'.[22] The oath was taken by the Queen kneeling at the altar, with her right hand on the Holy Gospel in the Bible which she kissed before signing the oath.

After returning again to her chair, the Queen was presented with the Holy Bible by the Moderator of the General Assembly of the Church of Scotland, who said:

> Our gracious Queen: to keep your majesty ever mindful
> of the Law and Gospel of God as the Rule for the whole
> of life and government of Christian Princes, we present
> you with this Book, the most valuable thing that this
> world affords. Here is Wisdom; This is the royal Law;
> These are the lively Oracles of God.[23]

In previous coronations the presentation of the Bible, which
was first introduced into the coronation service in 1689, had
been made by the Archbishop of Canterbury. In his recent
study of coronations Roy Strong is highly critical of the
introduction of the Moderator into the service, writing: 'it
posed more problems than it solved, for he had no reason
to be part of a ceremony installing the Supreme Governor
of the Church of England.'[24] This seems to me to display a
curiously limited view of the purpose of the coronation. The
involvement of the leader of the other national established
church in the United Kingdom, with which the monarch has a
close relationship, was surely a welcome innovation and introduced an ecumenical dimension which is likely to be greatly
extended in future coronations.

The singing of verses 9 and 10 of Psalm 84 heralded the
beginning of the communion service which in recent coronations has come to frame the anointing, enthronement and
investiture. The Collect for Purity and *Kyrie Eleison* were
followed by a special prayer asking God to grant Elizabeth

> the spirit of wisdom and government, that being devoted
> unto thee with her whole heart, she may so wisely
> govern, that in her time thy Church may be in safety, and
> Christian devotion may continue in peace; that so perse-
> vering in good works unto the end, she may by thy mercy
> come to thine everlasting kingdom.[25]

Next came the Epistle (1 Peter 2.13-17), the second verse of
Psalm 141 sung as a gradual, the Gospel (Matthew 22.15-22)
and the recitation of the Nicene Creed.

In previous coronations there was often a sermon at this point but the 1953 service moved straight into its most solemn and holy stage, the anointing, preceded, as it has been in every coronation of which a record survives, by the singing of the great ninth-century Latin hymn, *Veni,Creator Spiritus*, to its original plainsong tune. Since James II's coronation it has been sung in John Cousin's English translation which begins, 'Come, Holy Ghost, our souls inspire'. This hymn, which is regularly used at the election of popes, the consecration of bishops in both the Roman Catholic and Anglican churches and the ordination of priests and ministers in a large number of different denominations, refers specifically to the anointing work of the Holy Spirit with its 'blessed unction from above'. It was followed by this prayer said by the Archbishop of Canterbury:

> O Lord and Heavenly Father, the exalter of the humble and the strength of thy chosen, who by anointing with Oil didst of old make and consecrate kings, priests and prophets, to teach and govern thy people Israel: Bless and sanctify thy chosen servant Elizabeth who by our office and ministry is now to be anointed with this Oil, and consecrated Queen: Strengthen her, O Lord, with the Holy Ghost the Comforter; Confirm and stablish her with thy free and princely Spirit, the Spirit of wisdom and government, the Spirit of counsel and ghostly strength, the Spirit of knowledge and true godliness, and fill her, O Lord, with the spirit of thy holy fear, now and for ever; through Jesus Christ our Lord.[26]

The ampulla which held the oil for Queen Elizabeth II's anointing is one of the very few items of the coronation regalia which survived the period of the Commonwealth and Protectorate. Most of the other items are replicas made for the coronation of Charles II. The actual anointing took place behind a canopy with the Queen hidden from view and seated on King Edward's chair while the choir sang the anthem

'Zadok the priest and Nathan the prophet', vividly recalling Solomon's consecration. The Archbishop also made direct reference to Solomon's anointing as he spooned oil from the ampulla. For the anointing, the Queen was stripped of her crimson robe and uncovered, symbolizing the setting apart and consecration. After pouring a small quantity of oil on to the palms of both hands, her breast and her head, with the sign of the cross being made at each stage, the Archbishop said a second prayer which alluded to the anointing of Jesus and picked up the quotation of Psalm 45 in Hebrews 1.9:

> Our Lord Jesus Christ, the Son of God, who by his Father was anointed with the Oil of gladness above his fellows, by his holy Anointing pour down upon your Head and Heart the blessing of the Holy Ghost, and prosper the works of your Hands: that by the assistance of his heavenly grace you may govern and preserve the Peoples committed to your charge in wealth, peace and godliness; and after a long and glorious course of ruling a temporal kingdom wisely, justly and religiously, you may at last be made partaker of an eternal kingdom, through the same Jesus Christ our Lord.[27]

The anointing over, the canopy was borne away by the Knights of the Garter and the Queen vested in the *colobium sindonis* and the *supertunica* or close pall of cloth of gold together with a girdle. These garments are based on priest's vestments and are designed to emphasize the sacerdotal character of monarchy. The *colobium sindonis* is to all intents and purposes an alb made of white linen with a lace border, while the *supertunica*, which is put on over it and fashioned in rich silk ornamented with a pattern of green palm leaves interspersed with red roses, green shamrocks and purple thistles, corresponds to a tunicle or dalmatic. The striking similarity with episcopal consecration was not lost on a witness to Henry VI's coronation, who noted that 'they rayed him lyke as a bysshop should say masse with a dalmatyk and a stole about his necke, and also with hosen and shoon and copys and gloves like a busshop'.[28]

Next came the presentation of the spurs and sword, the former a sign of knightly virtue, and the latter carrying a wealth of symbolism conveyed in the Archbishop's prayer:

> With this Sword do justice, stop the growth of iniquity, protect the Holy Church of God, help and defend widows and orphans, restore the things that are gone into decay, maintain the things that are restored, punish and reform what is amiss, and confirm what is in good order.[29]

The Queen herself offered the sword as an oblation on the altar and a peer redeemed it by paying the price of 100 shillings, drew it out of its scabbard and carried it naked before her during the remainder of the service. Following usual practice, the Queen was then invested with the bracelets, or armills, which were put on her wrists by the Archbishop with the words:

> Receive the bracelets of sincerity and wisdom, both for tokens of the Lord's protection embracing you on every side; and also for symbols and pledges of that bond which unites you with your Peoples: to the end that you may be strengthened in all your works and defended against your enemies both bodily and ghostly.[30]

The investiture continued with the Queen being vested in the stole royal and the royal robe of cloth of gold, the Archbishop saying, 'the Lord clothe you with the robe of righteousness, and with the garments of salvation'.[31] Again, there are clear similarities here with the ordination of priests and episcopal consecration. The stole, a band of cloth of gold about three inches wide with a square panel at either end worked with the red cross of St George on a silver background, which is placed around the sovereign's neck, is similar to that worn by priests, while the robe, sometimes referred to as the imperial

mantle or pallium regale, is essentially a cope embroidered
with the national emblems of rose, shamrock and thistle as
well as golden eagles, silver coronets and fleurs-de-lis. Next
the Archbishop put into the Queen's right hand the orb or
globe, a ball of gold surmounted by a large cross thickly
studded with diamonds, a symbol of sovereignty under the
cross and a reminder 'that the whole world is subject to
the Power and Empire of Christ'.[32] He then placed on the
fourth finger of her right hand a ring inlaid with a ruby and
engraved with St George's cross. Particularly associated with
Edward the Confessor and known as 'the wedding ring of
England', this ring also has obvious episcopal connotations
and is presented to symbolize the marriage of monarch and
country and as 'the ring of kingly dignity and the seal of
Catholic faith'.[33]

The final and perhaps most important symbols with which
Elizabeth was invested were the two sceptres, known in Latin
as the *sceptrus* and *baculus*. These may well represent the
rod and the staff of Psalm 23. One is surmounted by a cross
and stands for kingly power and justice, the other, longer
one is surmounted by a dove, signifying equity and mercy.
They also provide a link to pre-Christian inauguration rites
when monarchs were invested with a rod which was white to
represent truth and purity, and straight to symbolize justice
and uprightness.

It was only at this comparatively late stage of the ceremony
that Elizabeth was actually crowned. The crown used in recent
coronations is known as St Edward's crown but is in fact a
copy made for Charles II's coronation of the diadem that was
broken up on the orders of the Long Parliament. The Queen
was crowned sitting on King Edward's chair, the Archbishop
having first placed the crown on the altar and blessed it. As
he 'reverently put it upon the Queen's head' all present made
loud and repeated shouts of 'God save the Queen', trumpets
sounded, and a signal was given for the firing of guns at
the Tower of London. The acclamation having ceased, the
Archbishop said:

God crown you with a crown of glory and righteousness, that having a right faith and manifold fruit of good works, you may obtain the crown of an everlasting kingdom by the gift of him whose kingdom endureth for ever.[34]

The choir sang, 'Be strong and of a good courage: keep the commandments of the Lord thy God, and walk in his ways', after which the Archbishop gave the Queen a solemn blessing ending with the words, 'may wisdom and knowledge be the stability of your times, and the fear of the Lord your treasure'.[35] A second benediction was then delivered to the people assembled.

For the enthroning, the Queen moved from King Edward's chair to the throne set up in the theatre to which she was, according to the order of service, to be 'lifted up by the archbishops, bishops and other peers of the kingdom', thus recalling the old custom whereby a new king was lifted on to a shield by his followers and exhibited to the people. In reality, the supporters surrounded her as she made her own way to the throne. The Archbishop, after delivering an exhortation, led the assembled bishops and peers in making their homage to the Queen, which they did by kneeling before the throne and declaring that they would be faithful and true. This pledge of fealty, which was also made by Philip, Duke of Edinburgh, was accompanied by the singing of the anthems 'Rejoice in the Lord' by John Redford, 'O clap your hands' by Orlando Gibbons, 'I will not leave you comfortless' by William Byrd, 'O Lord our Governor' by Healey Willan and 'Thou wilt keep him in perfect peace' by Samuel Sebastian Wesley, and ended with the beating of drums, sounding of trumpets and shouts of acclamation from the people.

The last part of the coronation service continued with the communion, celebrated according to the Book of Common Prayer and preceded with the singing of 'All People That on Earth Do Dwell'. The Queen left her throne to kneel before the altar where she offered to the Archbishop first bread and wine and then her oblation of a pall or altar cloth and an ingot of gold weighing a pound. This oblation is described in the *Liber Regalis* as being made in direct imitation of the actions of the priest-king Melchizedek. At this point special prayers were offered for Philip, Duke of Edinburgh, who then joined the Queen, the Archbishop of Canterbury and the Dean of Westminster in receiving communion. At the end of the service the choir sang the *Te Deum Laudamus* and, in a final change of garment, the Queen was divested of the robe royal and arrayed in a robe of purple velvet which she wore during the procession out of the abbey and on her return journey to Buckingham Palace. Purple was, of course, the colour associated with Roman emperors and had by the fourth century come to have sacramental and mystical significance.

I have outlined the form of the 1953 coronation in some detail both because it shows the clear sacramental view of monarchy which prevailed when our present Queen was crowned and also because it may be the last of its kind. The pressures from various quarters to change the shape of the next coronation have grown to the point where they are probably irresistible. The nature of those pressures, and their likely effect, are discussed later in this book. At the conclusion of this chapter, I wish just to make a plea that we ensure we do not throw the baby out with the bath water and lose something very special and very sacred by stripping out of our national life what may strike many now as simply medieval mumbo-jumbo.

There is a danger that coronations, certainly on the scale and of the splendour that we have had in recent centuries, encourage monarcholatry and turn sovereigns into gods. It is certainly true that they load significance on to the person of the monarch in a way that derives as much from primal concepts of sacred kingship as from the Christian understanding of monarchy. This tendency perhaps reached its apogee at the coronation of Charles II in 1651 where the new monarch was variously compared to Jove crowned, Saul crowned, the sun on Easter Sunday, Apollo, Christ as king, priest and prophet, and St Paul finishing the race and gaining his crown. But it has also been a feature of more recent coronations, as Kingsley Martin has observed:

> Extravagant views of monarchy are usually expressed at coronations. So notably rational a prelate as Archbishop Temple, for instance, declared that at his coronation George V became the 'incarnation of his people', a phrase which might at first suggest that the king was a scapegoat who bore in his royal persons the sins of the people and whose ritual death would be a condition of their posterity. ... Another cleric declared that the coronation was 'a miracle that might save civilisation'.[36]

Yet in a sense these statements are justified. Coronations do symbolize sacrifice. The monarch is offered to the people, and to God, and dedicated to a life of selfless service and duty. They also involve a hallowing and consecration, a dedication to God of an individual and a nation, a setting apart and an invocation of divine blessing. They express particularly vividly the difficult and unfashionable Christian themes of vocation, discipleship and obedience. In the absence of a written constitution in the United Kingdom, coronations have also proclaimed the basis on which our government rests and our laws are cast.

Coronations are occasions for reflecting on and affirming the spiritual dimension of monarchy. If we lose them, or if we strip away too much of their symbolism and mystery, we take away much of the sacred significance of the Crown and we also lose a key moment of reconsecration and rededication in the religious life of the nation. Symbolism and metaphor are rightly much in vogue in contemporary postmodern culture and theology. It would be both ironic and tragic if we were to strip out of our national life one of its most transcendent and metaphysical moments.

5

The Protestant project

For the past 450 years Protestantism has been the single most important influence on the spiritual character of the British monarchy. Among the positive legacies of this influence have been a continuing emphasis on the biblical roots of kingship, the close involvement of the Crown in the production of the Book of Common Prayer and the Authorized Version of the Bible and the association of the monarchy with the virtues of duty and sacrificial service. More negatively, it has led to a pervasive anti-Catholic ethos and a somewhat exclusive relationship between the Crown and the established churches.

The modern British monarchy is as much the product of the Reformation as the Churches of England and Scotland to which it has been so strongly tied. The notion of a state church with the country's ruler as its supreme governor essentially derives from the Reformation, even if it was anticipated to some extent in ancient Israel and in the Middle Ages. The principle of royal supremacy over national churches was hammered out by Martin Luther and other sixteenth-century reformers who promoted the ideal of a godly prince ruling a godly nation to counter papal claims of absolute sovereignty over a universal church. It was taken up with particular enthusiasm in England where kings had long been engaged in tussles with the papacy over control of ecclesiastical affairs and appointments. The seventeenth- century doctrine of the divine right of kings was another product of the Reformation. So, indeed, was the counter-doctrine of the people's right to rebel against tyrannical rule, which provided the justification for the overthrow of the monarchy and the institution of the Commonwealth and Protectorate, although this principle had its origins in the claim of Pope Gregory VII and his successors that unworthy rulers could legitimately be removed despite the biblical injunctions to obey the powers that be.[1]

The most impressive spiritual title that has been held by English monarchs since the sixteenth century does not, however, derive from the Reformation. The title *Fidei Defensor*, or Defender of the Faith, which appears abbreviated as FID. DEF. on the £2 coin and simply as F.D. on other coins of the realm, was granted to Henry VIII by Pope Leo X in 1521 in recognition of the king's defence of the seven traditional sacraments of the Catholic Church in a theological pamphlet which appeared under his name but which had effectively been ghost-written for him by his Chancellor, Thomas More. Fourteen years later More went to the scaffold for refusing to recognize Henry VIII as head of the English Church. It is highly ironic that this title given by a pope to the king who later made the breach with Rome should have continued to be used by all monarchs until the present day and to have become associated very specifically with the defence of the Protestant faith.

The crown played a crucial part in the Reformation in England. As generations of schoolchildren have learned, the ending of papal supremacy and the establishment of a reformed national church came about principally because of Henry VIII's need for a divorce from Catherine of Aragon so that he could marry Anne Boleyn and attempt to produce an heir to the throne. Together with his loyal lieutenant Thomas Cranmer, Henry VIII was in many ways the architect of the English Reformation. They created what was effectively a nationalized state church of a moderately Protestant hue with the king at its head, bishops and a conservative liturgy in English. Subsequent sovereigns made their influence felt on the emerging Church of England, with Edward VI steering it in a very much more Protestant direction and Elizabeth steadying it to produce the characteristic Anglican *via media* which has remained one of its most distinguishing character-istics to this day.

The monarch's headship of the Church of England was a key part of the Reformation settlement. It was established in three acts passed by Parliament in 1534: the Annates Act which deprived the Pope of his power to appoint bishops, the Act for the Submission of Clergy by which the church in England surrendered its legislative independence to the Crown, and the Supremacy Act which declared the king 'the only supreme head in earth of the Church of England' with full authority to deal with abuses and intervene in its affairs. These acts effectively gave the English Crown caesaropapal powers similar to those which had been exercised by Holy Roman emperors from the time of Constantine. Royal supremacy over the Church was abandoned by the Catholic Queen Mary but reinstated by Elizabeth I, who modified the monarch's title from 'Supreme Head' to 'Supreme Governor', which it has remained ever since. The extent of the authority conferred by this role is clearly spelled out in the 37th of the 39 Articles drawn up in their final form in 1563 as the Church of England's principal statement of belief:

> The king's majesty hath the chief power in this realm of England, and other his Dominions, unto whom the chief Government of all Estates of this Realm, whether they be Ecclesiastical or Civil, in all causes doth appertain. ... We give not to our Princes the ministering either of God's Word, or of the sacraments, but that only prerogative, which we see to have been given always to all godly Princes in holy Scriptures by God himself; that is, that they should rule all estates and degrees committed to their charge by God, whether they be Ecclesiastical or Temporal.

While it is clear from the above that monarchs had no sacerdotal authority, they enjoyed considerable power with regard to ecclesiastical appointments and liturgical matters. Tudor kings and queens pursued an active, 'hands-on' approach in their dealings with the Church, personally appointing and removing bishops and promoting reforms in the field of worship, while at the same time enthusiastically reviving the Arthurian cult and medieval ideals of chivalry and Christian monarchy. The Royal Injunctions Act of 1536 which required all parish churches to acquire and display a copy of the newly authorized English Bible reflected Henry VIII's personal commitment to using the vernacular language in services. His intervention was probably also behind the demand that from 1543 onward all lessons in matins and evensong were to be read in English. Edward VI played a key role in the preparation of *The First English Prayer Book* of 1549. Diarmaid MacCulloch's book, *Tudor Church Militant*, has shown just how far Edward's own boyish enthusiasms (he was only 9 years old when he began his six-year reign) progressed the advance of Protestant practices and the disappearance of Catholic ones in the English church. On a visit to Westminster Abbey shortly after his coronation he ordered that the number of candles used at communion be reduced to two, the ringing of bells be limited to before and after the service and discontinued at the moment of consecration, the choir give up tonsures and the clergy cease wearing monastic habits. The young king took an active lead in promoting the singing of metrical psalms in church services and, more regrettably, signalled his approval for the wave of iconoclasm which destroyed chantries and parish churches. Elizabeth, while less zealous, also took a strong and active interest in church affairs and frequently interrupted preachers if she felt they were wandering off the subject.

For their part, the bishops and clergy of the Church of England honoured their royal governors. *The First English Prayer Book* of 1549 established a tradition that continues to this day by including a prayer for the sovereign to be said in parish churches every Sunday. The collect for the monarch in the communion service of the 1549 book asked God 'so to rule the heart of thy chosen servant, our king/queen and governor, that s/he, knowing whose minister s/he is, may above all things seek thine honour and glory'.[2]

Much appeal was made to Old Testament texts and precedents by churchmen preaching and writing about the Tudor monarchy. Images of the king as the Lord's anointed and God's deputy on earth were frequently invoked. Edward VI was inevitably compared with Josiah, an earlier boy-king who had purged his land of idols and whose discovery of the 'Book of the Law' was taken as a direct precedent for the production of the prayer-books of 1549 and 1552. In his coronation sermon, Cranmer described Edward as 'a new Josiah' who would put aside idolatry, guard against vice, reward virtue and practise righteousness. Solomon was also taken as a model for Edward VI because he had been allowed by God to build the temple of Jerusalem, a privilege denied to his father David with whom Henry VIII was compared. As well as being hailed as a Virgin Queen and even as the bride of the Church, Elizabeth was regularly compared to David in her struggles against papacy. Preaching before her in 1570, Edward Dering, a Puritan divine, took as his text verses from Psalm 78 referring to the election of David and spelt out his understanding of the monarch's spiritual responsibilities:

> It is true that the prince must defend the fatherless and the widow and relieve the oppressed. ... But this is also his duty, and his greatest duty: to be careful for religion, to maintain the gospel, to teach the people knowledge and build his whole government with faithfulness.[3]

Dering drew special attention to the monarch's responsibility for the priesthood, citing the example of the great reforming kings of Judah, and suggesting that in Elizabeth's case this meant taking away her authority from the bishops. In the event, Elizabeth chose to keep episcopacy not just as an integral part of the English Church establishment but as a key prop in the ever closer relationship between church and Crown.

In appealing to the model of the Israelite monarchy to support the notion of royal supremacy over the Church,

Anglican divines were acting very much in the spirit of the wider European Reformation. As Norman Sykes has observed,

> There can be no doubt that the rediscovery in the historical books of the Old Testament of the 'godly prince', and the argument therefrom *a fortiori* to the authority of the Christian sovereign, was one of the most important and significant themes of the Reformers, alike Lutheran, Calvinist and Anglican.[4]

Continental reformers also made much of New Testament texts enjoining unconditional obedience to the potentates and powers of this world and were prompted by their reading of them to support monarchy in general and royal headship over the Church in particular. The Strasbourg reformer Martin Bucer argued in his *De regno Christi* (1550) that kings rather than bishops would restore the rule of Christ to both churches and nations, while the Swiss reformer, Thomas Erastus, gave his name to the doctrine that the Church should be subordinated to and directed by the secular power.

If England took a broadly Erastian course, the Reformation in Scotland proceeded with very different consequences for the relationship between church, monarchy and state. There the impulse for religious reform came from below rather than above and produced a strong Protestant antipathy against hierarchies and authorities rather than an attachment to them. As James VI remarked wistfully in 1600, 'the reformation of religion in Scotland' was wrought 'by a popular tumult and rebellion ... not proceeding from the Princes ordour (*sic*), as it did in our neighbour country of England'.[5] While there was general enthusiasm among the Scottish reformers for the notion of a Godly commonwealth ruled by a Godly prince, they were strongly opposed to the monarch being head or governor of the Church. This was partly due to their reformed emphasis on the Lordship of Christ, and therefore their belief that Jesus alone was head of the Church. It also reflected an anti-Erastian Genevan emphasis on the Church exercising its own discipline and having complete autonomy and independence from the civil magistracy.

Experience of persecution and exile under the Catholic Mary Queen of Scots led the Scottish reformers to become even less enthusiastic about Crown control over the Church. Their shift of views may be clearly seen in the case of John Knox. Initially, he subscribed to the view that the temporal powers were ordained by God and that subjects owed unstinting obedience to their rulers. He also believed, with the English Puritans, that the Christian prince had both the duty and the authority to reform a corrupt church and to restore 'the true, pure, and sincere Christian religion'. He did not, however, feel that this extended to active regulation of the affairs of an established Protestant church. In the mid-1550s, as an exile in Geneva, Knox changed his position and argued that subjects had the right to rebel against a tyrannical or ungodly monarch, a theme that he developed most vigorously in his famous *First Blast Against the Monstrous Regiment of Women* with its vitriolic attack on Mary Tudor. By 1559 he was arguing that in a godly commonwealth both monarch and subjects alike are equally members of the Church and subject to its disciplines.

The General Assembly of the reformed Church of Scotland held that the title of supreme head or governor belonged to Jesus Christ alone. In 1568 it ordered the pulping of all copies of a recently published book on the downfall of the Roman Church because it referred to the recently crowned James VI as 'supreme head of the primitive kirk'. When a Scottish Oath of Supremacy was drawn up in 1572, it avoided the English formula that the monarch was supreme governor 'in all spiritual or ecclesiastical things or causes as in all things temporal' and spoke rather of him as 'the only supreme governor of this realm, as well in things temporal as in the conservation and purgation of religion'.[6] The most crushing blow to monarchical pretensions was delivered by Andrew Melville, the true architect of Scottish Presbyterianism. In a celebrated encounter with James VI at Falkland Palace in 1596, he took hold of the king's gown, called him 'God silly vassal' and expounded in the clearest possible terms what became known as the 'two kingdoms theory':

> I must tell you, there are two kings and two kingdoms in Scotland: there is King James the head of this Commonwealth, and there is Christ Jesus the King of the Church, whose subject James the Sixth is, and of whose kingdom he is not a king, nor a lord, nor a head, but a member.
>
> We will yield to you your place, and give you all due obedience; but again I say, you are not the head of the church: you cannot give us that eternal life which we seek for even in this world, and you cannot deprive us of it. When you were in your swaddling clothes, Christ Jesus reigned freely in this land in spite of all his enemies.[7]

This Presbyterian put-down had little effect on the one to whom it was directed. James VI and I, the first sovereign to be crowned in both Scotland and England, took a high view of the sacred dimension and authority of kingship and his writings set out the theory of the divine right of monarchy with which the Stuart dynasty that he inaugurated was to be particularly associated. In his treatise *The Trew Law of Free Monarchies* (1598) he noted that 'kings are called Gods by the prophetical David because they sit upon God his throne in the earth and have the count of their administration to give unto him'.[8] This sentiment was versified in his next work, *Basilikon Doron* (1599):

> God gives not kings the style of Gods in vain,
> For on his throne his sceptre do they sway,
> And as their subjects ought them to obey,
> So Kings should fear and serve their God again.[9]

James gave the fullest exposition of his understanding of the divine aspect of monarchy in a two-hour lecture to the Lords and Commons assembled in 1610:

The state of monarchy is the supremest thing upon earth; for kings are not only God's lieutenants upon earth, and sit upon God's throne, but even by God himself they are called Gods. ... Kings are justly called Gods, for that they exercise a manner or resemblance of divine power upon earth. For if you will consider the attributes of God, you will see how they agree in the person of a king. God has power to create, or destroy, make, or unmake at his pleasure, to give life, to send death, to judge all, and to be judged nor accountable to none. ... And the like power have kings. They make and unmake their subjects; they have power of raising and casting down; of life, and of death. Judges over all their subjects, and in all causes, and yet accountable to none but God only.[10]

James' exalted view of monarchy was accompanied by a strong sense of his own religious responsibilities. Brought up as a devout Presbyterian, he regarded himself as the benevolent 'nursing father' of the Scottish kirk. The Scottish reformers for their part also had high expectations of him in this respect. At his Scottish coronation in 1567, the infant king was compared by John Knox to the Israelite king Joash, and when he entered Edinburgh at the age of 14 he was hailed as another David and as the godly prince of a Protestant people. Initially James gave strong support to the reformed church in Scotland and to its Presbyterian government and structures. All parish ministers were instructed to ensure that their parishioners subscribed to the 'King's Confession', a statement of Protestant principles drawn up by his chaplain and assented to by the king in 1581. The so-called Golden Act of 1592, which recognized the Presbyterian system of church government, gave the king the right to decide the time and place for future meetings of the Church of Scotland's general assemblies. James attended every general assembly from 1597 until his departure south to ascend the English throne in 1603 and took a hands-on approach to ecclesiastical affairs which led to increasingly strained relations between Crown and church through the 1590s. James found the Anglicanism which he encountered as King of England rather more to his royal taste than the Presbyterianism in which he had been reared in Scotland. To the consternation of his erstwhile supporters in the Scottish kirk, he sought to establish in his northern kingdom the Church of England's doctrine of royal supremacy and episcopal system, famously declaring his belief in its particular compatibility with the institution of monarchy in the maxim 'no bishop, no king'.

This first Stuart sovereign's most lasting and precious contribution to the religious life of the newly united kingdom of Scotland and England over which he ruled was his patronage of the authorized version of the Bible. Recent studies have confirmed that its alternative title of the King James version is highly appropriate and justified. The king did not just call the Hampton Court conference which commissioned the new translation but laid down clear instructions for the methodology, staffing and timetable of the project and continued to take a keen interest in it until its completion. He was concerned that the new Bible should not be a narrow reflection of a single theological position. However dogmatic his views on monarchy, in the wider theological context he strove for breadth and moderation, maintaining 'I am for the medium in all things'. He deliberately brought together Puritan and High Church translators to collaborate on what he genuinely hoped would be an *irenicon*, or instrument of peace and unity founded on his own divine authority. Adam Nicolson, who has written the most eloquent recent book on the subject, refutes convincingly the notion that the King James Bible is 'any kind of propaganda for an absolutist king':

Its subject is majesty, not tyranny, and its political purpose was unifying and enfolding, to elide the kingliness of God with the godliness of kings, to make royal power and divine glory into one indivisible garment which could be wrapped around the nation as a whole. Its grandeur of phrasing and the deep slow music of its rhythms – far more evident here than in any Bible the sixteenth century had produced – were conscious embodiments of regal glory. It is a book written for what James, the self-styled *Rex Pacificus*, and his counselors hoped might be an ideal world.[11]

Subsequent Stuart monarchs shared James' high view of the divine aspect and religious responsibilities of monarchy. Charles I continued his father's crusade to impose the English prayer book and episcopal system on the Scottish church, provoking the so-called 'Bishops' war' in Scotland which in turn led to the English Civil War. Charles II took a close personal interest in the restoration of the established church, the episcopacy, the Book of Common Prayer and the festivals of the Christian year which had been swept away together with the institution of monarchy during the period of the Commonwealth and Protectorate. James II sought to return his realms to Roman Catholicism through the medium of religious toleration, provoking a Protestant backlash which ensured that no Roman Catholic would subsequently occupy the British throne.

Alongside their ill-judged and high-handed attempts to impose their own religious preferences on unwilling subjects, the Stuart monarchs also had a fascination with the romance and tradition of medieval sacred monarchy. Perhaps because they were the first dynasty since the Norman Conquest to be free of competing claims to the throne, being heirs to the houses of Tudor and Plantagenet as well as to all Scottish kings since Bruce and responsible for uniting the thrones of Scotland, England and Wales, the Stuarts had a strong quasi-religious sense of their role in renewing and uniting the British people. In taking the oak as the royal symbol they emphasized the regenerative powers of the Crown and appealed to both pre- and post-Christian Celtic notions of sacred kingship. In giving the name Britain to the new united kingdom over which he presided, James VI and I was widely seen as consciously comparing himself to Arthur. The fact that the execution of a Stuart king in 1649 brought about the apparent end of monarchy before its restoration eleven years later further encouraged parallels with the ancient motif of the dying and rising king, and indeed with the death and resurrection of Christ. As we have already noted, Stuart monarchs were particularly enthusiastic in touching for the king's evil and recovered this highly visible manifestation of sacred monarchy which the Tudors had largely neglected.

This conscious cultivation of the sacred dimension of monarchy was accompanied by a fascination with iconography. The Stuarts were keen to be represented in paintings in the guise of Old Testament monarchs or with other symbols of sacred monarchy. James I was depicted as Solomon in Rubens' portrait for the Banqueting Hall in Whitehall. Charles I was especially interested in iconic representations of himself as a sacred king. The editor of a recent book on the subject notes that he 'promoted and stimulated a court culture that projected regal splendour with a refulgence unmatched in English history'.[12] Much of this projection and representation had a distinct religious dimension. The court masques of which Charles was so fond regularly portrayed monarchs as gods and goddesses. Silver coins struck during his reign carry the legend *'Christo Auspice Regno'* ('I reign by Christ's favour'). The famous portrait by Van Dyck depicts him seated on a white horse, representing the Word of God, 'faithful and true,' as described in the Book of Revelation 19.11-14.

The promotion of the divine and sacred aspects of monarchy in the seventeenth century was not confined to monarchs and their immediate court circles. Churchmen joined in the process. The sermon preached at James I's funeral included a long panegyric describing him as the British Solomon and Archbishop Laud had no qualms about describing Charles I as 'the beauty of holiness'. Poets and playwrights enthusiastically added their eloquent tributes. Shakespeare is believed to have inserted the passage about the king's miraculous powers into *Macbeth* (quoted on p. 86) to flatter James I. Kathleen Raine has argued that 'Shakespeare's historical plays are, in a sense, the foundation of the English concept of Kingship'.[13] A speech in *Richard II* comes close to encapsulating the Stuart theory of divine right:

> Not all the water in the rough-rude sea
> Can wash the balm from an anointed king.
> The breath of worldly men cannot depose
> The deputy elected by the Lord.
>
> (*Richard II*, act III, sc. 2)

Abraham Cowley, perhaps the first great Royalist poet, who significantly wrote an epic poem on the biblical story of King David, described Charles I as a 'blessed alchemist' who could transmute base metal into gold through his holy power.[14]

Of all those who hymned the spiritual character and divine aspects of the Stuart monarchs, perhaps none reached the poetic heights of John Dryden. His *Absalom and Achitophel* (1681) cast Charles II in the role of David and gave more than a hint of his Christlike qualities as well as placing him firmly in the tradition of the sacred patriarchs and kings of ancient Israel:

> Auspicious prince, at whose nativity
> Some royal planet rul'd the southern sky;
> Thy longing country's darling and desire;
> Their cloudy pillar and their guardian fire:
> Their second Moses, whose extended wand
> Divides the seas, and shows the promis'd land:
> Whose dawning day in every distant age
> Has exercis'd the sacred prophet's rage:
> The people's prayer, the glad diviner's theme,
> The young men's vision, and the old men's dream!
> Thee, Saviour, thee the nation's vows confess,
> And, never satisfied with seeing, bless:
> Swift unspoken poems thy steps proclaim,
> And stammering babes are taught to lisp thy name.
>
> (lines 229–43)

Dryden drew on classical and pagan images as well as Christian comparisons in his panegyrics to the later Stuart kings. His poem on the coronation of Charles II represented the new monarch as the type of God, the type of the Sun and the soul of the nation. His 1685 'funeral-pindarisque' in memory of Charles, *Threnodia Augustalis*, described the departed king as 'the type of Him above' (line 258), a saint and a martyr. He was equally extravagant in his language about James II whom he described as 'God's image, God's Anointed' and 'a second Constantine', this last appellation being accompanied by a reminder that 'the former too, was of the British line'. Dryden's *Britannia Rediviva*, written in 1688 to celebrate the birth of James II's son, contains an extraordinary couplet in which the baptism of the infant prince is portrayed as having atoning significance and effecting the cleansing of the whole nation:

> Let his baptismal Drops for us atone;
> Lustrations for offences not his own.
> Let Conscience, which is Int'rest ill disguis'd,
> In the same Font be cleans'd, and all the Land Baptiz'd.
>
> (lines 188–91)

It is true that this last poem also includes a warning to kings to remember where their power comes from:

> The power from which all kings derive their state,
> Whom they pretend, at least, to imitate,
> Is equal both to punish and reward;
> For few wou'd love their God unless they fear'd.
>
> (lines 343–6)

Its overall tendency, however, is to portray the monarch as having metaphysical powers and partaking in some measure at least in the special nature and atoning work of Christ.

Comparisons with Christ were, indeed, a common feature

of the royalist iconography and literature of the seventeenth century. The medieval notion of the king's two bodies or natures was revived and often explicitly linked to the Christian understanding of the two natures of Christ. At the time of his English coronation in 1661, Charles II was frequently likened to Christ, a comparison which was encouraged by the story that an especially bright star had shone at his birth as well as by the obvious associations prompted by his restoration or resurrection of the monarchy and established church after the dark days of Puritan rule. One of the arches through which he passed on his journey to Westminster Abbey was decorated with verses written by Sir James Ogilby:

Comes not here the King of Peace,
    Who, the Stars so long foretold,
From all woes should us release
    Converting Iron-times to gold[15]

Other poems published at the time of Charles II's coronation applied to him the phrase 'he led captivity captive', first found in Psalm 68 and later used of Jesus by Paul in Ephesians 4.8, and portrayed him as the one who would fulfil the prophecy in Isaiah 11 and inaugurate a new age when the lion would lie down with the lamb.

Following his flight and exclusion from the throne in 1689, James II was regularly described in Jacobite propaganda in Christlike terms:

Would you see the Man of Sorrows,
    Then behold great James the just,
Tho' grief his cheeks hath plowed in furrows,
    Yet in him still put your trust.
His Majesty's divinely sacred,
    Which your conscious hearts must own,
'Twas your blind misguided hatred,
    Drove him from his lawful throne.[16]

In later Jacobite poems, continuing well into the eighteenth century, Stuart pretenders were portrayed as messiahs whose return to their rightful thrones would signify resurrection and renewal.

The Stuart monarch most frequently compared to Christ was Charles I, following his execution in 1649. His death aroused conflicting emotions. Puritan radicals, for whom Charles had been a tyrant and archetype of the Antichrist, saw it as an act of deliverance which would usher in the reign of King Jesus and the inauguration of God's kingdom on earth. For royalists, however, and for those in the crowd outside the Banqueting Hall who pressed forward to soak their handkerchiefs in royal blood, Charles died a martyr to the Christian faith and to the Church of England in particular. The widespread cult which grew up around him in death was given a powerful stimulus by the publication on the day of his burial of the *Eikon Basilike: The Portraiture of His Sacred Majesty in His Solitudes and Sufferings*. The cover of this collection of meditations and prayers depicted Charles kneeling and grasping a crown of thorns, his eyes fixed on a heavenly crown and his earthly crown lying discarded at his feet. In the book Charles' words merge with those of David. The *Eikon Basilike* provided a manual of prayers, supposedly written by the king although this has never been clearly established, which enabled people to join him in the community of believers. Here was a new version of the Old Testament model of the king leading his people in worship, with the dead king summoning his people to prayer and devotion. The *Eikon Basilike* established Charles in the role of the martyr king who imitated Christ in the depth of his devotion and suffering. Poems published after his death portrayed him in this light:

'Twas a far more glorious thing
To die a Martyr, than to live a King,
When he had copied out in every line
Our Saviour's Passion (bating the Divine).[17]

Signs and wonders which occurred at the time of Charles' funeral were taken as further evidence of his Christ-like qualities. A fall of snow which covered his coffin with a white pall as it was being carried into St George's Chapel, Windsor, was seen as a sign that heaven was declaring his innocence. A teenage girl near Deptford was apparently cured of the king's evil by a handkerchief dipped in Charles' blood. Devotion to Charles, king and martyr, was widespread in the Church of England for the next 200 years. Until 1859 his martyrdom was commemorated with a special service in the Book of Common Prayer on 30 January, coincidentally the date on which the reading prescribed in the Lectionary was the chapter in Matthew's Gospel dealing with the crucifixion of Christ. Although no longer in the Prayer Book, services are still regularly held on 30 January to commemorate Charles I, and as recently as 1986 an Anglican clergyman was closely comparing him to Christ:

> First, just like the Messiah who, from the beginning of his time on earth, as on several occasions He told His Disciples, knew that He would have to die the death on the Cross, so Charles I had a premonition of what his own end would be. ... Indeed, for him, as in the case of the Redeemer, in his doom was his duty; since he was predestined to regenerate the faith in his realms and to manifest to his own people through his personal belief, example and sacrifice, the truth and value of Christian doctrines. ... So like Christ sold to the Sanhedrin by one of His Disciples, was Charles sold to the Parliamentarians by the closest of his people, the Scots ... the royal and anointed incarnation of Scotland, England and Ireland.[18]

If the sacred nature of seventeenth-century monarchy was enhanced by the comparisons made between individual kings and Christ, it perhaps received its most consistent boost from the theory of divine right. The four propositions on which this theory rested have been admirably stated in the classic work on the subject by Neville Figgis – they are that monarchy is a divinely ordained institution, that hereditary right is indefeasible and the right acquired by birth cannot be forfeited through any circumstance, that kings are accountable to God alone, and therefore 'a mixed or limited monarchy is a contradiction in terms', and that non- resistance and passive obedience are enjoined by God.[19] The origins of the theory of divine right go back to medieval times and may be found in such works as the anonymous twelfth- century tract quoted on page 82. Figgis identifies its first great protagonist as the proto-Reformer John Wycliffe, who in his *De Officio Regis*, written to counter both papal and clerical claims to supremacy over the Church, developed the notion of the king as God's vicar on earth and as a reflection of the godhead of Christ where the priest reflected only his manhood. In its full form, however, divine right was essentially a post-Reformation theory, worked out in sixteenth- and seventeenth-century England and France in opposition to the claims of papal supremacy and closely allied to the development of nation states. In many ways it was also a particularly Anglican theory, opposing the clericalism found in both Roman Catholicism and Presbyterianism which sought to limit the sovereign's power over the Church.

Drawing heavily on Old Testament texts and especially on an understanding of the monarch as the Lord's Anointed, the theory of divine right held that the sovereign was above human criticism or judgement and could not be resisted. This principle of passive obedience is well conveyed both in the speech that Shakespeare wrote for the Bishop of Carlisle in *Richard II* and in the opening verse of the popular song *The Vicar of Bray*, which refers to the time of Charles II:

> What subject can give sentence on his king?
> ... Shall the figure of God's majesty,
> His captain, steward, deputy elect,
> Anointed, crowned, planted many years,
> Be judg'd by subject and inferior breath?
> (*Richard II*, act IV, sc.1, lines 121, 125–8)

In good King Charles' golden days,
When loyalty no harm meant,
A zealous High Churchman was I,
And so I got preferment
To teach my flock I never missed,
Kings were by God appointed,
And lost are those who dare resist
Or touch the Lord's anointed.

A brief review of the arguments of the two leading exponents of divine right theory in the mid-seventeenth century underlines its biblical basis. For Robert Filmer, kingship belonged to the natural order of society which God had established when he first created Adam, and which embodied the patriarchal system that underlay the life of families and nations. The king ruled as patriarch or father of his people. Filmer's theory of divine right was based on a rather selective and truncated reading of the fifth commandment as 'honour thy father' and on tracing a direct link from Adam through the judges and kings of the Old Testament to contemporary rulers. He held that subordination of children to their fathers was the basic law of God and argued that this principle applied equally to the relationship between people and their rulers. His thesis is neatly encapsulated in the headings of the three chapters in his book *Patriarcha*: 'That the first kings were fathers of families. It is unnatural for the people to govern or choose governors. Positive laws do not infringe the natural and fatherly power of kings.'[20]

Thomas Hobbes similarly based his argument for the comprehensive and exclusive rights of the sovereign in matters of religion and politics on his reading of the Bible. In Chapter 16 of his *De Cive* he traced the monarchical system in Israel back to Abraham, whom he saw as the first ruler appointed by God with full rights to legislate in secular and domestic matters. The system reached its full expression with the election of Saul as king. From this point, and throughout the monarchical period, Hobbes saw God as ceasing to rule his people directly and governing through kings who alone had the right to interpret his word or even to issue the books which constituted his word. In the following chapter of *De Cive* Hobbes turned to the New Testament and argued that Christ's kingly rule only begins with his second coming and has no status or existence prior to that event. In the meantime it is earthly monarchs who have all power and authority in matters spiritual and temporal, expressed through their sovereignty over the state church.

The absolutist concept of divine right was not the only theory of monarchy worked out in the seventeenth century on the basis of appeals to the Old Testament. A very much more limited concept of sovereignty was developed by those who took their stand on the covenant theme in Israelite kingship and argued that it was the nation rather than the monarch on which God looked with special favour. This theory was taken up especially in Scotland and underlay the King's Confession made in 1581 by James VI, the National Covenant of 1638, which Charles I refused to sign, and the tract *Lex Rex* by the academic theologian Samuel Rutherford, which was ordered to be burned in 1661.

The essence of this covenant theory was perhaps never better expressed than in the three-hour sermon preached by Robert Douglas at the Scottish coronation of Charles II at Scone in 1651. The Moderator of the Church of Scotland took as his text 2 Kings 11.12-17, which describes the crowning of Joash and the role of the priest Jehoiada in making a double covenant, first 'between the Lord and the king and the people that they would be God's people' and then between the king and his people. Douglas' sermon, which was followed by Charles being called on to take the coronation oaths, sign the Solemn League and Covenant and swear to maintain the Reformation in Scotland and the Presbyterian government of its national church, spelt out a very different doctrine of the monarchy from that held by the proponents of divine right:

> When a king is crowned and received by the people, there is a covenant or mutual contract between him and them, containing conditions mutually to be observed. ... It

is good for our king to learn to be wise in time and know that he receiveth this day a power to govern – a power limited by contract; and these conditions he is bound by oath to stand to, for a king's power is not absolute but is power limited by covenant.[21]

This Presbyterian sermon was noticeably free of the adulation and flattery with which most clergymen in the established Church of England addressed the Stuart monarchs. It exhorted Charles to embark on both a personal and a family reformation and directed him to seven specific duties – to seek God in frequent and earnest prayer (Douglas having observed that 'prayers are not in much request at Court'), to be careful of the kingdom, to make much of faithful servants of Christ, whether ministers or laymen, to be very careful whom he put in places of trust, to be moderate in his use of authority, to be strenuous against the enemy and, above all, to be constant. Charles was reminded that there were three categories of monarch in the Old Testament – those who did evil in the sight of the Lord, those who did what was right but not with a perfect heart, and those who did right in the sight of the Lord with a perfect heart. 'Let us neither have the first nor the second but the third written upon our King' preached Douglas, before adding a ringing reminder of the impermanence of earthly kingship:

A king should always bear in mind that even the firmest of earthly crowns is but a fading crown after all: and therefore that he should have an eye upon the 'crown of glory that fadeth not away', and 'the kingdom that cannot be shaken': that crown and kingdom belongeth not to kings as kings, but unto believers: and a believing king hath this comfort that when he hath endured for a while, and been tried, he may receive the crown of life, which the Lord hath promised to them that love Him.[22]

The dramatic events of 1688 to 1689, when James II was forced to flee his kingdom and William of Orange was invited by Parliament to occupy the vacant throne, effectively signalled the triumph of the covenant theory of monarchy, albeit in a more secularized form than its Scottish proponents would have wished, over that of divine right. The interruption in the succession which brought William and his wife Mary to the throne and the conditionality imposed on their accession broke two of the cardinal principles of divine right theory. The Glorious Revolution, as it came to be known, replaced the iconography and mystery of Stuart sacred kingship with a monarchy that was more prosaic, popular and Protestant. Significantly, William of Orange had little time for the ritual of touching for the king's evil, telling one sufferer who approached him for a cure, 'God give you better health, and more sense.'[23] W. B. Yeats' comment that in Ireland the events of 1688 to 1690 'overwhelmed a civilisation full of religion and myth and brought in its place intelligible laws planned out upon a great blackboard' well describes the new spirit that applied throughout the United Kingdom.[24]

The constitutional settlement that followed the Glorious Revolution rested on a concept of limited monarchy where sovereignty lay with the Crown in Parliament. It was based on an essentially secular Whig concept of social and civil contract, as propounded in the writings of John Locke. After 1689 there were far fewer appeals by either monarchs or churchmen to Old Testament texts and the model of Israelite kingship. Contract rather than covenant became the guiding constitutional principle. In the words of Oliver O'Donovan:

> In the course of the seventeenth century, under the influence of contract-theory, an important shift of emphasis occurred in radical political thought: the ruler's primary responsibility ceased to be thought of as being to divine law, but rather to the people whose supposed act constituted him. This act of popular will came to be thought of as the source of all law and constitutional order.[25]

The Glorious Revolution did not, however, entirely sweep away the notion of the Godly prince ruling the Godly Commonwealth and the close connections between Crown and Christianity. In two respects, indeed, it strengthened them. The link between the monarch and the established churches of England and Scotland was confirmed. One of the conditions on which William had been offered the throne was that he would outlaw episcopacy in Scotland and maintain the Presbyterian government of the Church of Scotland. In England he retained the position of Supreme Governor of the established Church. The Crown and the Church of England had been brought closer together in the mid-seventeenth century through their banishment, along with other institutions like the House of Lords and the Book of Common Prayer, during the period of the Commonwealth and Protectorate and their joint restoration in 1660. Their close relationship was confirmed in the settlement that followed William's accession to the throne and was, indeed, exemplified in the reign of his successor, Anne, the last of the Stuarts, who was devoted to the Church of England and personally established funds to augment the stipends of poor clergy and to build new parish churches in London.

The second respect in which the Glorious Revolution strengthened the religious character of the monarchy was in its emphatic Protestantism. More so even than the constitutional arrangements which came out of the Henrician and Elizabethan reformations, the post-1689 settlement affirmed and secured the abiding Protestant character of the British monarchy. This was achieved through both ceremonial and legislative means. A new element was introduced into the coronation service whereby the English Bible was carried with the regalia into Westminster Abbey and presented to the new monarch during the service. An act of 1689 recast the coronation oath so that the sovereign now promised to maintain not just the laws of God, and the true profession of the Gospel, but also 'the Protestant Reformed Religion established by law'. An article in the 1707 Treaty of Union between England and Scotland added to the coronation oath a promise to 'maintain and preserve inviolably the settlement of the Church of England and the doctrine, worship, discipline, and government thereof', and also required that each new monarch should swear at the Accession Council to maintain the Protestant religion and Presbyterian government of the Church of Scotland.

The Revolution Settlement did not just harness the Crown positively to the Protestant cause. It also identified it with militant anti-Catholicism. The Act of Settlement of 1701 laid down in the clearest possible terms:

> That all and every person and persons that then were, or afterwards should be reconciled to, or should hold Communion with the See or Church of Rome, or should profess the Popish Religion, or marry a Papist, should be excluded, and are by that Act made for ever incapable to inherit, possess or enjoy the Crown and Government of this Realm.

In their determination to prevent a Roman Catholic from succeeding to the throne, those responsible for framing this Act passed over more than fifty close blood relations of Anne in order to arrive at the acceptably Protestant figure of Sophia, Electress of Hanover and her heirs. Similar concerns underlay the Treaty of Union with Scotland in 1707. The Scottish Parliament had not been consulted about the Act of Settlement and had passed an Act of Security in 1703 reserving Scotland's right to make its own choice with regard to the succession. There were fears on the English side that on Anne's death, the Scots might favour the accession of her exiled Roman Catholic half-brother James Edward Stuart, if they were not locked into a parliamentary union.

The 1689 Coronation Oaths Act, the 1701 Act of Settlement and the 1707 Act of Union remain in force to this day although there is now considerable pressure for their repeal. They have by no means been dead letters. George III forced the resignation of his prime minister in 1801 because he regarded

William Pitt's proposals for Roman Catholic emancipation in Ireland as contravening his coronation oath, and both he and George IV opposed Catholic emancipation in the rest of the United Kingdom on the same grounds. The only part of the Revolution Settlement that has been modified is the declaration required of a new sovereign at the first state opening of Parliament following his or her accession. As made by William III, this ran:

> I do solemnly, in the presence of God, profess, testify, and declare, that I do believe that in the sacrament of the Lord's Supper, there is not any transubstantiation of the elements of bread and wine into the body and blood of Christ, at or after the consecration thereof by any person whatsoever. 2ndly, That the invocation or adoration of the Virgin Mary, or any other saint, and the sacrifice of the mass, as they are now used in the church of Rome, are superstitious and idolatrous.[26]

This vehemently anti-Catholic statement of personal belief was made by every British monarch throughout the eighteenth and nineteenth centuries without demur. At his accession in 1901, however, Edward VII protested at its 'crude language' which he considered an insult to his Roman Catholic subjects. With the approval of the Cabinet he asked for it to be changed, but nothing was done, much to his annoyance. His successor George V refused to open Parliament until a less insulting form of words had been substituted. The Accession Declaration Act of 1910 substituted a considerably modified declaration which has been used ever since:

> I do solemnly and sincerely in the presence of God profess, testify and declare that I am a faithful Protestant and that I will according to the true intent of the enactments which secure the Protestant succession to the Throne of my Realm, uphold and maintain the said enactment to the best of my powers according to the law. [27]

It is hardly too much to say that during the eighteenth century the Protestant succession replaced divine right as the great bulwark and spiritual talisman of the British monarchy. The changing focus of loyalty was well appreciated by the ever-pliable Vicar of Bray who noted that with the accession of William and Mary, 'passive obedience was a joke, a jest was non resistance'. Throughout the reign of George I, the good Vicar 'almost every day abjured the Pope and the Pretender'. The final verse of his song nicely encapsulates both the priorities and provisionality of the post-Stuart monarchy:

> The illustrious house of Hanover
> And Protestant succession,
> To these I do allegiance swear,–
> While they can keep possession.
> For in my faith and loyalty
> I never more will falter,
> And George my lawful King shall be–
> Until the times do alter.

Linda Colley's important book, *Britons: Forging the Nation*, has demonstrated the extent to which, in the absence of any ethnic sense of nationhood, Protestantism, or perhaps more precisely anti-Catholicism, became the great uniting force in the creation of the new United Kingdom of the English, Welsh and Scots in the eighteenth century. The monarchy was a key focus of this Protestant national identity, much of which was achieved through the assiduous application of what we would now call spin and public relations. National days of commemoration were promoted to remind people of key events in the development of the Protestant monarchy – 30 January commemorated the execution of Charles I, 29 May the restoration of the monarchy in 1660, 1 August the accession of the Hanoverians in 1714, and 5 November was the occasion for a double celebration of both the foiling of the Catholic-inspired Gunpowder Plot against James I and the landing of William of Orange in 1688.

If the sovereign was now seen as being accountable as much to the people through Parliament as to God, there was still a strong sense of the divine ordination of the institution of monarchy and the importance of obeying the powers that be. The widespread prevalence of this view helps partly to explain why Britain did not go down the route taken by both the Americans and the French in the eighteenth century and espouse a wholehearted doctrine of popular rights and contractual government. Although biblical texts came to be quoted less frequently in discussions about government and kingship, their influence remained strong not just among Anglicans but among many in the new Dissenting communities. John Wesley remained a Tory throughout his progress from Anglicanism to Methodism because, he said, of his belief that power descends from God and not from the people. This made him a fervent monarchist. Indeed, he may well have gone through a pro-Jacobite phase but like many others he transferred his allegiance to the Hanoverians, acting pragmatically as well as out of principle, on the biblical maxim of 'fear God, honour the king'.[28]

In place of the theory of divine right to which the Stuarts had appealed, the Hanoverian dynasty was sustained by a notion of divine providence which saw Britain as a chosen nation over whom God had placed a Protestant ruler. The sentiment is well expressed in the opening line of 'Rule, Britannia', written by James Thomson around 1740, which speaks of Britain arising 'at heaven's command' out of the azure main. This sense of special providence was reinforced throughout the first half of the eighteenth century at least by the ever-present Jacobite threat. Numerous sermons were preached up and down the land in the aftermath of the 1745 Jacobite rebellion reminding churchgoers that George II owed his throne to divine providence. The Hanoverians may not have been compared to the Godly kings of Israel as often as their Stuart predecessors but their Jacobite rivals were regularly portrayed, not least by Presbyterian ministers in Scotland, as the Assyrians attacking the British Israel or indeed as the Antichrist.

Ironically, Jacobitism played a key role in both inspiring and popularizing the British national anthem, which stands as one of the most abiding monuments to the whole project of Protestant monarchy. In his fascinating study of the anthem, Percy Scholes traces its origins back to 1688 when 'God Save Great James our king' was sung by Stuart loyalists on the eve of William of Orange's invasion. The song may conceivably be older and have been sung during the reign of Charles II. Jacobite versions appeared on wine glasses in the early eighteenth century. At what stage the Stuart anthem was appropriated for the Hanoverians is not clear, but it was undoubtedly the threat of the Jacobite rebellion in 1745 that brought it into the public domain. 'God Save Great George our King' received its first known public performance at the Theatre Royal Drury Lane on 28 September 1745 following the theatre manager's announcement that he was raising a troop of soldiers to fight for the king with his actors as its nucleus. It was sung there by the men who had been enlisted and was conducted by Thomas Arne, whose tune for 'Rule, Britannia' had been heard in the theatre six months earlier. The anthem was taken up by other theatres and sung in public places. 'God Save the King' seems first to have been sung in churches during George III's bouts of illness when new verses were added, praying for the king's deliverance and thanking God for his recovery. The first coronation to include the national anthem was that of George IV in 1821, and by Victoria's reign it had become the invariable accompaniment to public appearances by the sovereign.

The national anthem was a peculiarly British invention, rapidly copied by other countries, twenty of which at one time or another adopted or adapted the tune of 'God Save the King' for their own national songs. What distinguished the British version was the fact that it was so clearly addressed to God rather than to the fatherland, the flag or some other symbol and that it focused very directly on the person of the sovereign rather than on the nation or people. While it clearly called on the Almighty to bless and protect the monarch, however, there was no hint of divine right theory. Indeed, the third verse introduced a note of conditionality indicative of a contractual view of monarchy:

> Thy choicest gifts in store
> On him be pleased to pour,
>   Long may he reign.
> May he defend our laws,
> And ever give us cause,
> With heart and voice to sing,
>   God save the king.

During Victoria's reign the national anthem was often turned into an anti-Catholic rallying cry. The widespread anti-papal demonstrations which followed Pope Pius IX's creation of a hierarchy of bishops for England and Wales in 1850 were accompanied by the singing of an amended version of the second verse with the line 'Frustrate their Popish tricks, confound their politics'. The following year a new verse provided 'for the use of her Majesty's loyal subjects in their social circles and public assemblies' and invoked divine protection for the anti-Catholic cause:

> Let now thine arm be seen,
> Guarding our gracious Queen
>   From papal power.[29]

If the emphasis on the Protestantism of the British monarchy in the eighteenth and nineteenth centuries had unfortunate negative consequences in fostering anti-Catholic prejudice, then it also had a more positive effect in promoting those qualities which are perhaps thought of as the characteristic Protestant virtues. The reign of George III in particular saw a new reverence for monarchy based on respect for the king's earnestness, conscientious exercise of his duties and absolute propriety. To some these might seem dull if worthy characteristics to find in the occupant of the throne but for those influenced by the Evangelical Revival which had brought a new mood of seriousness across the country, there was something both reassuring and even endearing about the fact that the monarch prayed regularly, was loyal to his wife and had no mistresses, and went about his business in a sober and solid way. Many would have agreed with John Wesley's verdict on George III: 'He believes the Bible ... he fears God ... he loves the Queen.'[30] George III and Queen Charlotte established a paradigm of a happy and fruitful royal marriage which was to be enormously important in maintaining public respect and affection for the British monarch after it ceased to have any major political role or influence. As a clergyman commented in a sermon after the queen's death, their life together provided a 'lofty example of conjugal affection, domestic religion, economy and virtue'.[31] He also suggested that it was the existence and display of these qualities in the British monarchy which principally explained its survival through a period that had seen the overthrow of most of the other royal houses in Europe.

George III and Queen Charlotte pioneered another important aspect of the modern British monarchy in their patronage and direct support of voluntary, philanthropic and charitable endeavours. Frank Prochaska traces the origins of what he calls Britain's 'welfare monarchy' to their activities and notes that they both distributed proportionately more of their own wealth to charitable purposes than any other British sovereign.[32] They especially favoured the Christian-inspired charitable societies established in the wake of the Evangelical Revival to promote missionary endeavour, education, poor relief, moral reform and the abolition of slavery. In their turn, leading figures in the revival like Hannah More extolled the crown as the focus of national morality and also commended its Christlike assumption of sacrificial dedication and service:

A Crown! What is it?
It is to bear the miseries of a people!

To hear their murmurs, feel their discontents,
And sink beneath a load of splendid care![33]

If George III was instrumental in establishing an association between the Crown and the virtues of domestic respectability, philanthropy, private morality and public duty, he also endeared himself to his subjects by his simplicity and vulnerability. His very ordinariness appealed, while his frequent bouts of insanity drew considerable popular sympathy and concern. As well as associating the Crown with domestic virtue and propriety, he also consciously promoted its more splendid and majestic elements. He rebuilt Buckingham Palace as a spectacular royal residence and centre for court ceremonial in London and went on frequent royal visits around the country, displaying the public face of monarchy to the people in a way that has been followed by all subsequent monarchs. Several of his public appearances involved religious ceremonies and church services, as when he led the nation in thanking God for the victorious outcome of the Napoleonic wars. For their part, the Church of England and other denominations regarded significant events in the personal life of the sovereign, such as the onset of or recovery from illness, as suitable occasions for special services. On the day that George III entered the fiftieth anniversary of his reign, a correspondent to *The Times* expressed the hope that 'my fellow citizens will throng into the sanctuaries of Divine Worship, there to present the offerings of their best praises, for the blessings of the long reign of one of the best of Kings'.[34] Reporting on the Jubilee celebrations the following day, the paper noted that:

the forenoon was dedicated to public worship and the acknowledgement of the Divine Providence (exemplified in the protection of His Majesty's person, and of the many national blessings almost exclusively enjoyed by the inhabitants of the United Kingdom) in every parish church and chapel.

It was not just the established churches which showed this enthusiasm for the royal jubilee. *The Times* noted with particular pleasure that

> among the various classes of Dissenters of all persuasions, we have heard of no exception to the general loyalty and piety of the day. The cathedral, the abbey, the parochial church, the meeting house of the dissenter, the chapel of the Methodist and the Catholic and the synagogue were alike opened.[35]

Another newspaper noted that 'the whole nation was like one great family ... in solemn prayer and thanksgiving for ... the Father of his People.'[36]

This reverence for the person of the sovereign has, perhaps, been one of the most long-lasting consequences of the Protestant character of the British monarchy since the Reformation. In the view of its critics, it has made the monarch what the Pope is for Roman Catholics. It is generally seen as an especially English and Anglican characteristic, exemplified in the prayers for the Royal Family traditionally said at matins and evensong in the Church of England, although the Church of Scotland has recently been accused of a similar tendency towards being over-reverential towards the monarchy in its latest prayer-book (p. 240). In his interesting analysis of established religion, the sociologist Werner Stark concludes a discussion of sixteenth- and seventeenth-century divine right theory by noting that 'this particular brand of loyalism and royalism has survived all the vicissitudes of history and is still profoundly characteristic of the English nation'. He presents it, indeed, as the reason why the Anglo-Catholic wing of the Church of England, which in other respects is more Catholic than the Roman Catholic Church, has not broken away from Protestantism. 'It remains Anglican because it cannot break loose from its deep anchor in a world-view which makes the king of England at least God's viceregent on earth, if not indeed even more.' Stark believes that this tendency to worship the monarch also explains the vein of virulent anti-Catholicism which has run through English life over the past 450 years: 'To accept a sovereign in the Vatican beside the sovereign in Buckingham Palace – what unthinkable treason and impiety!'[37]

The royal supremacy over the established Church of England which is perhaps the other major legacy of the Reformation in terms of the spiritual dimension of monarchy also has its critics who see it smacking of Anglican imperialism and privilege. Colin Buchanan, a former Bishop of Woolwich, has expressed particular unease about what he describes as the 'sentiment of romanticised affection towards the Crown' and has written that:

> Anglicans have felt both privileged and possessive in respect of their chances to indulge their romanticism. From one standpoint, this is witnessed at, for example, royal weddings at St Paul's, the Maundy Money rite somewhere in the country every Maundy Thursday, and the Royal Family's attendance at Sandringham parish church, and similar places. 'We' – the Church of England – host these events, and we walk tall when they are on.[38]

Seen in this light, the continuing existence of the so-called 'royal peculiars', namely Westminster Abbey, St George's Chapel, Windsor, and the chapels at St James' Palace, Hampton Court and the Tower of London, which come under the direct jurisdiction of the sovereign, seems to some to be unjustifiable. So does the procedure whereby all new bishops in the Church of England kneel and make homage to the sovereign after their consecration. Archaic as these customs may seem, however, they speak eloquently and movingly of the spiritual heart of the state and its embodiment in the person of the monarch. They may derive from the post-Reformation project of making the British monarchy a Protestant device but they exemplify a broader spiritual symbolism which is catholic in the fullest and best sense of the word.

It is true that only one church has the sovereign as its supreme governor. The Church of England, however, has by no means had a monopoly in its attachment and loyalty to both the institution of monarchy and the persons of individual sovereigns. The Church of Scotland has also had a close relationship with the Crown and has been held in particular affection by several sovereigns, not least Queen Victoria, as the next chapter illustrates. If Anglicanism and Presbyterianism have both played a significant part in moulding the Protestant character of the British monarchy, then another major influence, often overlooked, has been Lutheranism, the original religion of the Hanoverians and of Prince Albert who did so much to revive and re-model the institution of monarchy in the mid-nineteenth century. The United Kingdom may not itself have any strong native Lutheran tradition but several of its monarchs have been influenced by and have themselves exemplified the Lutheran values of solidity, liturgical dignity and a respect for tradition coupled with a willingness to reform. Lutheranism has, perhaps, played a rather greater role than we have realized or acknowledged in shaping the character of the British monarchy.

The Protestant project of monarchy that has been so important over the past four and a half centuries may seem increasingly anachronistic and irrelevant as Britain becomes less and less a recognizably Protestant country. Yet it has produced institutions and fostered values which, with suitable adaptation and modernization, can still strike a deep and positive chord in a more secular, pluralistic, multi-faith society. Nor should it be forgotten that non-Protestants, and especially Roman Catholics and in more recent years adherents to other faiths, have also shown their loyalty to and affection for an institution which has kept an element of the sacred and trans-cendent at the heart of the nation and its government, and for those individuals who have exercised the heavy duties and responsibilities of sovereignty.

6

Duty, discretion and dignity – the Victorian legacy

While the political power of the British monarchy steadily diminished through the later nineteenth and early twentieth centuries, its moral and spiritual influence increased as its role became essentially symbolic and exemplary. Thanks in no small part to the firm personal faith and practical Christianity of Queen Victoria, the Crown maintained and strengthened its links with religion, philanthropic and charitable activity and public service. The monarchy came to embody and personify the values of duty, service, self-sacrifice, stability, dignity and moral principle. This was combined with a certain distance and reserve, a tendency to understatement and a commitment to discretion.

This style of monarchy, which to a large extent remains the dominant model to this day, derives in large part from the Protestant project outlined in the previous chapter. It is not about divine right or the assertion of national sovereignty over and against Rome but it does conform to a recognizably Protestant ideal of the serious-minded, philanthropically inclined, churchgoing and God-fearing sovereign. Its first clear exemplar, as we have already noted, was George III, well described by his biographer John Brooke as 'the first of the Victorians'.[1] It was during the reign of his granddaughter Victoria, however, that the key principles of modern British monarchy were consolidated in terms of its strong family emphasis, its high moral tone and its embodiment of Christian principle. The move away from the martial style which characterized earlier sovereigns to a more domestic and spiritual emphasis is often portrayed as a feminization of the monarchy and it is perhaps not without significance that for more than 120 of the past 170 years the United Kingdom has had a female on the throne.

Queen Victoria epitomized this new face of Christian monarchy. Hating ostentation and show, she was far more at home opening a hospital than opening Parliament. In place of the medieval ideal of the Christian king as the valiant knight fighting for the right, or the Stuart model of the Lord's anointed, she established the role of the Christian queen as 'Bible lady' and district visitor. For several years while resident in Buckingham Palace, she personally conducted a Bible class for children of the staff. She frequently forsook Windsor Castle and Balmoral to undertake errands of mercy among sick or anxious tenants. A typical such visit was prompted by a report from one of her daughters, who had stopped to admire the flowers outside a cottage in Windsor Great Park, that the woman living there was ill and depressed. Victoria paid a visit to the cottage the following day, responding to the panic that greeted her arrival with the remark: 'Don't be put about. I come not as a Queen, but as a Christian lady.' She then asked for a Bible and read the fourteenth chapter of John's Gospel before kneeling in prayer with the sick woman and saying, 'Put your trust in Jesus and you will soon be in a land where there is no pain. You are a widow, so am I; we shall soon meet our beloved ones.'[2] This was not just a one-off visit. The woman's daughter reported that thereafter when in Windsor the queen regularly visited the cottage once or twice a week.

Victoria's natural charitable impulses were much encouraged by her husband Albert, who once declared that he believed the purpose of royalty to be 'the headship of philanthropy, a guidance and encouragement of the manifold efforts which our age is making towards a higher and purer life'.[3] He lived out this ideal, spending himself sacrificially in tirelessly promoting schemes of social and scientific reform. Together, husband and wife devoted themselves to the welfare of their subjects while at the same time seeking to transmit their own exalted sense of duty and service to their children, with the result, as Frank Prochaska puts it, that 'royal descent became not so much a title to enjoyment as a summons to duty. ... Members of the royal family inherited charitable responsibilities the way poor children inherited clothes.'

In Victoria's own case good works and dedication to public service were the result of both an adherence to the gospel of duty and an eminently practical Christian faith. Brought up after the early death of her father, the Duke of Kent, by a devout evangelical mother, she imbibed as a girl many of the principles of the 'vital religion' that swept through England in the aftermath of the Evangelical Revival.[4] Characteristically, her first reaction on being woken in the middle of the night to be told that she had acceded to the throne at the age of 18 was to ask the Archbishop of Canterbury to pray for her, prompting an early biographer to comment that she 'thus began her reign with a prayer meeting'.[5] She maintained the religious tone in her first address to Parliament, saying, 'I ascend the Throne with a deep sense of the responsibility which is imposed upon me; but I am supported by the consciousness of my own right intentions, and by my dependence upon the protection of Almighty God.'[6] It is also evident in the journal entry on the day of her coronation:

> Since it has pleased Providence to place me in this station, I shall do my utmost to fulfill my duty towards my country; I am very young ... but I am sure that very few have more real good will and more desire to do what is fit and right than I have.[7]

During her reign Victoria lost no opportunity publicly to acknowledge God and forward the claims of Christianity. When her ministers submitted a royal proclamation to the people of India in 1859 she was appalled to find that it made no mention of God or the Christian religion and took up her pen to add at the beginning of the document the phrase 'Firmly relying on the truth of Christianity, and acknowledging with gratitude the solace of religion' and, at the end, 'May the God of all power grant to us, and those in authority under us, strength to carry out these, our wishes, for the good of our people.'[8]

Under the twin influences of her mother's evangelicalism and her husband's Lutheranism, Victoria's Christianity exhibited a distinctly Protestant hue. She had a strong preference for plain 'low church' worship and a pronounced antipathy towards the High Church ritualistic tendency in the Church of England. Whatever their persuasion, clergy preaching before her were required to wear a simple black gown, and private services in her presence were conducted without the aid of vestments, candles, processions or other ornamental accessories. A journalist observed in 1888: 'It is no secret that, with her Lutheran sympathies, she feels more at home among Presbyterian than Episcopal surroundings. She is a very staunch Protestant and heartily dislikes all forms of ritualism and sacerdotal pretension.'[9]

Victoria did, indeed, find the worship in the Presbyterian Church of Scotland much more to her taste than that in the Church of England. She developed a particular affection for the Sunday morning services at Crathie Parish Church which she faithfully attended during her residence at Balmoral, much to the disapproval of the *English Churchman* which expressed the view that 'Her Majesty may, when she crosses the Tweed, doff Spitalfields silks and don Scotch tartan, but she may not put off her Churchmanship and adopt Scottish Presbyterianism without forfeiting her character as a member of the Catholic Church'.[10]

Leading Anglicans were horrified that when in Scotland the Queen not only attended a Presbyterian church but shared in the sacrament there. When she first received communion at Crathie Kirk in 1873, it was against the advice of senior English clerics. 'The Queen', her private secretary, Sir Henry Ponsonby, noted with some irritation,

> needless to say carried out her own decision, in spite of warnings and even objections from the Archbishop of

Canterbury, the Dean of Westminster and the Dean of Windsor. No report was allowed in the Court Circular but the ecclesiastical and legal side of the question produced a mass of correspondence with which her Private Secretary was very much bored.[11]

Scottish ministers not surprisingly took a rather different view. Preaching in St Giles' Cathedral the Sunday after her death, Dr Cameron Lees said, 'To see her at Crathie side by side with the poorest in the glen, taking with them the symbols of our common redemption, was a sight which those who witnessed can never forget.'[12] A Deeside farmer put it even more eloquently. On being assured by his minister that she had indeed received communion sitting unobtrusively with her tenants and servants around the Lord's table, he exclaimed: 'That would make a man die for her!'[13]

Victoria's partiality for the Church of Scotland extended to its preachers. Requiring that sermons preached before her be 'orthodox, short and interesting', she generally demanded that no preacher exceed 20 minutes. However, this was waived in the case of several Scottish ministers, notably her own favourite chaplain Norman Macleod, who once preached before her for 47 minutes only to be told that she wished he had gone on for longer. Other Scottish preachers who shared Macleod's combination of liberal broad churchmanship and vigorous muscular Christianity were similarly indulged. When Cosmo Gordon Lang, who as vicar of Portsea preached regularly at Osborne House and was himself the son of a Church of Scotland minister, complained of this favouritism, the Queen replied, 'When English dignitaries can preach as well as Scottish ministers, I will let them go on as long as they like.' She went on to spell out the main reason for her partiality to the established church north of the border: 'Thank God, the Scotch Church is a stronghold of Protestantism, most precious in these realms.'[14]

Victoria was keen to push the Church of England in a more Protestant direction. Ten days after first receiving communion at Crathie she composed a series of letters to Arthur Stanley, the Dean of Westminster, lamenting the fact that the Church of England had not been 'reformed as every other Protestant Church has been. ... We are in fact in form NOT Protestants though we are in doctrine.' She went on to express her own preference 'for the sweeping Reformation of the English Church'. If this were not possible, then at least 'the Archbishop should have the power given to him, by Parliament, to stop these ritualistic practices, dressings, bowings, etc.'.[15] The Public Worship Act, passed by Parliament the following year, and designed to strengthen the mechanism of ecclesiastical courts to deal with clergy accused of Romanizing practices, was widely seen as a result of her direct intervention and was one of the last measures resulting from a proactive use of the royal prerogative. Twenty years later she intervened to protect her beloved Church of Scotland, refusing to sanction the Queen's Speech to Parliament in 1894 if it included a commitment to its disestablishment which had been in the manifesto of the recently elected Liberal government. The religious affairs correspondent of the *Scotsman* commented, 'personally, I have no doubt that the Queen saved the historic Church of Scotland'.[16]

Although she abhorred Anglo-Catholic ritualism in the Church of England, Victoria had no animus against Roman Catholics. Indeed, a contemporary pointed out that 'she liked Roman Catholics very much better than Anglican Ritualists'.[17] She deplored the no-Popery riots which followed the restoration of the English hierarchy, declaring, 'I cannot bear to hear the violent abuse of the Catholic religion, which is so painful and cruel to the many good and innocent Roman Catholics.'[18] Towards the end of her reign she sent the Duke of Norfolk as her envoy to the Vatican to assure the Pope of her 'sincere friendship and unfeigned respect and esteem'. This personal gesture, apparently made at her own initiative, did much to thaw the traditionally frosty relations between the British Crown and Rome.

Victoria was moved by genuine faith and piety, especially

when it expressed itself in practical action, regardless of its denominational hue. What she disliked was the smooth superiority that she detected among the Anglican episcopacy. A reception for those attending the Lambeth Conference in 1897 provoked her to comment to one of her ladies in waiting, 'A very ugly party. I do not like bishops.' To the rejoinder 'Oh but your dear Majesty likes *some* bishops' came the royal reply, 'Yes, I like the man but not the bishop.'[19] Despite her dislike of the breed, however, the Queen took an active interest in episcopal appointments in the Church of England, using her influence wherever possible to secure the preferment of moderate Broad Churchmen rather than Tractarians or extreme Evangelicals. 'It is by such appointments alone,' she told Benjamin Disraeli, 'that we can hope to strengthen the tottering fabric of the established church. The extreme evangelical school do the established church as much harm as the high church.'[20] The Jewish prime minister, who was not particularly interested in matters ecclesiastical, found the Queen's hands-on approach to episcopal appointments somewhat frustrating. On one visit to Balmoral he telegraphed his secretary: 'Ecclesiastical affairs rage here. Send me Crockford's directory. I must be armed.'[21]

For Victoria, being a Christian queen did not just involve regular churchgoing, visiting the poor and taking a keen interest in ecclesiastical affairs. It also meant being a devoted wife and mother. It was these domestic aspects of Christian monarchy that Victoria particularly emphasized and that were to have a major influence on the image of royalty in Britain. The whole idea of the Royal Family was in many ways a Victorian invention. Thanks both to the Queen's own interests and to the tastes of the new mass-circulation press with its insatiable appetite for gossip and personality-led stories, the lives of the Royal Family became matters of huge national interest. New technology also helped, with the development of photography and colour printing allowing images of the Queen and her family to be widely and cheaply distributed. While this iconography generally encouraged the long-standing British tendency to worship the monarchy, it also threatened to diminish its mystique and awe. As a recent study of public discussion of the monarchy during Victoria's reign points out, 'veneration of the Royal Family and preoccupation with the trivial detail of their lives' went hand-in-hand.[22]

Victoria herself preserved her dignity and distance, setting a tone of reserve for the sovereign which has been maintained by the Windsor dynasty. It was more difficult for younger members of the Royal Family and those more distant from the throne to remain set apart and detached. This was to prove an increasingly tricky issue in the twentieth century, especially as the standards of the popular press fell and the levels of public prurience rose. During Victoria's reign the new interest in the lives and personalities of the members of the Royal Family and the popular identification with some of their most intimate moments and experiences was kept within bounds, in large part, perhaps, because it was effectively harnessed to and expressed through religion. The domestic life of the Royal Family stood at the apex of the sentimentalized Victorian religion of hearth and home. It also provided a significant boost to the civic religion of the nation and to the public face of Christianity as expressed through major state services. Where previous monarchs and their offspring had opted for quiet private services for their christenings, weddings and funerals, for Victoria and her family these events were turned into great state occasions loaded with symbolism and atmosphere.

Victoria herself was by no means enthusiastic about this development. Her natural instincts inclined her to eschew large and showy religious observances. At the same time she believed strongly in commemorating significant events in the life of her family with elaborate monuments filled with morally uplifting and improving images. Perhaps the most striking of these eloquent sermons in stone is the chapel at Windsor which she fitted out as a memorial to Albert after his death in 1861. The Albert Chapel stands as a magnificent testament to the ideal of Christian monarchy. There are striking murals of Moses blessing the Israelites and Solomon receiving the gifts of the kings of the earth. A bas-relief depicts the wisdom of Solomon, and the theme of sacrifice is underlined by panels showing the betrayal, arrest and crucifixion of Christ, the bound figure of Isaac and the symbol of the pelican. The Prince Consort's cenotaph is surrounded by statues of the principal saints of the British Isles together with the Virgin Mary and St Michael the Archangel. The immense mausoleum which Victoria ordered to be built at Frogmore to house Albert's remains further emphasized the sanctity of monarchy and proclaimed the Queen's sure and certain Christian faith, not least through the text which she chose to have inscribed above the entrance doors: 'Farewell, best beloved, here at last I shall rest with thee, with thee in Christ I shall rise.'

Victoria's mourning for Albert displayed depths of conjugal piety and respect for the dead which both fitted and to some extent moulded the religion of the family and the funerary obsessions espoused by many of her subjects. Its excessive and prolonged nature, however, seriously weakened popular support for the monarchy. It was largely in an effort to counter this that the government decided to make the recovery of the Prince of Wales from typhoid fever the occasion for a spectacular service of thanksgiving in St Paul's Cathedral in 1872. Victoria herself was characteristically uneasy about the procession and ceremonial which was to accompany this event, making clear her own feeling that 'no religious act ought ever to be allied to pomp and show'.[23] The views of the government, and specifically of the Prime Minister, Gladstone, prevailed, however, and in her first major public appearance since her husband's death ten years earlier, the Queen attended the service at St Paul's, which was echoed in smaller scale acts of thanksgiving in churches and chapels throughout the land and in a huge performance at Crystal Palace of a specially commissioned and suitably triumphant Te Deum by Sir Arthur Sullivan, who changed the last line to 'God save the Queen'. These events mark a significant development in the linking of episodes in the domestic life of the royal family – in this case the recovery of the Queen's son from the illness which had

killed his father – to organized religion and state ceremonial.
How far the focus was Christian rather than civic religion was
a moot point, but the evangelical Earl of Shaftesbury for one,
having witnessed his countrymen's reaction to the St Paul's
thanksgiving service, was not going to quibble on this point:

> I rejoice in this manifestation of feeling. It is something
> gathered out of the wreck of all hereditary attachments,
> and may be (God may be merciful to us!) the seed
> plot of better things in this ancient Kingdom. There is
> something, too, in the spectacle of a whole nation not
> ashamed, in these days, to join in a great national act of
> religion. In the vast majority there may be no sentiment
> of the kind, but, at any rate, there is a willing acceptance
> of it, and not, as there would be in Paris, a satanical
> rejection of it.[24]

Five years earlier, the importance of the family aspect of
monarchy had been identified by Walter Bagehot in his classic
work, *The English Constitution*. Bagehot realized that, lacking
political power, modern monarchy would survive and indeed
thrive by appealing to the heart rather than the head. 'So long
as the human heart is strong and the human reason weak,' he
wrote, 'Royalty will be strong because it appeals to diffused
feeling, and Republics weak because they appeal to the understanding.'[25] On this view, the domestic and familial aspects of
monarchy assumed particular importance.

> A family on the throne is an interesting idea. It brings
> down the pride of sovereignty to the level of petty life.
> ... The women – one half the human race at least – care
> fifty times more for a marriage than a ministry. ... A royal
> family sweetens politics by the seasonable addition of
> nice and pretty events.[26]

Bagehot's chapters in *The English Constitution* on the value
and purpose of monarchy were studied by both George V and

George VI as part of their preparation for kingship and are still regularly quoted today. They rightly make much of its spiritual heart. For Bagehot the two great features of monarchy are its intelligibility and the fact that 'it strengthens our government with the strength of religion'.[27] After providing a fascinating historical exegesis of sacred monarchy in Britain through all the vicissitudes of the seventeenth and eighteenth centuries, he concludes that it constitutes 'the solitary transcendent element' in the body politic. 'Commonly hidden like a mystery, and sometimes paraded like a pageant', monarchy 'consecrates our whole state' and provides a visible symbol of unity.[28] Bagehot goes on to commend the situation prevailing in his own time whereby the Crown had come to be regarded as 'the head of both our society and morality'.

> The virtues of Queen Victoria and the virtues of George III have sunk deep into the popular heart. We have come to believe that it is natural to have a virtuous sovereign, and that the domestic virtues are as likely to be found on thrones as they are eminent when there.[29]

Bagehot's most quoted dictum concerns the importance of maintaining the mystery and magic of royalty:

> Above all things our royalty is to be reverenced, and if you begin to poke about it you cannot reverence it. When there is a select committee on the Queen, the charm of royalty will be gone. Its mystery is its life. We must not let in daylight upon the magic.[30]

Although this remark was made in terms of the constitutional understanding of the monarch's influence and prerogative, it clearly has a wider applicability and touches on the very heart of the spiritual dimension of modern monarchy. Much of the strength and popularity of the British monarchy in the early part of the twentieth century derived from the fact that not too much daylight was let in on the magic. The churches played a key role in maintaining the element of mystery and encouraging a reverential attitude towards those occupying the throne through providing highly colourful and elaborate rituals for coronations, royal weddings and funerals. In an important essay the historian David Cannadine has pointed to the decisive change which took place in the image of the British monarchy in the period between the late 1870s and 1914.[31] Its ritual and ceremonial aspects, which had hitherto been largely low-key, private, often ineptly organized and of little popular appeal, became splendid, public and popular. Among the reasons for this change was a new enthusiasm on the part of the clergy in the Church of England for ritual and stage management. Victoria's longevity encouraged the national Church to organize large-scale services to celebrate her Golden and Diamond Jubilees and bask in her reflected glory. For the service in 1887 to mark the fiftieth anniversary of her accession, Westminster Abbey was transformed by the rebuilding of the organ, the remodelling of the choir stalls and the introduction of electric lighting. The officiating clergy were dressed for the first time in copes and coloured stoles, hailed by a journalist present as 'a novel and picturesque innovation' even if they may have raised the Queen's anti-ritualistic hackles. In the Jubilee celebrations the Church and the monarchy were indissolubly linked and jointly promoted. The cheering crowds which greeted the Queen as she drove through the East End of London in May 1887 were taken by Edward Benson, the Archbishop of Canterbury, as an indicator that the Church as well as the monarchy was loved and valued. 'They are not a church-going race,' he noted in his diary of the English, 'but there is a solemn quiet sense of religion for that in their sayings and doings.'[32]

The Church's reverential attitude towards the monarch is well captured in the hymns written for Victoria's Jubilees. The Golden Jubilee hymn written by John Ellerton, the vicar of Crewe best known for 'The Day, Thou Gavest, Lord is Ended', painted a vivid picture of the varied peoples of the British Empire uniting in the national anthem:

Dusky Indian, strong Australian,
Western forest, Southern sea,
None are wanting, none are alien,
All in one great prayer agree –
God save the Queen!

The official hymn for the Diamond Jubilee, written by William Walsham How, the Bishop of Wakefield, with an appropriately hearty tune by Sullivan, and commanded to be sung in every parish church in the land on Sunday, 20 June 1897, focused almost as much on the matriarchal majesty of Victoria as on the glory of God:

Oh Royal heart, with wide embrace
For all her children yearning!
Oh happy realm, such mother-grace
With loyal love returning!
Where England's flag flies wide unfurl'd,
All tyrant wrongs repelling,
God make the world a better world
For man's brief earthly dwelling.

This level of devotion to the Queen was by no means confined to the Church of England. A recent study has noted that of all Victorian periodicals, 'the leading Catholic newspaper, *The Tablet*, showed perhaps the most reverence towards the monarchy because of its belief in the divinely sanctioned nature of royal authority'.[33] A Church of Scotland minister described the Queen as 'the nursing-mother of a Christian population'.[34] After 60 years of presiding over a period of unexampled prosperity during which the British Empire had grown by more than ten times to encompass a quarter of the earth's land mass and one-third of its population, it was hardly surprising that Victoria had become an icon if not actually a goddess to many of her subjects. Her own strong Christian faith, firm moral rectitude, unwavering attention to duty, high seriousness and simple, unpretentious bourgeois tastes did nothing to diminish the attitude of reverence. One of the many poems written after her death links Crown, Cross and expansion of empire in a somewhat unorthodox trinity:

> A Righteous Ruler! Thou Thy throne hast planted
> Beneath the Cross, where love was crucified,
> Thy prayer for grace, in deep abundance granted,
> Hath spread Thine Empire, far as flows the tide.[35]

Close as they may sometimes have come to it, however, churchmen fell short of idolatry in their attitude towards Victoria. She was rather held up as an example, a model of Christian monarchy, an ally of all working for good and noble causes, and as one who had been especially blessed and favoured by God. 'As to Solomon of old,' wrote the clerical author of one tribute on her death, 'so to her God gave not only wisdom and knowledge, but also riches, and wealth, and honour, such as none of the kings of England ever had before her.'[36] Norman MacLeod lauded her 'noble calling as a Queen and the value of her life to the nation'.[37] Hensley Henson, preaching in Westminster Abbey after her death in 1901, was among many who alluded principally to her philanthropic activities:

> Every clergyman, philanthropist and social reformer has had, these sixty-three years past, an ally and sympathizer on the throne of his country. ... We thank Almighty God for the gift of that gracious and serviceable life, we add to our national treasures the priceless jewel of a pure and lofty tradition bound about the ancient and famous English Crown, and henceforth we connect our civic duty with a dear and honoured name.[38]

The pattern of Christian monarchy established by Victoria and predicated on the values of duty, discretion and dignity held throughout the twentieth century and is still largely normative today. As practised by the Windsors, it has had four main prongs: civic duty expressed principally through philanthropic and charitable activity; spiritual leadership demonstrated through attendance at religious services and public exhortation; the development of ceremonial and ritual to emphasize the splendid and mystical aspects of monarchy; and personal example through private lives lived according to high moral principles and family values.

Of these four main features of modern Christian monarchy, civic duty expressed through philanthropy has been the most important. A Mass Observation survey carried out in 1964 found that people were more than twice as likely to encounter a member of the Royal Family in a 'welfare' context than in any other situation. Yet there is also much truth in Frank Prochaska's comment that the main contribution of the monarchy to national well-being in the twentieth century has been 'largely ignored or misunderstood. ... It may sound curious to those obsessed by constitutional niceties or royal spectacles, but the humdrum day-in day-out charitable activity of the monarchy may be far more important than the "dignified" duties.' Prochaska, who has written more than anyone else about this activity of the monarchy, rightly points out that it 'serves the country by propping up civil society, that commonwealth of citizenship outside the state'.[39]

Royal philanthropy has been strongly supportive of what might be called the voluntaryist ethic which emphasizes the promotion of social welfare through private charity, local cooperation and self-help rather than through government agencies and legislative action. This voluntarist tone was set at the very beginning of the twentieth century by Edward VII, who, as Prince of Wales, had been deeply involved in supporting numerous voluntary welfare associations and launched a fund to support the London hospitals. *Punch* published a cartoon entitled 'Our New Knight Hospitaller' showing him as a medieval knight on horseback with the cross of St George on his tunic and a banner in his hand inscribed with the words 'Loyalty' and 'Charity'. King Edward's Hospital Fund for London, as it became known on his accession in 1902, later changed its name to the King's Fund and continues to this day to support medical and health research. George V was equally if not more assiduous in his charitable activities. Prochaska comments that his 'industrial tours, hospital work, visits to poor cottagers, speeches, broadcasts, subscriptions and fundraising were better known to the common man than his opinion of the Versailles Treaty or the gold standard'.[40] Characteristically, he ended his Silver Jubilee speech to the empire in 1935 with a call to voluntary service and the most enduring monument of that Jubilee was a trust set up in his name to provide camps and clubs for young people.

George V expected good works from all members of the Royal Family. He kept a map in Buckingham Palace into which little flags were stuck to show the places where his children had opened hospitals, attended fundraising events or made visits. Later he had a chart drawn up, which was brought to Sandringham each Christmas, listing the public engagements and appearances by each member of the Royal Family during the year. His younger son Albert, later George VI, fully lived up to his father's expectations. In 1919, he took over the presidency of the Boys' Welfare Association, later the Industrial Welfare Association, which gave him considerable insight into factory conditions and industrial relations. As Duke of York, he was instrumental in setting up annual summer holiday camps which brought together public school and working-class boys and in which he himself participated. He was also closely involved with the establishment of the National Playing Fields Association. As king, George VI continued his charitable endeavours which sprang out of a deep practical Christian faith. His broadcast to the Commonwealth and Empire which followed his coronation in 1937 contained the moving statement that 'the highest of distinctions is the service of others, and to the Ministry of Kingship I have in your hearing dedicated myself, with the Queen at my side, in words of the deepest solemnity'.[41] His approach was shared by his wife Elizabeth, who in the words of Prochaska, 'had a marked preference for Christian kindness and voluntary service over the corporate and the abstract'.[42]

As more fully outlined in the next chapter which focuses on her reign, Elizabeth II and her family have continued to put the monarchy at the head of the vast voluntary sector in the United Kingdom by giving their patronage to hundreds of philanthropic associations and charities and actively promoting the ethic of community service. Particularly notable contributions in this area have been made by Prince Philip, Prince Charles and Princess Anne.

Alongside their philanthropic and charitable work, the Windsors have also demonstrated their commitment to the principle of Christian monarchy by exercising spiritual leadership. This has been particularly expressed through personal exhortation as well as through the more traditional role of leading the nation in prayer and thanksgiving. Relatively early on in the twentieth century the new medium of broadcasting enabled the sovereign to speak directly and intimately not just to his or her subjects in the United Kingdom but to the peoples of the Empire and Commonwealth. Since their inception in the early 1930s, royal broadcasts have become the main and most effective way in which monarchs have communicated with the people and expressed their own personalities. It is striking how many of them have included a strongly Christian message and indeed had a markedly sermonic character. This has been particularly true of the annual Christmas broadcast which early on in its life took on a ritualistic quality and became a key event in many families' Christmas Day celebrations. The idea for it came from John Reith, the fervently Presbyterian and staunchly monarchist first director of the BBC, who in 1932 persuaded initially reluctant palace officials that George V should make a live Christmas Day broadcast to the people of the Empire. Reith proudly recorded in his autobiography:

It was the most spectacular success in BBC history thus far. The King had been heard all over the world with surprising clarity; only in New Zealand were parts of the speech inaudible owing to atmospherics. It was sensationally starred in foreign countries; the *New York Times* in large type: 'Distant lands Thrill to His "God Bless You"'; two thousand leading articles were counted in Broadcasting House.[43]

Well might the *New York Times* single out the valedictory benediction. Here was the British monarch fulfilling one of the classic roles of the Old Testamental king and invoking God's blessing on his subjects, in this case not just at home, but throughout the dominions of his empire. The audience for the first royal Christmas message was an estimated 20 million. George V continued to make a live broadcast every Christmas Day until his death in 1936. The tradition was nearly abandoned the following year when the Prime Minister, Neville Chamberlain, expressed the view that it was impossible to produce something new and interesting to say every year. 'How pathetic,' Reith characteristically noted in his diary, 'almost unbelievable. How typical of the attitude of politicians.'[44] He insisted that the broadcast become an annual fixture, and so it has remained, moving to television in 1957 and from live transmission to being recorded in 1960, but always going out at the sacrosanct hour of 3p.m. on Christmas afternoon, originally chosen as the best time for reaching the countries in the Empire through short-wave transmitters from Britain but also ideal for those at home rising from the festive lunch table.

Reith, who was determined to make the BBC an arm of the church militant, was keen that royal homilies should not just be confined to Christmas. He found a powerful ally in Queen Elizabeth, whom, he noted after sitting next to her at a dinner in Buckingham Palace in 1940, ' agreed emphatically with me that the Christian ethic should be the basis of post-war policy and thought the King ought to make a pronouncement about it – "he believes it, you know", she added'.[45] After conquering the stammer that had so inhibited his earlier attempts at public speaking, George VI found broadcasting an ideal medium through which to express his own deep Christian faith. His Empire Day broadcast in 1939 ended with a characteristically moving message for young people:

> Hold fast to all that is just and of good report in the heritage which your fathers have left to you, but strive also to improve and equalize that heritage for all men and women in the years to come. Remember too that the key to all progress lies in faith, hope, and love. May God give you their support, and may God help them to prevail.[46]

It was the annual Christmas broadcast which really established the monarch in the role of preacher. The broadcasts made by George VI during the Second World War carried a strong Christian message which made a deep impression on the millions who listened. His 1939 Christmas broadcast memorably set the tone when he spoke of the war being fought for 'the cause of Christian civilization' and went on to quote the words which are now engraved at the entrance to his tomb in St George's Chapel, Windsor:

> I said to the man who stood at the Gate of the Year, 'Give me a light that I may tread safely into the unknown.' And he replied, 'Go out into the darkness, and put your hand into the Hand of God. That shall be better to you than light, and safer than a known way.'[47]

If broadcasting gave monarchs a platform for preaching to the nation, it also played an important role in presenting them to the public in their religious and churchgoing roles. It is hard to overestimate the impact of first radio and then television's coverage of coronations and royal jubilees, weddings and funerals.

Once again, John Reith deserves much of the credit for establishing British broadcasting's love affair with the monarchy and especially with its spiritual dimension. He has been well described as 'Gold Microphone Pursuivant'.[48] In 1923 he masterminded the first-ever radio outside broadcast to cover the Duke of York's wedding to Lady Elizabeth Bowes-Lyon. Microphones were positioned so that listeners could hear the sounds of the processional horses and carriages, the cheering crowds and the bells ringing as well as the church service itself. In this way an 'audible pageant' was created that did much to enhance the magic and aura of monarchy and established a pattern for future broadcasts of royal occasions. For the semi-Jubilee of George V's reign in 1935 Reith mounted the first-ever religious service in the concert hall of Broadcasting House in which the Archbishop of Canterbury, the Moderator-designate of the Church of Scotland, and the Moderator of the Free Church Federal Council all took part, with an orchestra and choir conduced by Adrian Boult and Walford Davies and George Thalben Ball at the organ. At Reith's specific request all the clergy wore scarlet cassocks for this radio service, which, he noted with characteristic self-congratulation, was generally judged to have been more impressive than the official thanksgiving service in St Paul's Cathedral the following day.

Although the BBC played a major role in projecting the ceremony and splendour of Christian monarchy in the twentieth century, a new emphasis on these aspects had, in fact, marked royal services some time before the arrival of microphones and television cameras. It was clearly evident in the first coronation of the century. Jocelyn Perkins, the sacrist of Westminster Abbey, noted how 'the attainment of a lofty standard of worship and ceremonial at the solemn sacring of Edward VII was felt on all sides to be imperative'. He went on to contrast the magnificence of the 1902 coronation with the skimpiness of previous coronations:

> From end to end did the altar blaze with a display of alms dishes, flagons, chalices. ... Upon the amateur ritualist of the nineteenth century, with his tailor made vases,

his feeble floral decorations, the scene bestowed a sorely needed lesson.[49]

The Edwardian era, traditionally associated with the full flowering of British imperialism, saw a conscious revival of the chivalric aspects of medieval Christian kingship. The investiture of the future Edward VIII as Prince of Wales in Carnarfon Castle in 1911, a wholly novel event yet packed with medieval language and symbolism, was infused with Christian references. The 17-year-old prince ended his speech saying (in Welsh), 'Without God, without anything; God is enough' and the hymn sung, *Marchog, Iesu, yn llyddianus* ('Lord, ride on to triumph glorious'), had strong associations with the great Welsh revival of 1904 to 1905. Imperialism encouraged reverential feelings towards the monarchy, as exemplified in the 1911 Indian Durbar where George V appeared to a quarter of a million of his Indian subjects as 'a semi-divine figure' clad in purple robes and wearing a crown valued at £60,000. It also inspired a revival of the medieval system of knightly honours and orders of chivalry centred on and deriving from the person of the monarch. The Order of the British Empire was instituted in 1917 to embrace the 99 per cent of the population who did not qualify for the medieval orders of the Garter, Thistle and Bath, and to honour especially those involved in philanthropic work, literature, science and art. Modelled on the old chivalric orders, the new order had a clear Christian dimension, symbolized in its motto 'For God and the Empire' and the fact that it had both a prelate, the Bishop of London, and (eventually – the location was not finally established until 1957) a chapel in the crypt of St Paul's Cathedral. The role of the monarch as the fount of the honours system, presiding over civil and military investitures as well as at long-standing survivals from the medieval era like the Garter service at St George's Chapel, Windsor, confirmed the close association of the Crown with the values of heroic sacrifice and knightly virtue.

This association was powerfully reinforced during and in the immediate aftermath of the First World War. Much has been written about the intermingling and intertwining of the themes of Christian sacrifice and secular nationalism during this period.[50] The Crown, traditionally embodying both themes, inevitably played a key role in the symbolic linking of Christianity and patriotism. This was not, of course, a new phenomenon. It had been powerfully demonstrated in the tribute placed beside Queen Victoria's tomb in Frogmore by her daughter-in-law Queen Alexandra, which took the form of a cross resting on the Union flag. The experience of the Great War considerably heightened the link between monarch, Christian sacrifice and patriotism. It was perhaps supremely expressed at the funeral of the unknown warrior in Westminster Abbey in 1920 when King George V walked behind the coffin on which a wreath bore a card written in his own hand. In the words of Piers Brendon and Phillip Whitehead, 'The funeral was a consecration of chivalry whose apotheosis was the Crown.' The inscription on the tomb concluded: 'They buried him among the kings because he had done good towards God and towards his house.'[51]

The years following the First World War saw a significant shift in the arrangements made for royal weddings and other rites of passage. Increasingly these became big state occasions focused on a major church service. The wedding of Princess Mary and Viscount Lascelles in 1922 took place not in the privacy of the chapels at St James's Palace or Windsor, the venues for most previous marriages in the royal family, but in Westminster Abbey with a full-scale procession through the streets of London beforehand. The following year the Duke of York became the first royal prince to be married in the Abbey for 500 years. His wedding procession was watched by more than a million people who lined the streets of London. Since then, virtually all royal weddings have taken place in either Westminster Abbey or St Paul's Cathedral and have involved spectacular processions through the capital as well as increasingly elaborate television coverage.

The two major Anglican churches in London have also been the venues for other highly public services where monarchs have given thanks for particular anniversaries or led the nation in acts of thanksgiving or remembrance. Twentieth century sovereigns have generally entered into the spirit of these occasions with markedly more enthusiasm than their nineteenth-century predecessors. Partly due to her age, Victoria felt unable to leave her carriage and enter St Paul's Cathedral for the service to commemorate her Diamond Jubilee in 1897. George V, by contrast, was an enthusiastic and active participant in the service at St Paul's which marked the high point of his Silver Jubilee celebrations in 1935 and was marred only, according to some observers, by a superfluity of clergy. In an address relayed through loudspeakers to the cheering multitude outside, the Archbishop of Canterbury declared that the national spirit of unity had found its centre in the throne and that King George was 'the Father of his People'.[52] The king and queen appeared on the balcony of Buckingham Palace every night for a week to acknowledge the rapturous applause of the crowds below and drove through the East End and docklands of London. The spiritual dimension of the Jubilee celebrations was commented on by several of those who took part. After attending a reception for Dominion prime ministers, the Labour politician Ramsay Macdonald noted, 'We all went away feeling that we had taken part in something very much like a Holy Communion.'[53] Harold Nicolson reflected:

> There was pride in the first place, pride in the fact that, whereas the other thrones had fallen, our own monarchy, unimpaired in dignity, had survived for more than a thousnad years. Reverence in the thought that in the Crown we possessed a symbol of patriotism, a focus for unison, an emblem of continuity in a rapidly dissolving world. Satisfaction in feeling that the sovereign stood above all class animosities, all political ambitions, all sectional interests. Comfort in the realisation that here

was a strong, benevolent patriarch, personifying the highest standards of the race. Gratitude to a man who by his probity had earned the esteem of the whole world. King George represented and enhanced those domestic and public virtues which the British regarded as specifically their own. In him, they saw, reflected and magnified, what they cherished as their own individual ideals – faith, duty, honesty, courage, common sense, tolerance, decency and truth.[54]

Reverence for the monarchy reaching this quasi-religious level has perhaps been most publicly evident on the occasions of royal deaths and funerals where public mourning has allowed the expression of pent-up grief and sorrow and supplied a language of transcendence not normally available to most people. More, perhaps, than other public events, royal funerals allow people to make contact with latent religious impulses and take stock of both their own lives and the life of the nation within a framework of overarching metaphysical values. Once again, broadcasting has made a significant contribution to heightening the spiritual atmosphere of these occasions. When George V died in 1936 the BBC implemented an 80-page policy document entitled 'Procedures on the Death of a Sovereign' and broadcast only solemn music, tolling bells, religious services, elegiac poetry and lapidary orations. There were those who felt that it went over the top. One journalist exclaimed, 'I am beginning to think that the death of the King is the greatest event in human history since the Crucifixion.'[55] The heavy official Court mourning from which the BBC took its cue almost certainly affected the public's mood. As Brendon and Whitehead observe, 'Probably the official mourning both inspired and expressed popular sorrow. Unquestionably it was orchestrated to promote veneration for the throne and to enhance the spiritual dimension of monarchy.'[56] Yet it is also true that there was a strong latent folk religion of reverence for the monarchy, tied in no small part to its identification with Christianity as well as with a more civic religion, which needed little official prompting and expressed itself in genuine grieving over the death of a deeply loved king.

It was in the aftermath of George V's death that the British monarchy went through its most serious crisis in the twentieth century. The circumstances surrounding the abdication of Edward VIII showed the dangers inherent in basing part of the monarchy's appeal on personal example and high moral principles. For once, a sovereign received neither popular nor ecclesiastical approbation. Following the abdication an American journalist observed that for the first time royal personages were being spoken of as human beings, not deities: 'The Hallelujahs have been soft-pedalled; the taboo is off.'[57] The churches' opposition to divorce undoubtedly played a major part in forcing Edward off the throne. In a broadcast shortly after the abdication the Archbishop of Canterbury, Cosmo Gordon Lang, expressed his disappointment that Edward had abandoned his sacred trust and 'sought happiness in a manner inconsistent with the Christian principles of marriage, and within a social circle whose standard and way of life are alien to all the best instincts and traditions of his people'.[58]

After this serious but short-lived wobble, George VI restored to the Crown its essential decency, dignity, self-discipline and conscientiousness which sprang, in his case, from a deep Christian faith. Personal example and high moral standards exemplified through a happy family life once again became one of the central features and definining characteristics of modern British monarchy. *The Times* leader on the morning of his coronation noted that successful kingship relies 'not upon intellectual brilliance or superlative talent of any kind, but upon the moral qualities of steadiness, staying-power and self-sacrifice'.[59] The Second World War provided a context for the exercise of monarchical fortitude and forbearance which both set an example to and moved the nation. George VI and Queen Elizabeth insisted on remaining in Buckingham Palace throughout the Blitz. Describing the environment in which their two daughters grew up in the 1940s, their nanny, Marion

Crawford, noted that 'in the Palace, discretion and self-control – and I feel I must add genuine self-sacrifice – are carried to lengths quite unbelievable to the world outside'.[60]

It was in this atmosphere with its essentially Victorian values that Princess Elizabeth was reared. She had a happy childhood. Unlike his own father, George VI was demonstrably affectionate with his children and they were surrounded by love and affection from both their parents. They were brought up in the Christian faith and schooled in the Victorian virtues of duty, discretion and dignity. There is some evidence that the young Elizabeth felt that she was at the receiving end of rather too much religious teaching. According to Lord Dawson who attended George V during his final illness in 1936, the 10-year-old princess, visiting her grandfather at Sandringham, was asked by the Archbishop of Canterbury, Cosmo Gordon Lang, whether she would like to walk in the garden with him. 'Yes, very much,' she replied, 'but please don't tell me anything more about God. I know all about him already.'[61] The following year she wrote an account of her father's coronation, describing it as 'very, very wonderful' but complaining that 'at the end the service got rather boring as it was all prayers'.[62]

These early protestations aside, however, Princess Elizabeth soon showed that she had the same strong faith and moral qualities as her father, her grandfather and her great-great grandmother. In her very first broadcast, made at the age of 14 from Windsor Castle during the darkest days of the Second World War in October 1940, with her younger sister Margaret at her side, she spoke directly to children who had been evacuated from their homes or moved abroad, and told them, 'We know, every one of us, that in the end all will be well; for God will care for us and give us victory and peace.' After listening to the broadcast, Jock Colville, private secretary to the Prime Minister, wrote in his diary, 'Her voice was most impressive and, if the Monarchy survives, Queen Elizabeth II should be a most successful radio Queen.'[63] So she has been, excelling the earlier Windsors in the role of bringing spiritual exhortation to the nation. In her case, the exhortation has been consistently coupled with and backed by manifestly exemplary behaviour, a high sense of self-dedication and a sincere Christian faith. Her reaction to unexpectedly ascending the throne at a young age was very similar to that of Victoria in not dissimilar circumstances over 100 years earlier – to turn herself to prayer and ask for the prayers of her people. This was what she said in her first Christmas message as Queen in 1952, broadcast live from Sandringham:

> At my Coronation next June, I shall dedicate myself anew to your service. I shall do so in the presence of a great congregation, drawn from every part of the Commonwealth and Empire, while millions outside Westminster Abbey will hear the promises and the prayers being offered up within its walls, and see much of the ancient ceremony in which Kings and Queens before me have taken part through century upon century.
>
> You will be keeping it as a holiday; but I want to ask you all, whatever your religion may be, to pray for me on that day – to pray that God may give me wisdom and strength to carry out the solemn promises I shall be making, and that I may faithfully serve Him and you, all the days of my life.[64]

7

The past 60 years

The past 60 years have seen massive changes in British culture and society, three of which in particular have impacted upon the standing of monarchy in both its institutional and personal aspects. There has been a steady decline in deference and respect for authority and institutions of all kinds. The hold of Christianity in Britain has considerably weakened, leaving a nation and society variously described as post-Christian, secular, pluralistic or multi-faith. Perhaps most corrosive to the spiritual heart of monarchy has been the ever-growing and largely unchecked power of the mass media, notably television and the tabloid press, with their relentless pursuit of the sensational and the trivial, and their combination of intrusiveness and untrustworthiness well summed up by the Prince of Wales in his parody of the hymn 'Immortal, invisible, God only wise':

> Insistent, persistent, the Press never end,
> One day they will drive me right round the bend,
> Recording, rephrasing, every word that I say,
> It's got to be news at the end of the day.[1]

The monarchy is, of course, by no means the only institution to suffer in recent decades from these intertwined trends. The range of those affected was well summed up by the broadcaster Robin Day shortly before his death in 2000:

> Look at all our great traditional institutions – the Monarchy, the Church, the judges, the police, the Bar, the BBC – every pillar of the established order. They seem now to inspire more ridicule than respect. It is due to an

overwhelming sea-change in attitude to authority, institutions, history, religion, tradition, law and ceremony. The age of deference, the age of reverence, is over.[2]

In part this loss of respect for institutions springs from the cult of novelty and the dismissal of tradition and history. It is also the result of the steady drip-drip effect of the muck-raking, debunking, cynical mentality that has prevailed in Britain, and especially in the British media, since the late 1960s. The monarchy has been particularly vulnerable to assault because it is so personal and because it cannot hit back. Much of the satire directed against members of the Royal Family over the past 50 years now seems very tame – *Private Eye* calling the Queen Brenda and *Spitting Image* depicting the late Queen Mother waving a gin bottle – and some of it has been highly perceptive – the portrayal of Prince Charles as the 'Heir of Sorrows' – but its cumulative effect has undoubtedly been to sap respect for the monarchy and strip away the mystique and magic which Bagehot so rightly saw as central to its survival. It has to be said that certain members of the Royal Family have not helped by giving tabloid journalists and satirists plenty to write about.

The nature and effects of this assault were well identified by Eric Evans, the Dean of St Paul's Cathedral, in a letter to *The Times* in April 1996 following the publication of a MORI poll showing a slide in popular support for monarchy. The issue, he rightly noted, 'is not that members of the Royal Family are without fault. In each generation some member will have erred and strayed and one could take the line right back to Edward the Confessor to realise the truth of this.' Rather the problem lay in the overall loss of respect for institutions and for those who carry responsibilities: 'The institution of the monarchy, like that of any corporate body, if it is to work properly, demands respect. ... Without that it can wither and become a mere shadow of what it was intended to be.'[3] As Clifford Longley has observed, 'deference and dignity cannot long survive in a tabloid culture: those institutions which depend on the maintenance of deference and dignity are therefore doomed.' He points to the similar predicament of the closely interrelated institutions of church and Crown, both central to defining the identity and character of the United Kingdom in the absence of a written constitution and equally dependent on what he calls 'the body armour of mystery', and to the dire consequences of their loss of status as a result of the effects of salacious gutter journalism.

> Because they are two of the fundamental bearers of the meaning of statehood, profound damage is done to the nation below the water line. If neither its Crown nor its Church is held in respect, and nothing else is placed at the centre of the national altar, how long can Britain itself hope to be respected?[4]

The assault of the tabloids on the spiritual heart of monarchy has been multi-pronged. It is driven in part by a blatant anti-monarchical agenda, most evident in the newspapers owned by Rupert Murdoch. Then there is the prurient obsession with sexual peccadilloes and the intrusive activities of the paparazzi which have invaded the privacy of members of the Royal Family, put them on a par with showbusiness celebrities and pop stars, and encouraged a whole generation to think of them first and foremost in terms of scandals and sensational revelations. To quote Clifford Longley again,

> We have arrived at a job specification for a hereditary head of state which is well nigh impossible to fulfil. He or she, as Supreme Governor of the Church of England and symbolic representative and figurehead of the nation, has to be seen to live a life that is a shining model of private and public virtue. But the monarch has to do this at a time when the tabloid press has abandoned any pretence of deference for position or respect for privacy (or even truth) and in the context of persistent public ridicule and scandal.[5]

At its height in the 1980s and 1990s, the incorporation of the Royal Family into the prevailing celebrity culture had a particularly debilitating effect on the spiritual status of monarchy. For a time the dominant pictorial images of royalty in newspapers and magazines were more likely to be snatched photos taken with long lenses of bikini-clad female figures cavorting beside a swimming pool or on a luxury yacht,or blurry-eyed princes leaving fashionable nightclubs than the more traditional posed shots of weddings, christenings and state occasions, informal gatherings around the Christmas tree or on the lawn at Balmoral, church parades at Sandringham or Crathie, or stern-faced duty at the Cenotaph. This trend towards turning royalty into showbusiness stars and personalities was encouraged by the behaviour of certain members of the Royal Family and by the misguided enthusiasm of certain advisers and courtiers for media exposure and image building. The past decade has seen a return to more respect on the part of the press and more dignified behaviour on the part of the royals, but there is no doubt that much of the mystique and spiritual aura around monarchy has gone.

It is all very different from the state of affairs in the early years of Queen Elizabeth II's reign when fears were expressed in a number of quarters that, if anything, the monarchy had become too sacred and was held in too much reverence. In the aftermath of the coronation, critics argued that 'monarcholatry' was indeed in danger of becoming the national religion in Marx's sense of providing an opium for the people. Malcolm Muggeridge wrote in 1956 that 'the monarchy has taken the place of religion in the minds of the masses' and that 'true religion is in danger of being driven out by the royal soap opera ... a sort of substitute or ersatz religion'.[6] Three years later a Sunday newspaper concluded from a survey of its readership that 'reverence for royalty has become the new national religion'.[7]

Other critics of monarchy in the 1950s and 1960s complained of an over-emphasis on its sacred and spiritual dimension. In 1957 Lord Altrincham, a radical Tory peer, attacked the stuffiness and 'tweediness' of the Queen's image. He described her style of speaking as 'a pain in the neck' and observed that 'the personality conveyed by the utterances which are put in her mouth is that of a priggish schoolgirl, captain of the hockey team, a prefect, and a recent candidate for Confirmation'. The nub of the problem was that 'the Coronation had emphasized the priestly aspect of her office, and in the ensuing period she had continued to appear more sacerdotal than secular'.[8] In similar vein, Kingsley Martin suggested in 1962 that the Crown belonged to a pre-scientific society ruled by magic and superstition:

> With the growth of science and democracy, people begin to realize that monarchy is a survival, surrounded by superstitions which must be outgrown along with haunted houses, being thirteen at table and the disastrous effects of walking under ladders. An ideological battle is then joined in which the ruling class, whose position depends on retaining the existing social structure, use all the resources of propaganda to persuade the uneducated and the half-educated that in some mysterious way the monarchy is still sacrosanct and essential to the safety of the realm.[9]

The monarchy withstood these attacks just as it withstood the later and more damaging assaults of the tabloid press. It is true that it did go through a particularly bruising decade in the 1990s, which I described in the first edition of this book as the *decem anni horribiles*, expanding the Queen's own memorable description of 1992, the year which saw three of her children facing highly publicized marital difficulties as well as a disastrous fire at Windsor Castle, as her *annus horribilis*. Yet the fact is that the monarchy has ridden out that particular storm and come through it, albeit slightly battered. Overall, opinion polls suggest that public support for monarchy is not at a significantly lower level now than it was 60 years ago. Almost certainly, fewer of the population would now agree to the proposition that the sovereign is directly chosen by God than was the case in the 1950s or 1960s. It is itself indicative of changing mores that, as far as I am aware, that question has not been asked in recent decades. However, the institution of monarchy continues to command widespread popular support despite all that has assailed it. This is so is in no small measure due to the Queen's own steadiness and the way in which she and other senior royals have led what they are wont to call 'the firm' in the four key roles of philanthropy, spiritual leadership and exhortation, ceremonial splendour and personal example.

The Queen's tireless championship and patronage of voluntary public service stands very much in the tradition of the welfare monarchy anatomized by Frank Prochaska and discussed in the last chapter. In the face of an increasingly celebrity-driven and star-struck culture and media, she has resisted the temptation to turn the monarchy into a branch of the celebrity industry and infuse it with showbusiness values. Rather, she has given strong and consistent support to what she herself has called 'the quiet sort of public life'. In its leading article on her 1998 Christmas broadcast, the *Daily Telegraph* commented on the 'rather unfashionable organizations' that she had singled out for commendation, like the Scouts and Guides, the Red Cross and St John's Ambulance Association:

> These groups, and the volunteers who serve them, are far removed from glitzy, media-based circles. Their work is conducted not under the glare of television lights nor in fashionably minimalist salons in west London, but in local churches, schools and sports clubs. It could almost be characterized as the contribution of 'Uncool Britannia', but it involves, as Her Majesty reminded us, the time and effort of millions of people 'unpaid and usually unsung'.[10]

This support for quiet, faithful public service has been demonstrated through the honours system of which the Queen is the fount and head, through active royal patronage given to causes which might otherwise go largely unrecognized, and through the steady and dedicated way in which the Queen and other senior members of the Royal Family have gone about their demanding and unending routine of public engagements and visits. In the words of *The Times* columnist Libby Purves, 'At its best, British royalty honours the unfashionable, bedrock virtues and rewards solid, long-lasting, humble service to the public good.'[11]

Prince Philip revitalized the National Playing Fields Association, set up the Duke of Edinburgh's Award in 1956 to instil into young people social obligation through community work and has done much with the Worldwide Fund for Nature. Princess Anne has presided over the charity Save the Children since 1970, working tirelessly across the world for the relief of poverty and the improvement of health and well-being. It was significant that the Queen's Silver Jubilee in 1977 should be marked by the launch of a scheme to encourage voluntary service by young people in their own communities, fulfilling her own specific request that it be used 'to help young people help others'. The 2002 Golden Jubilee similarly saw the introduction of a new annual award for voluntary service by groups in the community. In her Jubilee address to both Houses of Parliament, the Queen underlined the theme of service, characteristically using the prayer-book phrase, 'honour one another and seek the common good,' and saying, ' I would especially like to thank those very many people who give their time voluntarily to help others.'

The supreme contemporary exponent of royal philanthropy is the Prince of Wales who has committed much of his adult life to practical good works, acting not just as a patron of voluntary and charitable bodies but also in a much more pro-active role, setting up a host of agencies and piloting major initiatives in the fields of employment, homelessness and social and physical disadvantage. As early as 1978, Anthony Holden estimated that Prince Charles' 'social work', as he called it, consumed one-third of his working hours. Since then his involvement has grown so that he has become, in the words of the author of a major study of this much underrated aspect of his life, 'the executive chairman of an enormous charitable conglomerate' and 'a seed capitalist for social issues'.[12] The Prince's Trust, set up in 1976 with his own money to give grants directly to young people to help themselves and inspired by a probation officer's description of the cycle of alienation suffered by young people who were without jobs, family and other support, is now among the biggest youth charities in Britain, with an annual income of £40 million, and has brought tangible improvement to over 600,000 lives. In 2010 it supported 12,864 young people through xl clubs, a team-based programme of personal development for those facing difficulties at school, 9,452 through Team, a course for those out of work, offering work experience, qualifications, practical skills and community projects, and 11,164 through the Enterprise Programme which provides money and support to help young people start up in business.

Prince Charles' 'hands-on' commitment to philanthropic projects has been driven by a restless idealism, a passionate concern for the disadvantaged and a vision of voluntary community service binding together a fractured and divided nation. It also has deep spiritual roots and is strongly influenced by the example of Jesus. Speaking to the Cambridge Union in 1978, he shared his vision of a nation of individuals

> modelled on the example set by the greatest expression of an individual life in service in Palestine some 2,000 years ago. This example ... challenged the human being to recognise that he had within him a personal obligation towards the life of his time which was peculiarly his own and in the service of which he found a meaning that made his life, no matter how hard or cruel, more than worthwhile.[13]

Closely allied to the philanthropic activity of both the Queen and the Prince of Wales has been their spiritual leadership of the nation through exhortation and reflection. In the Queen's case, as we have already noted, this leadership has also been exercised through the personal example of a quiet but deeply held faith and regular churchgoing. On a number of occasions she has emphasized the importance of spiritual values in an increasingly secular society. Instances include her concern that the focus of celebrations of the dawning of the third millennium should be Christmas 2000 as much as New Year's Eve 1999 and that the fiftieth anniversary of her ascent to the throne in 2002 should be marked primarily by church services and seen as an occasion for religious observance as well as partying. The celebration of her eightieth birthday in 2006 centred around a family service of thanksgiving at St George's Chapel, Windsor, and a national service of thanksgiving in St Paul's Cathedral. She has maintained a lively interest in church affairs and has personally inaugurated several sessions of the Church of England's General Synod and twice attended the General Assembly of the Church of Scotland as Lord High Commissioner.

While faithfully and conscientiously discharging her constitutional role as Supreme Governor of the Church of England, the Queen has acted as a spiritual leader in a much broader sense. Particularly striking has been her close relationship with and openness to Roman Catholics. It was highly significant that the last foray made by Cardinal Basil Hume from his sick-bed during his final illness in 1999 was to visit Buckingham Palace and receive the Order of Merit from the Queen in person. The first monarch to attend a service in Westminster Cathedral, the Queen made a generous personal donation to the giant millennium cross erected in the piazza outside the mother church of English Catholicism. She also invited Hume's successor as Cardinal Archbishop of Westminster and leader of English Catholics, Cormac Murphy O'Connor, to preach before her at Sandringham. It was widely reported that she had very much hoped to pray with Pope John Paul II during her visit to the Vatican in October 2000 but that this had been vetoed by senior figures in the Church of England because of the fear that it would alienate some Protestants and reopen sensitivities concerning her role vis-à-vis the established Church. In September 2010 she warmly welcomed Pope Benedict XVI to the palace of Holyrood in Edinburgh at the start of his state visit to the United Kingdom, telling him, 'your presence here today reminds us of our common Christian heritage' and paying tribute to the Catholic Church's 'special contribution' to helping the poorest and most vulnerable around the world.

Even more significant has been the Queen's outreach to other faiths. This was particularly apparent in her 2001 Christmas broadcast when in the aftermath of the 9/11 attack on the World Trade Center in New York she reflected on the values of communities and a sense of belonging:

> A sense of belonging to a group, which has in common the same desire for a fair and ordered society, helps to overcome differences and misunderstanding by reducing prejudice, ignorance and fear.
>
> We all have something to learn from one another, whatever our faith – be it Christian or Jewish, Muslim, Buddhist, Hindu or Sikh – whatever our background, whether we be young or old, from town or countryside.

In his book *Chosen People* Clifford Longley contrasts this broadcast with Rudi Giuliani's farewell speech as mayor of New York just two days earlier. While Giuliani explicitly invoked patriotism, saying that the test of Americanism is how much you believe in America ('because we are like a religion really. A secular religion. We believe in ideas and ideals'), the Queen never mentioned Britain or Britishness but rather spoke in broad terms of the importance of faith and of communities and, in the Christian context, of the Church's role 'to give meaning to moments of intense human experience through prayer, symbol and ceremony'.[14] Her quiet and calm plea for tolerance and respect, emphasizing the importance of learning from others rather than crudely banging the patriotic drum, epitomizes the very British qualities of the sovereign who has ruled over the United Kingdom so wisely for the past half century.

This emphasis continued in her speeches through the 2000s. Her address to both Houses of Parliament on the occasion of her Golden Jubilee in April 2002, said to have been more personal and revealing of her own feelings than many of her speeches, expressed particular pride in 'our tradition of fairness and tolerance,' and noted that 'the consolidation of our richly multicultural and multi-faith society, a major development since 1952, is being achieved remarkably peacefully and with much goodwill'. In her address she characterized the British as ' a moderate, pragmatic people, outward-looking and open-minded', a phrase that could describe her own position on many issues, and identified fairness and tolerance as the two enduring traditions in which the country should take most pride. Her 2004 Christmas broadcast reiterated this theme, affirming that 'tolerance and fair play remain strong British values'. It was noticeable that the service of thanksgiving to mark the Queen's eightieth birthday in St Paul's Cathedral in June 2006 included a procession of world faith representatives and prayers delivered by the High Commissioners from Pakistan, Nigeria, New Guinea and Barbados, reflecting her own passionate commitment to the Commonwealth and its rich mixture of faiths, races and cultures.

There has been another, more nuanced underlying theme to the spiritual leadership consistently provided by the Queen throughout her reign. While scrupulously careful to avoid unconstitutional and inappropriate political partisanship, she has clearly identified herself with the promotion and defence of public service, and with a communal, consensual 'one-nation' approach to social issues. One senses, indeed, that likes James VI and I, although in a slightly different context, she might say, 'I am for the medium in all things'. Newspaper stories in the late 1980s suggested that she was deeply concerned about what she, and others, took to be the somewhat uncaring and divisive policies and style of Margaret Thatcher's Conservative administration. The Christian Socialist author and activist,

Chris Bryant, has pointed out that 'Throughout the materialistic Thatcherite eighties the Queen remained one of the few national institutions that spoke of public service as an absolute virtue'.[15]

A complementary role, even more explicitly focused on the spiritual dimension of royalty, has increasingly been carved out by the Prince of Wales. Accurately described by William Rees-Mogg as 'the first heir to the throne since the Stuarts to take an intellectual interest in religion', Prince Charles has manifested his passionate concern for the spiritual through ways as various as his attachment to the language of the Book of Common Prayer and Authorized Version of the Bible, his fascination with Orthodox spirituality and Islam, and his insistence that the Millennium should be a catalyst for reflection as much as an occasion for partying.[16] He chose to mark the dawning of the year 2000 with a retreat at a Greek Orthodox monastery on Mount Athos rather than at the Millennium Dome where his mother had to endure an essentially secular evening of light entertainment at which she was clearly not wholly at ease, especially when, after seemingly endless repetitions of the Beatles' 'All You Need is Love', she was forced by the Prime Minister into a premature round of arm-swinging for 'Auld Lang Syne'.

In publicly championing organic and sustainable agriculture, holistic medicine and classical architecture, Prince Charles has pursued a personal crusade against the rising tide of secular materialism and scientific reductionism. Although official photographs often show him clad, like previous princes, in military uniform or double-breasted suit, he has also been caught on camera garlanded while visiting a Hindu temple, dressed in native fashion singing an eco-anthem in Guyana or striding across a Hebridean island with a huge shepherd's crook like a latter-day Columba.

In many ways Prince Charles takes us back to the early medieval model of king as philosopher and wise man. Like Alfred, he has surrounded himself with advisers and spiritual counsellors and has a vision of spearheading national spiritual revival through promoting basic literacy and cultivating learning, music and the arts, as well as in his case through more human-scale architecture, holistic medicine and organic agriculture. There is also something in him of the Lutheran Prince Albert with his thirst for social improvement and determination to put his reforming principles into practice. At a deeper level, he harks back to a more primal understanding of the monarch as representing order and taking on the forces of chaos, and, indeed, to the tragic, sacrificial dimension of royalty. Serious commentators and satirists alike have noted that the major theme of the speeches and conversation of this 'heir of sorrows' is the deep disintegration of the modern world and the need for it to be rebalanced and reordered. He himself has movingly expressed this driving passion in his life:

> I have gradually come to realise that my entire life so far has been motivated by a desire to heal – to heal the dismembered landscape and the poisoned soil; the cruelly shattered townscape, where harmony has been replaced by a cacophony; to heal the divisions between intuitive and rational thought, between mind, body and soul, so that the temple of our humanity can once again be lit by a sacred flame; to level the monstrous artificial barrier erected between tradition and modernity and, above all, to heal the mortally wounded soul that, alone, can give us warning of the folly of playing God and of believing that knowledge on its own is a substitute of wisdom.[17]

It is no coincidence that Prince Charles makes a recurring appeal in his speeches to the concepts of wisdom and order so strongly associated with sacred monarchy and Christian kingship. In his 2000 Reith Lecture, for example, the word 'wisdom' figured seven times, coupled variously with the adjectives 'ancient', 'instinctive', 'practical' and 'intuitive'. The appeal to order is very evident in a 1996 speech extolling the virtues of tradition:

Tradition is not a man-made element in our lives – it is a God-given awareness of the natural rhythms and of the fundamental harmony engendered by the paradoxical opposites in every aspect of nature. Tradition reflects the timeless order, and yet disorder, of the cosmos, and anchors us into a harmonious relationship with the great mysteries of the universe.[18]

For Prince Charles, restoring order and harmony to our disintegrated world involves refinding and reasserting a sense of the sacred. This is the overarching theme of the religion page on his website – and it is, of course, significant in itself that religion should have a prominent place on the heir to the throne's website. It is also the theme that recurs more than any other in his recent speeches. In 1996, for example, he chose to speak to an audience of businessmen 'about a subject which I suspect is not often discussed on occasions like this – the importance of the sacred in the modern world'. His speech went on to lament the separation of science from religion and the separation of the natural world from God, 'with the result that it has fragmented the cosmos and placed the sacred into a separate, and secondary, compartment of our understanding, divorced from the practical day to day world of man'.[19] The need to rediscover a sense of the sacred in dealing with the natural world surfaced again in the Prince's reflection on the 2000 Reith Lectures which had explored the theme of sustainable development:

If literally nothing is held sacred any more – because it is considered synonymous with superstition, or in some way 'irrational' – what is there to prevent us treating our entire world as some 'great laboratory of life', with potentially disastrous long-term consequences?

Fundamentally, an understanding of the sacred helps us to acknowledge that there are bounds of balance, order and harmony in the natural world which set limits to our ambitions and define the parameters of sustainable development.[20]

The Prince's *Thought for the Day*, broadcast on Radio 4
on 1 January 2000, made a heartfelt plea that 'in the new
millennium we will begin to rediscover a sense of the sacred
in all that surrounds us', and included a characteristic observation that 'it is a sacred thing to compose harmony out of
opposites' as well as a commendation of the teaching of 'our
Lord Jesus Christ ... that this life is but one passing phase of
our existence'.[21] The fact that it was the heir to the throne
rather than the Archbishop of Canterbury or some other
church leader whom the BBC invited to give the first 'Thought
for the Day' of the new millennium on the *Today* programme
could be taken to indicate a recognition both of the continuing
spiritual dimension of monarchy and the particular religious
interests of the Prince, who also found himself nominated in a
poll carried out for a Channel 4 programme in March 2001 as
the third most powerful religious figure in Britain.

Like the Queen, Prince Charles has become noticeably
more overt and 'up-front' in his references to religion and
spirituality over the years. It is striking, for example, how his
opposition to genetic modification has increasingly rested on
theological rather than scientific grounds.

> I happen to believe that this kind of genetic modification
> takes mankind into realms that belong to God, and to
> God alone. ... We live in an age of rights – it seems to me
> that it is time our Creator had some rights too.[22]

Libby Purves commented that many people would

> be outraged by the shameless fundamentalist way that
> the Prince brings God into the argument. ... Fashionably
> agnostic thinkers will be horribly annoyed that a
> pragmatic, rational argument should be defaced by this
> embarrassing mention of a creator with a capital 'C'. I
> was rather struck by it.[23]

Several academics did, indeed, object to the Prince's theological emphasis when dealing with what they took to be essentially neutral scientific topics. David Voas, a geographer at Liverpool University, complained that 'listening to the Prince of Wales is like going to church; having avoided it for a time you forget how dreadful it can be', and dismissed the heir to the throne as 'a self-indulgent preacher'.[24] The Roman Catholic columnist, William Oddie, by contrast, saw the Prince's intervention in the GM debate as a welcome reassertion of royalty's traditional role 'as having an authority which was in some sense spiritual as well as temporal'.

> The reason why Prince Charles is listened to on moral issues is twofold. Not only is the monarchy a more spiritual institution than we have come to suppose: we for our part are a more spiritual people.[25]

In a letter to *The Times* I concurred with his analysis and took it further:

> At a time when its constitutional role is coming increasingly into question, I suspect that the spiritual dimension of monarchy may come to assume increasing importance. In his stand against genetically modified crops, Prince Charles has shown himself not so much the defender of faiths as the supreme exponent of an essentially religious perspective on life in the prevailing climate of secular and scientific rationalism.[26]

The strongly spiritual perspective introduced by Prince Charles into discussions about contemporary issues perhaps has a greater appeal abroad than it does to church leaders at home. On a visit to Guyana in 2000, he was singled out for commendation by the Mayor of Georgetown who prayed: 'I ask the Creator to give you the strength and wisdom to remain in the vanguard helping keep the world safe, clean, good and green.'[27] In 2002 a statue was erected in the Brazilian town of Palmas in the middle of the Amazonian rain forest depicting him as an angel and, in the words of the local state governor, 'saving the world'. It shows the Prince, with wings outstretched, hovering over a sea of humanity with his arms in open embrace. Leaders of the Church of England, by contrast, seem to have found his attitudes rather confused. The Archbishop of Canterbury, Robert Runcie, apparently found him a mass of confusions and contradictions in respect of religion, one moment extolling the 'epic language of the Prayer Book' and the next 'exploring Hinduism with people in the inner cities'.[28] It is true that his personal and to some extent idiosyncratic spiritual quest is altogether more fitting for a prince than for a king. Yet Prince Charles is perhaps closer than many bishops to what a lot of people in Britain actually believe, both in terms of his own spiritual seeking and his desire not to give up on tradition, as reflected in his passionate commitment to the preservation of the Book of Common Prayer as 'a touchstone of our ability as a society to value its spiritual roots, its liturgical continuity, and its very identity as a nation of believers'.[29]

Alongside this spiritual leadership has gone the steady exercise of the more conventional monarchical role in terms of ceremony and spectacle. The Queen's reign has seen a host of dignified state occasions, royal and state funerals, royal weddings and jubilees, all centred around church services and reverentially covered by the BBC. The size of the television audiences for these events and the number of people who have turned out to see them 'live' suggests that there has been relatively little diminution in the public appetite for royal spectacle. In April 2002 more than a million people lined the route of the Queen Mother's funeral procession, following a Lying in State which was rich in medieval chivalric imagery with Guards officers posted at each corner of the coffin. Two months later an even greater number were back on the streets of London to cheer the Queen as she travelled in the Gold State Coach to the national service of thanksgiving at St Paul's Cathedral for her Golden Jubilee and to watch the great Jubilee procession down the Mall which illustrated British life through the years of the reign.

Those two events, the traditional Christian cathedral service and the exuberant colourful carnival procession, both deeply spiritual in their different ways, somehow caught the national mood of celebration and thanksgiving for the Queen's reign much better than the other, more secular features of the Golden Jubilee weekend, like the classical and pop music concerts in the grounds of Buckingham Palace and the somewhat dreary and repetitive simultaneous singing of 'All You Need is Love' in 200 towns and cities across the UK. For me, and I suspect for many others, the most memorable and joyful aspect of the whole Golden Jubilee weekend was the 5,000-strong Gospel choir led by Patti Boulaye, the Nigerian-born singer, which danced and sang its way down the Mall at the head of the carnival procession. The choir, predominantly black and drawn from Pentecostal, Apostolic, Methodist and Catholic churches with members of the Metropolitan Police Gospel Choir in the front row, sang Patti Boulaye's own specially written Jubilee anthem, 'Celebrate Good News', with its message 'It's been so long since we felt so strong', along with Gospel standards like 'Michael Row the Boat Ashore', 'He's Got the Whole World in His Hands', 'Oh Happy Day' and 'This Little Light of Mine'. These upbeat Gospel numbers and the West Indian steel bands which also paraded down the Mall appeared to catch the mood of the day and the imagination of the crowds more than the traditional national airs played by military bands. One of my most abiding memories of the Jubilee celebrations is of seeing Pearlie kings and queens dancing in front of Buckingham Palace to the black Gospel songs being belted out by the Kingdom Choir with members of the Treorchy Male Voice Choir enthusiastically joining in. Here was an exuberant black-led celebration of British identity and of the Queen's reign which enthused and embraced cockneys, Welshmen and many others, and did so on the basis of carnival, revivalist Christianity and fervent monarchism. It was the Gospel songs that really expressed the joyful patriotism of the crowds celebrating the long reign of their beloved monarch.

The whole emphasis of the Golden Jubilee procession was heavily tilted towards ethnic minorities. The first parade down the Mall represented the Notting Hill Carnival and the last was a Commonwealth Parade with four rainbow arches containing 1900 handwritten wishes sent in by children from every country in the Commonwealth. Both of these parades were almost entirely made up of recent Commonwealth immigrants to the United Kingdom. Indeed, the Commonwealth rightly played a very significant role in this celebration of a monarch who has done so much to promote it and its values. A potent image caught by the television cameras during the closing moments of the day when the Queen stood alone on the balcony of Buckingham Palace was that of an Asian woman vigorously waving the Union Jack and pouring her heart and soul into a rendering of 'Land of Hope and Glory'. As she sang 'Wider still and wider shall the bounds be set', it seemed to presage not so much nostalgic longing for an imperialistic past as the dawning of a new carnival and rainbow Britishness, diverse and pluralistic yet focused on traditional symbols of unity like the Union flag and the monarchy.

In more traditional vein, the churches did their best to encourage communal celebration of the Golden Jubilee. A booklet of worship material produced by Churches Together in Britain and Ireland for the use of Christian congregations throughout the United Kingdom invoked the biblical theme of jubilee and suggested as readings extracts from the Queen's 2000 and 2001 Christmas broadcasts as well as her twenty-first birthday speech as a princess to the youth of the Empire in 1947. The prayers of intercession were imaginatively based around symbols used in the coronation service – the Bible for faith, oil for anointing and a towel and bowl (in fact from the Maundy service of foot-washing rather than the coronation, although this was not acknowledged) for service. The booklet also included a fine hymn written for the occasion by June Boyce-Tilman which hit a contemporary note and picked up several of the themes dearest to the hearts of both the Queen and Prince Charles.

Jubilee sets us free!
Work for community;
Value diversity
Held in a unity.
Act justly with respect today!
We hear God's call and we obey.

Jubilee sets us free!
Weep with the damaged earth
Losing fertility,
Longing to find rebirth.
Show mercy to the world today!
We hear God's call and we obey.

Jubilee sets us free!
Walk with the silent poor;
Share with humility;
Open the freedom door.
Come, prophets, shout your words today!
We hear God's call and we bey.

Jubilee sets us free!
Sing of security
Served by a monarchy
In its integrity.
Come celebrate our Queen today!
She heard God's call and she obeyed.[30]

In contrast to the colourful carnival atmosphere of the parades down the Mall a year earlier, the service of thanksgiving held at Westminster Abbey in June 2003 to mark the fiftieth anniversary of the Queen's coronation seemed staid and over-wordy. No use was made of visual symbols, such as the royal regalia, which would have dramatically illustrated and pointed up the importance of the themes of faith, service, responsibility and respect around which the service was built. There was no active participation from Commonwealth representatives, nor from non-Christian faiths. It was all very clerical and very wordy and, apart from the choirboys, all those taking part were white, male and middle-class. In an article in the *Guardian* reflecting on how dull, static and unimaginative the service had been, I reflected:

> The monarchy can still speak in a profound way of deep values – unity in diversity, the defence of faith and tolerance, respect and loyalty, disinterested public service. To put these themes across cries out for recourse to the symbolic and iconic – all the more so in our visual culture in post-modern age, where image and metaphor are all important.
>
> The churches, and the Church of England in particular, have a key role to play in providing symbolic and iconic expression of these deep, transcendent values and linking them with the purposes of God. I hope it is not losing its nerve.[31]

The fourth element of modern monarchy, personal example through living according to high moral standards and the projection of a happy family life, has proved much more difficult to sustain over recent decades. The behaviour of the Queen herself has been exemplary, but certain other members of the Royal Family have at times been self-indulgent and have fallen from the perhaps unrealistically high standards expected of them. Early on in the Queen's reign there was, in fact, an example of considerable sacrifice when her sister, Princess Margaret, forsook marriage to the man she loved for the sake of her Christian faith and loyalty to the throne. After a meeting with the Archbishop of Canterbury in 1955, she announced that 'mindful of the Church's teaching that marriage is indissoluble, and conscious of my duty to the Commonwealth', she had decided against a civil marriage to Peter Townsend.[32] Since then there have been rather fewer displays of such sacrificial behaviour, and a combination of poor judgement and advice, changing mores, the relentless pressure of the tabloid press, and sheer bad luck, has produced a rather messy series of divorces, ill-conceived relationships and scandals, all played out in the full glare of publicity. The protracted breakdown of the Prince of Wales' marriage with Diana, Princess of Wales, which led to their separation in 1992 and divorce in 1996, was particularly unfortunate and unhappy, especially, of course, for those principally involved but also for the standing of monarchy, not least in terms of its spiritual and sacred dimension. Undoubtedly the *annus horribilis* of 1992, with the publication of the so-called 'Camillagate' tapes, marked a particularly significant stage in the desacralization of monarchy. Colin Buchanan, the leading Anglican advocate of disestablishment, sensed a distinct change of attitude in the Church of England during that year. Writing in 1994, he noted that 'something very serious has been happening to "monarcholatry" ... the Royal Family has been de-divinized' and he went on:

> Until mid-November 1992, whenever I got involved in discussions or disputes about disestablishment, I knew that I could be as confrontational as I wished with most present features of the links between Church and State, but that the Queen's position was not only inviolable, but even unquestionable. ... If a change would not touch the Crown – it could be looked at. But if it would touch the Crown – then it was virtual treason to propose it, and only the imbecilic or b-minded or bomb-throwing anarchist could persevere with it. ... But overnight this changed. Suddenly I began to get calls from the daily tabloids and even the quality Sundays, and occasionally from the radio and television, and the questions now all took the same form: 'Do not the troubles of the Palace, and particularly of the Prince of Wales, mean that the Church of England will have to be disestablished?'[33]

Some of the loss of respect that the monarchy has suffered over the past 60 years is also undoubtedly due to the fact that some members of the Royal Family, egged on at times by ill-advised courtiers and publicity consultants as well as by the insatiable demands of the media, have succumbed to the temptation, which the Queen and the Duke of Edinburgh have sensibly and staunchly resisted, to make royalty a branch of the booming celebrity industry. The medium of television has perhaps played the most significant role in turning certain royals into celebrities just as it has also undoubtedly helped considerably to project the spiritual and sacred aura and role of monarchy. Its contribution to the whole modern monarchical project has, indeed, been complex and ambiguous. Relatively early on in the Queen's reign it was embraced as offering a new way of projecting the monarchy in its exemplary role by emphasizing its happy family image. The result of this embrace, 'Royal Family', a 'fly-on-the-wall' style documentary, made by Richard Cawston and screened by the BBC in 1969, attracted 30.6 million viewers, the third-highest British television audience ever, and was hailed as a great public relations triumph for the monarchy. But it broke Bagehot's cardinal principle by letting the daylight in on the magic of monarchy. Amidst the general chorus of praise, the television critic Milton Shulman uttered a percipient warning:

> Judging from Cawston's film, it is fortunate at this moment in time we have a royal family that fits in so splendidly with a public relation man's dream.
>
> Yet, is it, in the long run, wise for the Queen's advisers to set as a precedent this right of the television camera to act as an image-making apparatus for the monarchy? Every institution that has so far attempted to use TV to popularise or aggrandise itself has been trivialised by it.[34]

Shulman's fears were confirmed in 1987 when a public relations consultant dreamed up a ploy to present royalty on television in a way that turned out to be humiliating and embarrassing. *It's a Royal Knockout* involved teams led by younger members of the Royal Family clowning around and behaving like showbusiness stars. Michael Mann, the Dean of Windsor, spoke for many when he said, 'I think it was a disaster. ... The thing that came over to me was that it was actually pulling the whole of the royal family down. ... It was making it a clown affair, and that is not the right way to win respect.'[35]

By no means all television programmes have trivialized the monarchy. The television biography Elizabeth R, made in the *annus horribilis* of 1992, showed very clearly the Queen's strong sense of duty, sacrifice and commitment. Jonathan Dimbleby's 1994 film portrait, *Charles: The Private Man, The Public Role*, portrayed the Prince of Wales' strong spiritual interests and social conscience, although, inevitably, this was not the aspect picked up by the press which leaped upon his admission of adultery. The problem with portraying the monarchy on television outside the context of major state occasions and religious services is that the medium by its very nature is not conducive to putting across qualities like reserve, duty and discretion. Television thrives on sensation, novelty and personality-driven drama. As Piers Brendon and Phillip Whitehead rightly observe, 'What the Queen offers, year in year out, is dignity rather than magic.'[36] The Queen herself observed in the *Elizabeth R* programme: 'If you live this sort of life, which people don't very much, you live by tradition and continuity.'[37] Unfortunately, in television terms tradition and continuity, like duty, do not make for very gripping viewing. Sensational revelation, gossip, innuendo and tittle-tattle of the kind normally lavished on celebrity superstars, on the other hand, does.

One member of the Royal Family did prove to be a shining star in the media firmament throughout the 1980s and 1990s. From her fairytale wedding to Prince Charles in St Paul's Cathedral in 1981, watched by a global television audience of 750 million and described by Robert Runcie, Archbishop of Canterbury, as 'the stuff that fairy tales are made of', to her funeral in Westminster Abbey in 1997, watched on television by three-quarters of the adult population of the United

Kingdom and a global audience which has been estimated at 2.5 billion, Diana, Princess of Wales, was seldom off the front pages of the tabloids or the television news bulletins. She became both the victim and the creature of the media. A global superstar, she was in the van of the transformation of royalty into soap opera and celebrity status. Hounded by the paparazzi whose attentions may have contributed to her death, she also encouraged media attention with her love of fashion and glamour. She felt at home in the world of showbusiness and was the first leading royal figure to be raised on and sustained by the pop music culture. She used her celebrity and glamour to promote the causes in which she believed, notably her courageous campaign against land-mines. In many ways she stood firmly in the tradition of the 'welfare monarchy', devoting herself to a huge range of charitable and philan-thropic activities. Her approach, however, epitomized in her self-description as 'the Queen of Hearts', was markedly more up-front and direct than that of the more reserved and distant Windsors.

Alongside her role as a celebrity and media superstar, Diana took on an iconic and spiritual status which at one level resembled nothing so much as the sacred aura of medieval monarchy with its magical healing touch. Her direct physical contact with sick children and with those suffering from Aids and leprosy was widely admired and summed up by the phrase 'she didn't wear gloves'. For some she was a Christian princess cast in the mould of a medieval saint, or even of Christ himself. The Roman Catholic journalist and historian Paul Johnson, who confessed to having prayed to her, noted after her death: 'The effect of Diana's short life did more to promote Christian values in this country than all the efforts of our state church in half a century. ... She was the grace of anti-materialism made flesh.'[38] Preaching in Lichfield Cathedral, Tom Wright compared to the actions of the Good Samaritan her role of reaching out as an establishment outcast to go to the rescue of those in the ditch. He went on to suggest another comparison:

She reminds us, if only subconsciously, of another young man, one with the tag of royalty, yet who didn't behave as royalty should; one celebrated by the masses, but deeply threatening to the establishment; one who brought healing and hope, but who was cut down, in his prime, by the forces he had challenged.[39]

For other observers, Diana epitomised an essentially postmodern and post-Christian spirituality. In the words of Grace Davie,

Diana herself was a seeker, beginning and ending her life in the Church of England – like so many of her compatriots – but in between a personification of religious consumption as she tried first this and then that, ending her life in the company of a prominent Muslim.[40]

In many ways she was, indeed, the supreme shopper in the postmodern spiritual supermarket, flirting with both Catholicism and spiritualism, and consulting a whole range of alternative therapists and New Age practitioners. Paul Heelas has identified her as the exemplar of the New Age quest for a religion within, and Linda Woodhead as the exponent of a 'religion of the heart' worked out in contrast to and out of disillusionment with institutional Christianity.[41] Andrew Billings identifies Diana with a new religion which is people-centred rather than God-centred, of the heart rather than of the head, and constructed by each individual rather than given. As he says, 'These three elements probably sum up the religion of many British people today.'[42] He describes it as a religion of autonomy rather than dependency and of self-love rather than self-sacrifice, based on feeling good about oneself, and therefore being able to do good to others, and needing neither priests nor churches. For Edward Norman, Diana's was a totally humanist faith:

the secularised love of humanity which is the modern substitute for religion ... it is a religion of empty sentiment, without doctrine and devoid of intellectual content. It is established on the needs of the individual, not on any commands of an external God.[43]

While Diana did seem to worship at the secular postmodern altars of fashion, beauty and hedonism, there was also a sacrificial and self-giving aspect to her life and character. Indeed, in many ways she takes us back to the archetype of the sacred monarch as a tragic figure, sacrificed for the people and the land. Glamorous as she was, Diana also fitted the paradigm of the wounded healer. It was her own vulnerability, candour and weakness that drew her to the suffering and them to her. She came to be recognized as the special friend, the patron saint even, of the marginalized.

Diana was widely interpreted both during her life and after her death as challenging the whole ethos and approach of the modern British monarchy as it had been described by Bagehot and practised since the time of Victoria. She was seen as being everything that the Windsors were not – available, glamorous, candid, vulnerable, disarmingly frank, sentimental, emotional and physical – and as such directly challenging the traditional Protestant monarchical values of reticence, reserve, restraint, formality, duty and discretion. For Linda Woodhead there was something deeply subversive about her self-styled role as 'Queen of Hearts':

> An ethic of duty and self-sacrifice was part and parcel of an established Anglicanism which has for at least three centuries legitimated an aristocratic social order in Britain. It teaches that virtue consists in obedience to higher powers, both religious and social. By contrast, Diana's Religion of the Heart encouraged spiritual independence and individual empowerment, and inspired Diana in her struggles against 'the Establishment'.[44]

I am not myself entirely convinced that this polarized distinction is quite right. Diana Spencer was herself brought up in and to a large extent continued to subscribe to a traditional aristocratic code of duty and loyalty. It was no coincidence that her favourite hymn, learned at school and sung both at her wedding and her funeral, was 'I Vow to Thee, My Country'. What is certainly true is that a significant proportion of the population, goaded on by the media, did identify her with a new more direct, open and 'touchy-feely' style of monarchy which contrasted with the restraint and discretion of the Windsors. This identification was particularly evident and divisive in the immediate aftermath of her sudden death when a section of the public and the media demanded instant demonstrative grief. The Queen's response in remaining in seclusion at Balmoral with the two young princes, sympathetically portrayed in the film *The Queen*, was in keeping with the dignified and reserved style of mourning which had long characterized British royalty. Yet it was widely interpreted as unfeeling and heartless by the tabloid press which shrieked at the Queen 'Show us you care' and 'Speak to us, Ma'am'.

At one level, the extraordinary outburst of demonstrative public mourning following Diana's death seemed to betoken a strongly populist sentiment which seriously challenged and possibly even threatened the traditional Christian view of monarchy as something consecrated and set apart. The mood was both caught and moulded by Tony Blair's description of Diana on the morning of her death as 'The People's Princess', a phrase that acknowledged her supreme availability and also suggested that it was to the public rather than to God that royalty belonged and owed primary allegiance. There was an unmistakably anti-royalist feel to many of the tributes which were left in the gardens of the royal palaces in London: 'The Princess of Wales to "royalty" – the Queen of Hearts to "The Commoners".' 'The Royals didn't deserve you. You showed the world what "Royalty" is about.' After analysing these and other aspects of the mourning for Diana, Anne Rowbottom and Gillian Bennett concluded that substantial numbers of people were 'rejecting Bagehot's sober model of the ideal monarch and looking for something more in tune with their needs'.[45]

The public mourning of Diana was a complex and even contradictory phenomenon from which it is difficult to draw clear conclusions. It was not universal and did not unite the nation in quite the same way as the coronation had 45 years earlier. At one level, Diana was mourned in death, as she had been regarded in life, as a medieval royal saint. The royal parks, piled high with flowers, candles, rosary beads, teddy bears and other votive offerings in the days following her death, took on a close resemblance to the shrines of medieval saints. People huddled quietly in small groups around candles, praying and meditating. It is clear from analysis that I have made of the books of condolence that many people thought of Diana as a saint, possessing intercessory powers and going straight to heaven. Her canonization, which reached its apogee in the appearance of statues of Diana as the Madonna, has been taken as representing both a Catholicization and a feminization of Britain. The Catholic emphasis seemed to be underlined by the holding of a Requiem Mass for Diana in Westminster Cathedral, a highly unusual event for a member of the Royal Family, and, indeed, for a Protestant. Yet if aspects of the mourning for Diana seemed medieval, continental and Catholic, there was also something very Victorian about the sentimental display of grief. In his book *Great Deaths*, John Wolffe has pointed to the spontaneous gathering of crowds in public places that followed the untimely deaths of Princess Charlotte in 1817 and Prince Albert in 1861, and noted more generally that 'throughout the nineteenth and early twentieth centuries, 'the deaths of the famous drew people to church in unusually high numbers and also stirred prolific religious and quasi-religious discourse'.[46] Viewed in the context of 'the religiosity of public grief' that Wolffe notes in the aftermath of the deaths and funerals of royalty and other prominent public figures in the Victorian and Edwardian era, the reaction to Diana's death fits into a recognizable pattern and testifies to the continuing way in which royal deaths in particular encourage people to confront their own mortality, ponder more deeply both their own situation and the life and times of the nation, and turn to the Church and to other sources of religious comfort.

Diana's funeral service was in many respects highly traditional and full of the ceremony and ritual usually associated with royal funerals. Nearly two million people stood in the streets of London to pay their respects as the coffin, draped with the royal standard, was carried from Kensington Palace on a gun carriage and borne into Westminster Abbey by uniformed pallbearers from the Welsh Guards. During the service itself, which was attended by forty-three members of the Royal Family, the lesson was read by the Prime Minister, the prayers led by the Archbishop of Canterbury and the hymns sung were in the main highly traditional, including 'The King of Love my Shepherd is', 'Guide Me, O Thou Great Redeemer' and 'I Vow to Thee, My Country'. The music included the funeral sentences set by Croft and Purcell, an extract from Verdi's *Requiem* and John Tavener's *Alleluia* from the Orthodox funeral liturgy. There were also significant departures from traditional practice, however. Elton John's rendering of 'Candle in the Wind', originally written for Marilyn Monroe and reworked by Bernie Taupin to apply to Diana, emphasized her celebrity aspect with its line 'Now you belong to heaven and the stars spell out your name'. Critics from both the evangelical and Catholic camps complained that the service appeared to be addressed to the deceased rather than to God. The princess was buried not alongside other royals in Westminster Abbey, nor at Windsor, but in a specially created island shrine on her family's Northamptonshire estate, to which she was transported in an extraordinary procession through the North London suburbs with thousands of flowers being strewn along the way.

Several of those who have written about the funeral argue that it was a post-Christian event. For Scott Wilson the spontaneous applause which greeted Earl Spencer's funeral oration turned it into a rock concert or even a political rally and announced 'that the locus of celebrity has decisively replaced the locus of sacred. The church no longer has any meaning; its rituals do not integrate traumatised subjects into its world of symbolised reality.'[47] Yet overall, the funeral had a strongly Christian and even monarchist focus, with the emphasis in the prayers being on the doctrine of resurrection and the qualities of wisdom and discernment found in the Crown. It may be indicative that in the index to one of the best studies of the mourning for Diana, Jesus Christ merits just two entries compared with nine for the next name, John, Elton. Yet a leading London record store reported that in the days following the funeral it had more requests for Tavener's *Alleluia*, a blend of Shakespeare's words from *Hamlet*, 'May flights of angels sing thee to thy rest' with lines from the Orthodox funeral service, than for 'Candle in the Wind'. For all its novelties, Diana's funeral, which formed the focal point for both national and international mourning, was still a Church of England ceremony which took place in an ancient abbey steeped in history and associated for more than 1000 years with the consecration of England's kings and queens.

There remains considerable disagreement over whether the canonization of and mourning for Diana represented an essentially religious or secular phenomenon. What it does surely point to is the continuing iconic power of monarchy. Whether seen as 'Queen of Hearts' or as 'The People's Princess', Diana's royal status was undoubtedly an important factor in her idolization. Her life, and more particularly her death, reinforced the deep cultural connections between monarchy, good deeds and sanctity. For some people Diana directly embodied the Arthurian ideal of sacred monarchy. A member of the British Order of Druids who fell into conversation with the social anthropologist Marion Bowman on the day after Diana's death suggested that her marriage to Charles had been engineered to reintroduce 'the ancient British bloodline' into the modern British monarchy:

The British people warmed so much to Diana because they instinctively recognized she was truly royal, their real monarch ... Prince William, whose name is William Arthur, was born on the summer solstice; if he were to follow the ancient custom of kings using their second name, he would become King Arthur. Thus, through Diana, the ancient British royal bloodline would be restored to power, with a new King Arthur for a new millennium.[48]

Even if not all went as far as this, there were many people who found in Diana, in Anne Rowbottom's words, 'a touch of magic, a glimpse of Camelot, a queen who made them proud to be British'.[49]

It was because she was a princess that her natural empathy and active good works led to her being described in religious language as a saint or an angel. As Ross McKibbin observed, the popular investiture of Diana with this imagery belongs to a tradition of attributing spiritual gifts and powers to royalty that is by no means dead:

We are surprised that so many people seemed to have a quasi-religious view of Diana. But throughout the twentieth century observers have been 'surprised'. In 1935, 1936 and 1937, years of many royal events, Kingsley Martin, the editor of the *New Statesman*, was astonished at the 'recrudescence of sheer superstition' surrounding the monarchy. People endlessly spoke of 'royal weather'; there was much publicity given to a crippled Scottish boy who learned to walk after having met George V; in 1939 it was alleged that the inhabitants of Southwold crowded around George VI to 'touch' him for his magical curative powers. These stories are very similar to those which have appeared about Diana and the effect she had on the ill. ... There is no reason to think that the enormous fund of popular religion has much diminished.[50]

The popular reaction to Diana both in life and death underlined the continuing religious dimension of royalty in terms
of its perceived association with quasi-magical powers and
spiritual qualities. It also showed the extent to which members
of the Royal Family still serve both as models and exemplars,
and as representative figures with whom people identify.
Diana was rightly seen as embodying and personifying the
noble values of compassion, kindness, love and reaching out
to the untouchable. She directly inspired imitative acts of
compassion and charity. The weeks following her death saw
a huge rise in the number of people volunteering to help in
hospitals and hospices. She powerfully reinforced the model
of 'welfare monarchy' established by George III and continued
by Victoria and the Windsors in which the emphasis was on
individual acts of charity and 'hands-on' good works. Like
George III, too, her own vulnerability and candour allowed
people to identify and empathize with her in a particularly
direct way.

Public reaction to Diana's life and death also seemed to
send a message to the monarchy. Asked in a poll to choose
between the way in which the Royal Family had traditionally
functioned and the way in which Princess Diana conducted
herself, only 13 per cent of respondents chose the 'Windsor'
model and 66 per cent the 'Diana' model. Tony Blair
predicted that in the aftermath of the trauma occasioned by
Diana's death the monarchy 'will change and modernize',
and the Queen herself promised in her live broadcast to
the nation on her return from Balmoral at the height of the
national outpouring of grief that the lessons of Diana's life
and death would be learned.

In the event, not that much has changed. Predictions that
Diana's death would fatally weaken the monarchy or at the
very least bring about its radical reform have proved wide
of the mark. It has not, thank goodness, led, as some feared
it would, to further attempts to align the crown with the
prevailing celebrity culture. Those responsible for the 1998
Demos pamphlet about *Modernizing the Monarchy* were

worried that this was going to be the post-Diana direction for the monarchy:

> Unfortunately, the signs are that the monarchy has learned the lessons of Diana 'the celebrity', rather than the 'Queen of hearts'. The Palace appears to have decided that the lesson of Diana's life and death concerns the power of glamour rather than the power of her adoption of active symbolism as her key role.[51]

In fact, despite some initial and ill-advised flirtations with populism in the immediate aftermath of Diana's death, on the whole 'the firm' has gone about its business much as before. Dignity has been substantially restored to the monarchy and the Royal Family, and public support largely won back for the 'Windsor' model with its essentially Victorian Protestant foundations and guiding principles. Perhaps the really important lesson from Diana's life and death was one for the media rather than the monarchy to learn, and they seem to have learned it. On the whole, there has been noticeably less press intrusion into the lives of the Royal Family in the 2000s than there was in the 1980s and 1990s – the generally restrained coverage of Prince William's romance with Catherine Middleton being a notable case in point. Perhaps, too, the public mood has changed – the impact of 9/11 and subsequent terrorist attacks and of the profound and prolonged economic recession has made dutiful public service and serious spiritual leadership, however dull and worthy, rather more appealing than celebrity glitz and glamour. Uncertain and rapidly changing times have enhanced the appeal of tradition and continuity.

Looked at in hindsight, the *decem annes horribiles* of the 1990s appear to be an abberant and atypical decade which marked the nadir of the fortunes of the British monarchy and from which a complete recovery has been made. Judging by opinion polls, the summer of 2000 represented the absolute low point of public support. A poll in the *Guardian* in June of that year chronicled a steep and relentless fall in the proportion of the population believing that Britain would be worse off without the monarchy from 75 per cent at the beginning of the 1990s to 44 per cent at its end. Among those aged 18 to 24 less than a quarter agreed with the proposition that the country would be worse off without a monarchy.[52] A MORI poll published in *The Times* two months later suggested that very nearly half the population expected Britain to be a republic within the next 50 years.[53]

Public opinion is notoriously fickle and easily swayed by events, and it is unwise to put too much weight on such findings. Nonetheless, it is clear that during the 2000s there was a substantial recovery of support for both the principle and the continuance of monarchy in Britain. Further underlining the significance of royal deaths, polls taken immediately after the death and funeral of the Queen Mother in 2002 showed just 12 per cent of respondents favouring the abolition of monarchy, compared with 34 per cent in polls taken a month or so earlier.

As I write this, the most recent available data, which come from an ICM poll carried out in early 2011, suggest that 82 per cent of the United Kingdom population would like the monarchy to continue after the death of the Queen. Even in Republican-inclined Scotland, another recent poll shows that the proportion of the population supporting the cessation of the monarchy with the end of the Queen's reign dropped from 33 per cent in 2006 to 24 per cent in 2011. Given all that has happened over the past 60 years, and especially given the deleterious effects of the three trends noted at the beginning of this chapter, it is a remarkable vote of confidence, from which the Queen and the Duke of Edinburgh should draw justifiable pride and satisfaction

8

Current debates

The past two decades have seen lively debate over several aspects of the monarchy's spiritual and ecclesiastical role. The main points at issue have been the bar on Roman Catholics succeeding to the throne, the nature of the coronation oath, the shape of the next coronation service and the monarch's role as Supreme Governor of the Church of England and Defender of the Faith. Proposals for change in these areas have arisen out of concern over the persistence of institutionalized religious discrimination in modern Britain, unease over the continuing existence of established churches, and a desire to provide appropriate constitutional arrangements for a pluralistic, multi-faith society. More fundamental questions raised in the 1990s about the desirability of maintaining a hereditary monarchy and a confessional Christian state were to some extent overtaken and overshadowed by debates in the 2000s on Britishness, national identity and multiculturalism in which the role of the monarchy was surprisingly little mentioned.

The ban on Roman Catholic succession to the throne is the subject that has attracted most publicity. At first sight it seems strange that this somewhat arcane measure imposed in the 1701 Act of Settlement, and confirmed in the 1707 Treaty of Union between England and Scotland, should have become such a live issue. It is not as if there is any serious prospect of a Roman Catholic coming to the throne in the foreseeable future. In fact, when such a prospect did seem a possibility, albeit a remote one, in the late 1970s, when there was press speculation that Prince Charles might marry Princess Marie-Astrid of Luxembourg, there was relatively little public or media interest in this aspect, although the Prime Minister,

Margaret Thatcher, did set up a Cabinet committee in 1980 to examine the implications of the heir to the throne marrying a Catholic.

Demands for repeal of the Act of Settlement have come particularly from Scotland where its historic association with the 1707 Treaty of Union makes it an obvious target for the Scottish National Party and others in the Scottish Parliament seeking to flex their political muscles, demonstrate their commitment to outlaw discrimination and find an issue on which to challenge and embarrass the Westminster Parliament and government. Vociferously urged by the late Thomas Winning, Cardinal Archbishop of Glasgow, and his successor as leader of the Scottish Catholic community, Keith O'Brien, Cardinal Archbishop of Edinburgh and St Andrews, repeal of the bar on a Roman Catholic succeeding to the throne has gained the support of all the major Scottish churches, including the Church of Scotland, and MSPs of all parties. It was, in fact, a Tory aristocrat, Lord James Douglas Hamilton, who initiated the first debate on the subject in the newly opened Scottish Parliament in 1999. 'My own passionate support for the monarchy,' he declared, 'does not alter the reality that the Act of Settlement contains anachronistic, discriminatory legislation.' Similar sentiments were expressed by another Tory, Lord Forsyth of Drumlean, who sought unsuccessfully to introduce a bill in the House of Lords to repeal the Act:

> The Act is deeply discriminatory. It does not constructively prescribe that the Sovereign's consort must belong to the Church of England; it is perfectly legal for a monarch to marry a Buddhist, a Hindu or even a Moonie, but not a Roman Catholic. It is the British constitution's grubby little secret and nobody wants to tackle it.[1]

In England David Hope spoke out in favour of repeal of the Act of Settlement when Archbishop of York, as have other Protestant church leaders since. The diaries of the former Liberal Democrat leader Paddy Ashdown, published in 2000, quoted Prince Charles as saying that he could not see why there could not be a Catholic on the throne. In 2002 the *Guardian* launched a campaign to have the Act repealed in advance of the Golden Jubilee celebrations. In the 2005 general election campaign Michael Howard, the Conservative leader, promised to work towards repeal if his party won. In the event, the election was won by Tony Blair, who, despite his own personal religious attachment to Catholicism, made no move to remove the ban on Catholics succeeding to the throne. When Gordon Brown took over as Prime Minister in 2007, he signalled that he was seriously considering repeal of the Act of Settlement and in 2009 he initiated conversations about it with Buckingham Palace and leaders of fifteen Commonwealth countries. Scottish political commentators suggested that Brown was strongly motivated by a desire to prevent the substantial Catholic vote in Scotland from being won over from Labour by the Nationalists. However, nothing was done before the election of 2010 and the new Prime Minister, David Cameron, let it be known soon after taking office that his coalition government had no plans to repeal the Act. In 2011 Keith Vaz became the latest in a line of MPs to introduce a private member's bill to amend the Act of Settlement to allow Catholic succession and also to permit the eldest daughter of a sovereign to succeed before a younger son. An academic book published in 2011, *The Rights and Wrongs of Royal Marriage: How the Law Has Led to Heartbreak, Farce and Confusion and Why it Must be Changed*, gained considerable publicity. Its author, Rebecca Probert, Professor of Law at Warwick University, described the Act of Settlement as 'absurd by twentieth century standards' and said, 'It's ridiculous that it has never been repealed.'[2] In October 2011 the leaders of 15 Commonwealth countries meeting in Perth, Australia, agreed that spouses of Roman Catholics should be allowed to succeed to the throne and females be given equal succession rights to males. They did not, however, lift the ban on Catholic succession.

The growing call to allow Roman Catholics on the British throne has not gone unchallenged. Not surprisingly, the strongest opposition has come from ultra-Protestants. The British Israelite body, the Kingdom Foundation, has declared apocalyptically that 'the repeal of the marriage provision in the Act of Settlement would bring the conflict between the Davidic Throne and the *antichristos* Papal Throne to a possible final conflict of authority'.[3] Christians Together in the Highlands and Islands have stated that 'by allowing any future monarch to be someone other than a Protestant Christian we would effectively be attempting to dethrone God as the overall sovereign in our land', and the Reverend Hugh Cartwright spoke in similarly trenchant terms to the Inverness branch of the Scottish Reformation Society in 2009:

> The single most significant contributory factor in the unity, security and prosperity of these islands has been a common commitment of the constituent nations to the Protestant constitution and throne. As this has declined so has a meaningful understanding of what it is to be British. The biblical and Protestant constitution of our nation and throne has been foundational to the values and freedoms which have characterised our nation and which are already seriously eroded as the nation departs in spirit and in practice from what is still the legal commitment.[4]

The *Daily Telegraph*, although edited by a Roman Catholic, Charles Moore, between 1995 and 2003, has consistently opposed repeal of the Act of Settlement on the grounds that it would be incompatible with the monarch remaining as Supreme Governor of the Church of England and would pave the way for its disestablishment. The newspaper delighted in pointing out in 2008 that repeal would make a 74-year-old German aristocrat, Franz Herzog von Bayern, the rightful claimant to the British throne under the Stuart line. Others have expressed concern about the anti-ecumenical sentiments of the Roman Catholic Church and predicted that its insistence on all children of mixed marriages being brought up as Catholics could lead to a permanent Roman Catholic monarchy. In an article in the *Spectator* in 2003, Adrian Hilton argued that 'it would be intolerable to have, as the sovereign of a Protestant and free country, one who owes any allegiance to the head of any other state' and that a Roman Catholic monarch would be obliged to view Church of England and Church of Scotland clergy as lacking the authority to preach or celebrate the sacraments and would therefore be unable to be crowned by the Archbishop of Canterbury. He also pointed to the example of other European countries with even tighter provisions about the religious positions of their heads of state, notably Denmark, Norway and Sweden, whose constitutions compel the monarch to be Lutheran, and the Netherlands, where the monarch must come from the Protestant House of Orange.[5]

Within the Church of England, the strongest proponent of maintaining the status quo has almost certainly been Michael Scott-Joynt, Bishop of Winchester from 1995 to 2010 and the Archbishops' spokesman on constitutional affairs, who has commended the 'constitutional sense' in restricting the freedom of movement of the heirs to the throne:

> Any alteration in that arrangement would call into question the ways in which the responsibilities of the Crown for Christian government have, since the Reformation, been closely linked to the position of the Church of England. Those who want to change the situation need to recognise the implications of doing so. I don't believe that any other body, in today's circumstances, would take the place of the Church of England – a constant pointer to the ultimately Christian character of government in this country. The result would be a state that was, in principle, secular.[6]

This remark, which drew the headline in the *Church Times*, 'RC on throne could mean secular state', seems to refer more to the monarch's role as Supreme Governor of the Church of England than to his or her own personal denominational affiliation which is, strictly speaking, a separate issue. It reflects, however, a widespread view in the hierarchy of the Church of England that the various issues concerning the relationship between monarchy, church and state are extremely difficult to disentangle and that once one thread is removed the delicate cord that binds them together may unravel.

The ban on a Roman Catholic acceding to the throne is usually presented as a straight case of religious discrimination. Leading human rights lawyers have pointed out that it breaches the Human Rights Act, which came into force in the United Kingdom in 2000, in two respects. It is clearly incompatible with both article 12, which gives everyone the right to marry whoever he or she wants, and article 14, which says that it is the right of everyone not to be discriminated against on religious grounds. Repeal of the Act of Settlement is a relatively low priority for the government, not least because it would be a highly time-consuming process, requiring complex legislation both at home and overseas. Eight statutes would have to be amended or repealed and legislation altered in 15 Commonwealth countries where the Queen is head of state. However, it is hard to argue with the conclusion of Stuart Reid, writing in the *Guardian* in 2009:

> The fact is that the Act of Settlement will be repealed. Its repeal will be seen as a triumph for toleration; but it will of course be a triumph for indifference and secularism and signal the end of the Protestant religion by law established.[7]

The call to repeal the Act of Settlement is often coupled with a demand for a change in the coronation oaths so that the next monarch will promise to uphold the Christian faith as a whole rather than just its Protestant branch. In an interesting article written at the time of the 2003 Golden Jubilee celebrations Adrian Leak argued that 'the disproportionate attention given in the wording of the oaths to the preservation of the Church of England and its rights is an embarrassment in urgent need of remedy,' and suggested that 'the ancient oath taken by King Edgar in 973 that "the Church of God and the whole Christian people shall have true peace at all times" would suffice.'[8] As we have already noted, the provisions of the coronation oath have been changed more than once (see pp. 141–2), and it would be open to Parliament to amend the Coronation Oaths Act of 1689, the Act of Settlement of 1701 and the Accession Declaration Act of 1910 to produce a more inclusive form of words, and indeed, to delete from both the oath and the accession declaration the monarch's specific commitment to uphold the Church of England and the Church of Scotland. There is a wider question about whether the oath should continue to favour Christianity over other religions. The report of the Commission on the future of multi-ethnic Britain set up by the Home Secretary and published in 2000 cited the coronation oath alongside daily prayers in the Westminster Parliament, the law of blasphemy and the Christian character of national memorial events as being discriminatory against other faiths.

Alongside these calls for a more inclusive coronation oath, there has also been a significant campaign over the past few years to promote not just its Protestant emphasis but also the moral responsibilities with which it charges the sovereign. In March 1999 a petition to the Queen was organized by Dr Clifford Denton, supported by Jesus is Alive Ministries and the National Council for Christian Standards, who declared themselves 'deeply concerned by the steady erosion of our historic Christian faith and the surrender of the commanding heights of the country to the advance of secular humanism and to a turning away from God'. It called on the Queen to remember her coronation oath, which had been framed 'to ensure that Britain's people would be governed and led by the ways of Almighty God'. The petitioners suggested that the Queen had broken the central part of the oath, where she had sworn that she would maintain the laws of God and the true profession of the Gospel in the nation, by signing 'the law that legalised abortion, the law that liberalised censorship, laws which liberalised divorce and laws which have led to an escalation of gambling in the nation'.[9] The petition drew this reply from the Home Office:

> I can assure you that the coronation oath is regarded as a solemn undertaking of the Sovereign which is binding throughout her reign. However in a constitutional monarchy such as we have in the United Kingdom, it is imperative that the Sovereign is politically impartial. The Queen therefore acts on the advice of Her Ministers, who would not wish to advise Her Majesty to sign into law any provision which contradicted the Oath. It follows that it is Government Ministers who are responsible to Parliament and the electorate for the matters to which your petition refers.[10]

It is good that the coronation oath is being taken seriously and that the National Council for Christian Standards is reminding us of the principles which underlie it. Quite apart from the constitutional point raised in the Home Office reply, however, there is, of course, no clear consensus among contemporary Christians as to the extent to which recent legislation in several of the areas mentioned in the petition is, in fact, contrary to the Word of God. The Council's view of the oath is set in the context of an application of the covenant theology at the heart of Israelite monarchy which many would now regard as anachronistic:

> The remarkable thing is that Britain, through leaders in past generations, set out to be, as a nation, in Covenant with Almighty God. The pivot of the Covenants is the Coronation Oath, which is based on the intention that all the institutions of the nation are to be governed according to the laws of God and the true profession of the Gospel. The means by which this has been achieved to a good measure is through the balance between Church, Government and Monarchy, whose subtle interaction can

allow God to be our King. This situation is remarkable in that a whole nation has endeavoured to be the people of God.[11]

The campaign of the National Council for Christian Standards and others to highlight the importance of the coronation oath does raise an important issue, which ought to be taken into consideration in any deliberations about its rewording. In the absence of a written constitution the oath stands as the most basic and solemn expression of the ultimate values of the British state. It is not without significance that the promises which it embodies are made by the sovereign not to Parliament or the people but to God, in the context of a religious service of consecration. Might the terms of the oath justify or even require the monarch on occasions to indicate disapproval of legislation? Should the central statement of the values of the nation continue to be couched in clearly Christian terms and involve a solemn promise to God by the sovereign? These questions need to be aired and discussed alongside many others in the current constitutional mêlée.[12]

The debate over the wording of a future coronation oath is inextricably linked with the question of whether the next monarch should retain the title of Defender of the Faith. This subject was raised most visibly in the 1994 television documentary *Charles: The Private Man, the Public Role*. In conversation with Jonathan Dimbleby Prince Charles discussed his long-standing belief 'that the Catholic subjects of the sovereign are equally as important as the Anglican ones, as the Protestant ones. I think that the Islamic subjects or the Hindu subjects or the Zoroastrian subjects of the sovereign are of equal and vital importance.'[13] He went on to provide his own novel interpretation of the monarch's traditional role as Defender of the Faith:

I personally would rather see it as Defender of Faith, not the Faith, because it (Defender of the Faith) means just one particular interpretation of the Faith, which I think is sometimes something that causes a deal of a problem. It has done for hundreds of years. People have fought each other to the death over these things, which seems to me a peculiar waste of people's energy, when we're all actually aiming for the same ultimate goal, I think. So I would much rather it was seen as defending faith itself which is so often under threat in our day where, you know, the whole concept of faith itself or anything beyond this existence, beyond life itself is considered almost old-fashioned and irrelevant.[14]

The Prince subsequently expanded on this definition by saying that for him Defender of Faith meant being 'Defender of the Divine in existence, the pattern of the Divine which is, I think, in all of us but which, because we are human beings, can be expressed in so many different ways'.[15]

This was by any reckoning a remarkable statement by the heir to the throne about the importance of the spiritual dimension of monarchy. It was also a very significant theological statement, both in terms of its inter-faith dimension and its strong emphasis on the value and importance of religious faith. These aspects were largely missed by commentators who almost without exception chose to take the Prince's remarks as suggesting that he wanted to sever the links between the monarchy and the Church of England, and was advocating disestablishment. The *Sunday Times*, which published an exclusive preview of the Prince's remarks before the Dimbleby documentary was shown, set the tone of press coverage by running under the headline 'Charles plans to break royal link with church' a front-page story which began:

> The Prince of Wales is planning to end the 450 year-old role of the monarch as head of the Church of England and defender of the faith. Charles believes that when he becomes king he should be a figurehead for all religions in Britain, including Roman Catholics and Muslims, and that the church should be disestablished.[16]

In fact there was nothing whatsoever about disestablishment, nor indeed about the royal relationship with the Church of England, in the Prince of Wales' remarks. The title 'Defender of the Faith', as we have seen, was given by the Pope to Henry VIII for his defence of the Catholic faith against Luther. It has continued to be adopted by successive monarchs and has come to be associated, at least in the popular mind and in the press, with the defence of the Protestant faith and the Church of England. In fact, it has no historical or legal connection with the monarch's role either in maintaining the Protestant religion, which is defined in the coronation oath and accession declaration, nor with respect to the Church of England, which is defined by the title of Supreme Governor, adopted by Elizabeth I in preference to that of Supreme Head which had been assumed by Henry VIII.

The titles of Defender of the Faith and Supreme Governor of the Church of England should, therefore, be treated separately and not confused, as they so often are. Jonathan Dimbleby is wrong to say in his book based on the television programme that Prince Charles' remarks about becoming Defender of Faith 'expressed strong sentiments about the relationship of the sovereign to the Church of England'.[17] They did nothing of the sort. The Prince made no allusion to the role of Supreme Governor, which is a constitutional responsibility undertaken by the sovereign as head of state and not dependent on the religious position or preferences of individual monarchs. The Prince of Wales was addressing not the monarchy's constitutional relationship with the established Church of England but its role in an increasingly secular and pluralistic society in promoting religious faith in the broadest sense.

Not surprisingly, this suggested new title for the monarch has not gone down well in Evangelical circles. A report on 'Faith and Nation' published by the Evangelical Alliance in 2006 called for it to be resisted 'on the grounds that such a change would too readily be interpreted as an endorsement of syncretism'.[18] This, too, is surely to misunderstand what Prince Charles had in mind. In the context of his lifelong crusade to champion the spiritual dimension of life, the title 'Defender of Faith' makes the religious dimension of the monarchy both more prominent and more inclusive without necessarily making for syncretism or the disestablishment of the Church of England. At a time when faith is becoming a demonstrably more important indicator of both individual and group identity among Britain's growing ethnic minorities and when there is much debate about how common values and cohesion can be preserved in a multi-faith society, the idea of giving the monarchy a particular responsibility for representing and defending the principle of faith and the interests of faith communities is one that is surely worthy of serious consideration.

Aside from Prince Charles' remarks about becoming 'Defender of Faith', the main way in which the multi-faith nature of modern Britain has been raised in connection with the monarchy has been in the context of discussion about the shape of the next coronation. Traditionally, coronations have been exclusively Christian services, regarded as sacramental in character and conducted by the bishops, and according to the rites, of the Church of England. At the time of the 1953 coronation this posed no particular problem, as Shils and Young suggest in their seminal article on the subject:

> Apart from the momentary appearance of the Moderator of the General Assembly of the Church of Scotland, the Church of England administers the entire ceremony, and yet there is no indication that this was regarded as an anomaly in a country where only a small proportion of the population actively adheres to that church. Britain is generally a Christian country, it is certainly a religious country, in the broad sense, and in the Coronation service the Church of England served the vague religiosity of the mass of the British people without raising issues of ecclesiastical jurisdiction or formal representation.[19]

Whether an Anglican coronation service conducted by the Church of England would still serve the 'vague religiosity' of the British people today is a moot question. Judged in terms of church membership and attendance, Britain is now a very much less Christian country than it was in 1953. Whether it is a less religious country is more difficult to say. There is still much interest in spiritual matters and, if the polls are to be believed, a strong persistence of belief in God and in other traditional tenets of religious belief, but there has been a sea change in the position of Christianity vis-à-vis other faiths, and of the established churches within the spectrum of Christian denominations. There are now considerably more Muslims than Methodists within the United Kingdom, and more Sikhs than Baptists. On Sunday mornings there are also almost certainly more Roman Catholics in church than Anglicans in England or Presbyterians in Scotland. There is widespread agreement that the next coronation should have an ecumenical character. Even if the central act of anointing and conse-cration, should it remain, is carried out by the Archbishop of Canterbury, there will almost certainly be a significant role in the service for leading figures in the Roman Catholic and Free Churches as well as from the main churches of Scotland, Wales and Northern Ireland. This has already happened at other royal and state occasions.

The question has also been raised as to whether the coronation should continue to be set in the context of a communion service. Several Anglican clerics have pointed out that the great spread of congregational communion throughout the Church of England over the past 60 years, with the Parish Eucharist rather than Matins becoming the main and best attended morning service, would make it difficult and anomalous to repeat the customary practice in the coronation service whereby only the sovereign and his or her consort receive. Adrian Leak has argued that, compared to the dazzling visual impact of the regalia and other rituals of the coronation, 'the sacrament of holy communion that follows is bound to appear less important' and that the litur-gical difficulty of combining two such unequal sets of symbols provides another reason for ditching the tradition of locating the coronation within the context of a celebration of the Eucharist.[20] David Edwards, a former canon of Westminster Abbey and provost of Southwark Cathedral, has suggested that while an Anglican eucharist might well be appropriate as a private act of devotion attached to the coronation when the monarch is a communicant, it should not form part of the televised public ceremonies.[21]

A much more contentious issue is the extent to which the next coronation should be a multi-faith ceremony involving the participation of leading representatives of non-Christian religions. At least two prominent Anglicans have indicated their enthusiasm for some such arrangement. Richard Harries, while Bishop of Oxford, expressed the view that 'at the next coronation the leaders of other faiths need to be significantly and symbolically present. They need to be much more than guests; they need to be present in the sanctuary, at the centre of things.'[22] Colin Buchanan, former Bishop of Woolwich, has similarly pointed to the desirability of inviting 'all religious groups in the country to pray for the monarch' and devising 'inaugural ceremonies, such as a Coronation, which both drew upon the loyalties of all the religious groups in the country and also allowed the monarch some special place for the public engagement of the rites of his or her own faith'.[23]

Such suggestions that the next coronation might in some way involve leaders of non-Christian faith communities have met with a predictably frosty response from several quarters. In the view of the British Israelite Kingdom Foundation:

> If the service took on a multi-faith character, it is unlikely to send a sweet smelling savour heavenward to Jehovah. Any Archbishop of Canterbury who embraced such a display of the religious multi-cult would undoubtedly place himself in a position not unlike Aaron, who made a golden calf for the people of Israel, bringing thereby the most severe Divine sanctions upon the nation.[24]

Similar unease surfaces regularly in the letters columns of the *Daily Telegraph*:

> The replacement of our 1,000 year-old coronation service with a multi-cultural, multi-faith pantomime deserves to be vigorously resisted. The prospect of Charles III arriving at Westminster Abbey, being greeted by the Islamic leaders who wanted to burn Salman Rushdie's books, and then declared 'Defender of Faiths' by the Archbishop of Canterbury and the chairman of the Commission for Racial Equality, is enough to send a shiver down the spine of anyone who believes that Britain should remain a basically Anglo-European nation, mindful of its traditional Christian heritage.[25]

In more temperate language, the Evangelical Alliance has urged that 'the Coronation should retain its historic character as an act of Christian worship, while being more ecumenical in form to reflect the growing diversity of Christian life and witness in the United Kingdom', and that it should include representatives of non-Christian faiths as guests while 'avoiding any suggestion of interfaith or syncretistic worship'.[26]

The merest hint that it might be desirable to open up the coronation to involve acknowledgement of the monarch by non-Christian faith groups tends to be seized on by the media and blown up into a full-scale repudiation of the United Kingdom's long tradition of Christian monarchy. A report commissioned by the Home Office from the University of Derby on religious discrimination in Britain, and published in 2000, raised the question in a very tentative way by noting that

> the religious composition of society has changed significantly since the last Coronation and the next Coronation will therefore highlight a series of very important issues and complexities, which it would be best to begin giving consideration to as soon as possible.[27]

This was the basis for a front-page story in the *Daily Telegraph* under the headline 'Multi-faith Coronation for Charles – plan could end 1,000 year tradition'. In fact, the report did not find a substantial feeling among leaders and members of minority faiths that the coronation as it stands is discriminatory, although they did strongly support Prince Charles' proposed change of title to 'Defender of Faith'. The *Telegraph*'s leading article on the report fulminated against the idea that 'our country should abandon altogether one of its most hallowed traditions at the behest of a few politically correct busybodies'. It provoked a salvo of letters in support of maintaining the existing form of the coronation service, including several from adherents of non-Christian faiths. Daoud Rosser-Owen, Amir of the Association of British Muslims, expressed the view that 'Muslims want the Coronation service and oath to stand', and a Jewish correspondent wrote in similar terms.[28]

Much of the thinking in senior ecclesiastical and court circles about the shape of the next coronation goes on behind closed doors but there does seem to be something of a consensus emerging that while the coronation itself should remain a Christian act of worship held in Westminster Abbey and conducted by and according to the rites of the Church of England, albeit with substantial ecumenical participation, there should also be a separate and further ceremony of recognition and inauguration which would involve the participation of other faith leaders. The idea of returning the act of homage to the new monarch to Westminster Hall, where it was often performed in the Middle Ages, has been widely championed by both ecclesiastics and constitutional historians. Roy Strong writes:

> The revival of the use of Westminster Hall may well provide a solution to many of the problems thrown up by what is now a multi-faith and multi-cultural society. There is no reason why the next sovereign, after anointing and crowning, should not process back to the hall to be blessed or saluted by the representatives of other faiths.[29]

At least two leading churchmen have promoted the idea of a 'rolling coronation' which would take in several locations. While Dean of Westminster Abbey, Dr Wesley Carr suggested that the ceremony might begin with the new monarch being presented to community leaders in the Great Hall of the Palace of Westminster. This 'could allow for the various religious groups and ethnic bodies that now constitute the nation to recognize their sovereign and offer a form of homage'. Following this act of recognition, the new monarch would 'then in the Abbey be able to present himself as carrying the unity of the nation as the basis on which the specifically Christian coronation would follow'. For Carr, the coronation in Westminster Abbey, centred around the ceremonies of anointing and crowning, should be 'according to the customary holy communion service of the Book of Common Prayer'. The monarch would then process to St Margaret's Church, Westminster, to receive the homage of the representatives of the people, Members of Parliament, and would then return to the Palace of Westminster for an interfaith inauguration ceremony.[30] In similar vein, while he was Archbishop of York David Hope suggested that the coronation might begin at Buckingham Palace, move on to the Houses of Parliament and then to Westminster Abbey, taking in a greeting ceremony involving the leaders of non-Christian faith communities. More radically, he also floated the idea that the new monarch should serve representatives of the poor and socially deprived in a series of banquets or garden parties following the coronation. Such an action, in some ways reminiscent of the ancient Maundy Thursday tradition of the monarch washing the feet of the poor, would, he suggested, 'be a clear sign of the monarch's commitment as a Christian to that fundamental insight into Christ's own power and authority – that of service'.[31]

Discussion of possible reform of the coronation is often linked with the question of whether the monarch should remain Supreme Governor of the Church of England. This complex constitutional responsibility has many ramifications and has been the subject of considerable debate over the past two decades. Several voices both from within and outside the churches have argued that it is now an anachronism but others have eloquently defended it. There have even been some suggestions that the monarch should exercise more direct 'hands-on' control and authority over the Church of England. A committee set up by the Church's General Synod in 1992 under the chairmanship of William van Straubenzee found that the sovereign's involvement in the appointment of archbishops, diocesan bishops and deans was greatly valued and it recommended that senior church appointments be made directly by the monarch and not by the prime minister through the mechanism of the prime minister's office and the Church's Crown Appointments Committee. The Committee felt that such a move would preserve the advantages of establishment and maintain the symbolic role of the sovereign as Supreme Governor, while bypassing the essentially political process and apparatus that many in the Church of England find offensive. Its recommendation was not accepted by the General Synod, however, and would, indeed, have been constitutionally improper. The sovereign can only act on the advice of a responsible minister and this principle applies to his or her role as Supreme Governor of the Church of England as much as to other aspects of being head of state.

There remains one area where the monarch still retains rather more direct control over appointments and other matters in the Church of England. The royal peculiars, which include Westminster Abbey and the chapels attached to the royal palaces, come under the direct jurisdiction of the Queen and not under the usual diocesan system. A committee set up to look into their management in 2001 recommended the establishment of a standing commission to which the Queen would delegate her visitorial functions and which would act as a permanent body to advise the sovereign on their management. Although the Committee's report was presented in the newspapers under such headlines as 'Queen may lose control of her five chapels' and 'Queen to loosen grip on Abbey', it specifically commended the principle of continuing independence for the royal peculiars and described them as 'a heritage that should be loved and preserved'. The royal peculiars remain independent, and provide a tangible reminder of the sovereign's close relationship with the established Church.

Debate over the desirability of the sovereign remaining Supreme Governor of the Church of England was clouded during the early 1990s by irrelevant speculation as to whether the Prince of Wales, as a divorced person, or in the event of remarrying after divorce, could properly assume that role on becoming king. The matter was admirably put into perspective by John Habgood, Archbishop of York:

> Sovereigns are not required to be saints. ... Nevertheless, is the Supreme Governor of the Church of England required to be at least as morally sober as an archbishop? If supreme governorship were the same as spiritual leadership the answer might be yes. But this would represent a serious misunderstanding. A monarch's personal involvement in the Church is welcome. The role of Supreme Governor, however, is not personal but institutional.
>
> The monarch is the visible representative of the unity and identity of the nation, and it is the Church's commitment to the nation, and responsibility for its spiritual welfare, which is symbolised by supreme governorship. It would be theoretically possible to hold to the symbol even if in personal terms the monarch only fulfilled the minimum requirement of belonging to the Protestant succession.[32]

There have been suggestions that the title 'Supreme Governor' should be changed to reflect a less authoritarian and more participatory relationship between sovereign and church. David Edwards, reviewing the first edition of my book in 2002, wrote:

> It seems right that the monarch should be a protector of the Church to which the majority of the English still turn when wanting a church (I mean the Church of England) – but isn't the role better described as being the Church's 'Senior Member'?[33]

Such a title would make the monarch's relationship with the Church of England more analogous to that with the Church of Scotland, although the word 'senior' might stick in egalitarian Presbyterian throats. While in Scotland, the Queen is a loyal and welcome member of the national Church whose General Assembly she symbolically attends, occasionally in person, and more often by deputing a Lord High Commissioner, but over which she has no jurisdiction.

The most vigorous recent defence of keeping the sovereign's role and title of Supreme Governor has come from Paul Avis, General Secretary of the Church of England's Council for Christian Unity. He points out that the royal supremacy is a constitutional fact that applies to all bodies and persons within the realm. The Church of England's Canon A7, which is part of the law of the land, states that 'the Queen's most excellent majesty, acting according to the laws of the realm, is the highest power under God in the kingdom, and has supreme authority over all persons and causes, as well ecclesiastical as civil'. Constitutionally, he points out, the sovereignty exercised by Queen in Parliament under God extends to all institutions, and among churches not just to the Church of England but to other Protestant churches and to the Roman Catholic Church. He enthusiastically lauds the specific relationship with the Church of England embodied by the sovereign's position as Supreme Governor because of the role it gives to a layperson.

> It is no embarrassment to a church profoundly touched by the Reformation that a lay person should hold large responsibilities in the church. It is simply an outworking of the doctrine of the universal royal priesthood of the baptized. But it also signals symbolically that in the

Church of England lay people have major responsibilities and significant privileges. A church that recognizes the spiritual competence of lay persons is likely to be a broad and tolerant church. The laity say the creeds in the context of the liturgy, but they are not subject to any other tests of orthodoxy. A church with a lay person as its Supreme Governor cannot be a church dominated by ecclesiastical niceties.[34]

The position of the sovereign as Supreme Governor is just one aspect of the established status of the Church of England, a bigger question which has also been the subject of much recent debate. It is not surprising that the strongest calls for the abolition of this particular role and title have come from those arguing for disestablishment. At their 2000 Assembly the Liberal Democrats became the first major political party in Britain to back disestablishment by passing a motion calling for the separation of church and state, removal of the ban on Roman Catholics succeeding to the throne, discontinuance of the practice of bishops sitting in the House of Lords and abolition of the sovereign's role as Supreme Governor. For Colin Buchanan, long one of the Church of England's foremost proponents of disestablishment, the supreme governorship is a key element in the church–state relationship which it is high time to sever:

I find it possible to be not only an Anglican Christian, but an Anglican Christian with a strong sense both that the Christian Churches should be united and that we have genuine good news which we ought to want to offer to other religions, and to believe it right to sit on no apparent advantage that might come our way through the slightly forced adherence of the Crown to the Church of England, and through the resultant Supreme Governorship, which actually binds us to the government in power as much as to the monarch's own person. ... The point of principle for which we strive is that the

Church should take responsibility for its own life, and
that the machinery of government, including the actual
office of Head of State, should formally and theologically
be divorced and distanced from any interference with
that life.[35]

The whole question of church establishment is strictly speaking
beyond the scope of this book, although it is clearly impossible
to write about the spiritual dimension of monarchy in the
British context without alluding to it. I have myself written
widely about what I regard as the strengths of establishment
and of the desirability of a re-establishment which has an
ecumenical dimension.[36] Some kind of relationship between
monarch and church is clearly an important aspect of establishment but, as the Scottish experience shows, it does not
have to be that of Supreme Governor. The Church of Scotland
provides an alternative model of establishment where the
monarch has a close and much valued involvement in the
life of the national Church but does not exercise any control
over its affairs or appointments. It acknowledges no supreme
head or governor other than Jesus Christ, and is by the terms
of the Church of Scotland Act 1921 entirely autonomous
and free to control its own affairs without any interference
or involvement from the state. At the same time, it has legal
recognition as the national Church and a special responsibility
to bring the ordinances of religion to everyone in the nation.
This is a model which I sense is gaining increasing favour
within the Church of England.

There has been much helpful thinking and writing on the
subject of church establishment over recent years which has
inevitably involved consideration of the religious position of
the monarchy. In a significant lecture given on St George's Day
2002 as Archbishop of Canterbury, George Carey commended
the constitutional principle of sovereignty being vested not
in Parliament alone, but in the monarch in Parliament, both
accountable to a divine authority, and promoted the idea of
what he called a hospitable establishment 'centred squarely

on the concept of service ... which helps to underwrite the commitment of a national church to serve the entire community and to give form and substance to some of its deepest collective needs and aspirations'.[37] The best recent defence of church establishment is in Paul Avis' 2001 book, *Church, State and Establishment*, which, as already pointed out, strongly supports the continuation of the monarch's role as Supreme Governor. Theo Hobson's *Against Establishment: An Anglican Polemic* (2003) provides a powerful counterblast. He is particularly contemptuous of the ritual surrounding coronations, seeing the 1953 ceremony representing 'the last gasp of our religious myth when the illusion of stability was most complete' and observing that 'royal personality cult suffused with vague religiosity is obviously the ideal religion of the English people'.[38]

It is interesting and ironic that while the call for disestablishment has come largely from the Christian or secular majority in Britain, the principle of church establishment has found some of its staunchest defenders among the religious and ethnic minorities. The most eloquent proponent of establishment has almost certainly been Jonathan Sacks, when he was Chief Rabbi of the United Hebrew congregations of the Commonwealth. In his 1990 Reith Lectures, he argued that established churches provide a 'sacred canopy', or overarching framework of shared meanings and moral landscape, create a sense of belonging and 'put faith at the centre of our national symbols'. The extent of minority support for the existence of established churches was demonstrated in a conference on 'Church, State and Religious Minorities' convened by the Policy Studies Institute in 1995. Here it was the Christian and humanist speakers who opposed establishment and the representatives of Judaism, Sikhism, Hinduism and Islam who supported it, albeit in a form which allowed the Church of England and Church of Scotland to speak on behalf of other faiths. The Home Office-commissioned report on institutionalized religious discrimination published in 2000 found, somewhat to the compliers' surprise, that far from being a major grievance among those from minority faiths, the principle of church establishment was generally supported, along with such rituals as the Christian coronation of the monarch, for putting religion at the heart of the state and national identity, and affirming the importance of the sacred and spiritual.

It is surely significant that two of the leading contemporary advocates of multiculturalism in Britain are also in favour of church establishment and indeed of close links between the monarchy and the Church. Tariq Modood suggests that far from being an obstacle to multiculturalism, an established church can broker greater recognition of and respect for religious minorities and the importance of faith in their identities. He commends the coronation of the monarch by the Archbishop of Canterbury. Bhiku Parekh similarly favours Christianity remaining the central part of British collective identity, provided that other religions receive adequate, though not necessarily equal recognition in the institutions, rituals and ceremonies of the state.[39]

It may indeed be that as with other traditional marks of Britishness, there is now as much if not more enthusiasm among the ethnic and religious minorities than among many of the majority nominally Christian white population for the maintenance of a close constitutional connection between church and Crown and a realization of what would be lost if this delicate and complex link was broken. There do also remain staunch advocates of maintaining this link from within the established Church, most notably Paul Avis:

> In the unwritten British constitution, the Crown is the linchpin of the system of checks and balances that gives us a legislature answerable to the electorate, a judicial system independent of the executive, and armed forces that do not owe their ultimate allegiance to politicians. The Crown guarantees the freedom under law enjoyed by British citizens. Yet at the same time the Crown is in some sense dependent on the Church. The Sovereign is seen

as answerable to a higher power. Crowned and consecrated by the archbishops and bishops of the Church of
England, she exercises her office as a duty and privilege
that comes from God. She thus has a constitutional role as
the guardian of higher civic values. It is arguable that the
unique relationship between the Crown and the Church
of England underpins the constitution of the United
Kingdom as a whole and its attendant civil liberties. The
link between Crown and church can therefore be said to
be on behalf of all persons, communities and institutions
that flourish under the constitution. The constitutional
position of the sovereign is understood in relation to
a church that is formally recognized by the state, The
Crown could become vulnerably isolated and exposed
without that link. Crown, church and constitution are
bound up together in a delicate ecology.[40]

In marked contrast to these sentiments, however, there has
been a growing call to distance the churches, and particularly
the Church of England, from the monarchy. This has taken a
number of forms. At an intellectual and ideological level, it has
been expressed through a questioning of the whole compatibility between Christianity and monarchy. In a recent pamphlet
advocating disestablishment, Chris Bryant, the Anglican Chair
of the Christian Socialist Movement, writes: 'It is a well-
concealed fact that the Bible is less than wholehearted in its
support for the idea of Kings and Queens.'[41] Media hostility
and public disaffection with royalty have also spilled over
into the churches, especially perhaps the Church of England,
anxious to repent of its previous tendency towards monarcholatry and to prove its 'Cool Britannia' credentials. In the words
of Martyn Percy, Principal of Cuddesdon Theological College:

> The alienation of the monarchy is something that affects
> the Church of England deeply. Coronations were once
> seen as mystical rites that symbolised the 'giving' of God's
> power to rule. From the monarch, divine government

flowed to ministers of the State, Crown and Church. Society was carefully ordered, so that only those with the right titles had the right to access. Bishops, as Lords, are part of that process, as are Royal Peculiars and the like. The collusion of the Church in this elitism, no matter what social good comes from it, looks an increasingly risky strategy. No-one seriously sees the Queen's rule as 'ordained' by God, irrespective of what St Paul had to say about temporal authority – the notion simply lends a spurious divine authority to a hegemonic status quo.[42]

This assault on the lingering echoes of monarcholatry is not confined to the Church of England. William Storrar attacked the Church of Scotland's 1994 *Book of Common Order* for its frequent prayers for the Queen and the High Court of Parliament which he found to be 'curiously old-fashioned in a British Unionist and twilight of the empire sort of way'.[43] I am conscious that I am now one of relatively few Church of Scotland ministers who regularly prays for the Queen at Sunday morning services. Even within the Church of England this practice seems to be becoming less common. The growing mood of disenchantment with the monarchy in both the national churches of England and Scotland has also led to a greater willingness within the churches to question the desirability of continuing with the institution itself, at least in its present form. The Church of Scotland's magazine, *Life and Work*, devoted its main feature in March 1997 to a debate on the merits of monarchy, with the editor, Robin Hill, who is now himself a parish minister, putting the case for a republic. In May 1998 Eric James, who served as chaplain to the Queen from 1984 to 1995, suggested in a lecture at Westminster Abbey that the time might be right to return to having an elected monarchy in Britain.

The problem of hereditary monarchy is obvious and simple. The monarch now may be above reproach but you can never tell what you are going to get. The question needs to be posed, again, in our own time, whether the mere accident of birth can ever now be expected to produce a man or a woman fit for the role that royalty requires. In our age, from birth, the fierce glare of publicity is directed on to the heir's upbringing, education, and development; followed by the investigative glare of the media on his making of friends, wooing and so on. The relation between the private person and the public role – it must be faced – now makes all but impossible demands. ... In England, until 1213, the monarch was elected. Maybe the time is returning for election to the task and role.[44]

Not surprisingly, this part of Eric James' lecture, which was inspired as much by a deep pastoral concern for those thrust into prominence by accident of birth as by his well-known radical political views, received considerable publicity. Perhaps more important, however, was his call for the churches to contribute to the whole debate on the future of the monarchy:

> I respectfully suggest that the archbishops should set up a broad-based Commission on Church and Nation, with special reference to the future of the monarchy. So far, the churches have been strangely silent on the modernising of the monarchy, though, surely, they have much to contribute through what the Bible says on monarchy – not least through the prophets, but most through the self-revelation of God in Jesus and the model He provides of leadership in His kingdom in contrast with our all too human requirements of distance, rank, status, possessions and hierarchy – which, of course, meant originally 'rule by priests' ... Such a commission would surely have valuable insights for our secular, multi-racial and multi-faith society.[45]

Four years earlier a similar call for an Archbishops' commission on the wider question of church–state relations had been made by David Edwards. Sadly the kind of church-initiated and inspired debate on the interrelated issues of monarchy, church and state that these two leading liberal Anglicans have called for has largely failed to happen. Theologically informed contributions to the debate on the future of monarchy are few and far between. One such came in a letter to *The Times* in November 1999 from Nigel Biggar, now Regius Professor of Moral and Pastoral Theology at Oxford University, who questioned the prevailing worship of the 'popular will' and argued that while democratic election provides the makers of laws and policies with political legitimacy, it does not endow them with moral legitimacy:

> What alone confers moral legitimacy upon a democrati-cally elected government is its obedience to the principles of justice, which are given in nature, and not invented by humans to suit their political purposes.
>
> It is therefore highly salutary for popularly elected representatives to be subject to a head of state who symbolises the givenness of justice precisely by not being chosen – directly or indirectly – by the people; and who at her coronation receives the symbol of authority, not from below, but from above.[46]

This extremely interesting argument from the natural law tradition in defence of the principle of hereditary monarchy is exactly the kind of thing it would be good to hear more of from church leaders and theologians. As it is, such serious thinking as there is about the desirability and the future of the monarchy in contemporary Britain has been largely pursued in overwhelmingly secular terms and without the input of the churches or university theology departments. A good example is the thoughtful manifesto for a modernized monarchy published by the think-tank Demos in 1998. It argues that the key problem for the British monarchy is the 'schizophrenic identity' that comes from trying to fulfil three different roles – the political/constitutional, the quasi-religious and mystical, and the symbolic. The Demos report proposes the curtailment of the political and religious roles and the reinforcement of the symbolic role. It outlines the attributes of a modernized monarchy:

> That the institution itself draws its legitimacy not from divine right, historical continuity, constitutional formula or parliamentary permission but popular assent expressed in a public ballot.
>
> That the monarch should be head of state and thus symbol of the nation but have minimal connection with the executive, legislature, or judiciary.
>
> That the monarchy should be organised in a fashion that allows for full accountability.
>
> That a symbol of unity cannot be exclusively associated with any one religion or organised religion at all.
>
> That the symbolic activities of the monarchy reflect the diversity of contemporary society.[47]

To attain these objectives, the Demos report suggests a referendum to determine who should succeed to the throne following the death or abdication of the sovereign and advocates a series of measures to depoliticize the monarchy, including removing the royal assent, abolishing the Privy Council and disestablishing the Church of England. The secularization of the monarchy should be brought about by repealing the Act of Supremacy of 1559 and all other legislation bonding together church and state, and requiring the sovereign to maintain the Protestant religion in England and the Presbyterian faith in Scotland. The monarch should be entitled to membership of any religious grouping and the Archbishop of Canterbury should be stripped of all state functions including his role at coronations. These reforms, the report suggests, 'would realign the monarchy with the reality of British society. This is a predominantly secular country.'[48]

What the Demos report champions is essentially a reinvigorated welfare monarchy. Arguing that 'the primary function of the monarchy should be the promotion of national unity and the cohesion of civil society through charitable endeavours', it offers some interesting suggestions as to how this might be achieved.[49] The Royal Family are enjoined to make a special commitment to schools and education, to increase their patronage of the arts and to promote the cause of international reconciliation by becoming ambassadors-at-large. They are also charged with the role of promoting British values and worth: 'The monarchy should stand for the whole gamut of British values – our openness to the world, our multiculturalism, our traditions of democracy and fair play, our creativity – and help to change perceptions of Britain where they are inaccurate.'[50] Overall, the function of monarchy is conceived of as acting as a symbolic focus of unity and of predominantly secular if worthy values. There is no room for a spiritual or sacred dimension since 'a symbol of unity cannot be exclusively associated with any one religion or with organised religion at all'.[51]

A similarly secular vision characterizes Vernon Bogdanor's important academic study *The Monarchy and the Constitution* (1995). Like the authors of the Demos pamphlet he believes that the future of the monarchy rests primarily on 'the practical employment of its symbolic influence', especially in the field of charitable and philanthropic work identified by Prochaska as propping up civic society. He also calls for the disestablishment of the Church of England and the severing of the links between crown and church, with fundamental changes being made to the coronation service and coronation oath to create an essentially secular monarchy.

> There can be no doubt that a secular monarchy would be a very different type of monarchy from that to which we have historically been accustomed, and this would involve a breach with its historic origins. But a secularized monarchy might nevertheless prove to be a monarchy more in tune with the spirit of the age.[52]

The idea that the future of the monarchy lies in making it more secular is also regularly canvassed in the broadsheet press. For *The Times*, 'the monarch's sole hope of survival rests in throwing off its political and religious roles', while the *Independent* has called for a new secularized constitutional monarchy which is not governed by the 'quasi-religious beliefs of another age and the mystical accretions of yore'.[53]

A similarly secular outlook and a strange and almost total neglect of the role of monarchy has characterized the debate on national identity and what it means to be British that has been a major feature of public discourse over the past decade or so. This debate, fuelled by concern about the loss of social cohesion and common identity as a result of immigration, the growth of political separatism and the pursuit of multicultur-alism, has actively engaged both Labour and Conservative politicians as well as academics and commentators. It has involved calls for a renewed definition and assertion of core British values, a new public holiday to be called UK Day, and a greater emphasis on a distinctively British, as well as a distinc-tively English, Scottish, Irish and Welsh cultural identity.

There has been very little discussion on the role and place of the monarchy in this debate. This is bizarre to say the least, given that it is one of the institutions which most clearly symbolizes British national identity. Its continuing iconic status in this regard was confirmed in a 2004 poll of school-teachers and pupils where the monarchy was rated second only to the Union flag in terms of symbols most associated with Britain. In another recent survey, Germans aged between 16 and 25 singled out the language, the monarchy and multi-culturalism as the aspects of Britain that they most admired. More than anyone else, the Queen personifies and exemplifies British identity, a fact that has been acknowledged much more readily by the monarchy's detractors and those opposed to the pursuit of Britishness than by enthusiasts for these two linked causes. Billy Bragg, the radical singer-songwriter, who has been a leading critic of the whole pro-British project and advocated instead a renewed and redefined English national identity, asked in his millennium song 'Take Down the Union Jack, It Clashes with the Sunset':

> Is this the Nineteenth Century that I'm watching on
>   TV?
> The dear old Queen of England handing out those
>   MBEs?

In similar vein, Jeremy Paxman, writing in anti-monarchical mode in his book *The English* before his Damascene conversion apparently evident in his later *On Royalty*, acknowledges that 'The supreme embodiment of the idea of Britain is the country's royal family. ... The institution of monarchy belongs to the world of red tunics and bearskins, the Union flag and the Gatling gun.[54]

These and other detractors link the monarchy with Britishness, believing that both are long past their sell-by date and should, in Bragg's words, be 'buried in the attic with the Emperor's old clothes'. By contrast, enthusiasts for redefining and reasserting British identity, among the most passionate of whom have perhaps been the last three prime ministers, Tony Blair, Gordon Brown and David Cameron, have made relatively little of the monarchy's potential role in this project. It is true that the Queen has been put at the centre of the new civic ceremonies introduced in 2004 to bestow British citizenship. In these naturalization ceremonies, where the Union Jack and the national anthem have a prominent place, it is the act of swearing eternal loyalty to the person of the Queen which officially imparts British citizenship. This reinforcement of the central link between the monarchy and British national identity has been curiously little commented on or championed by those seeking to develop a more cohesive society focused on a shared set of loyalties. This is particularly strange when the presence of the Queen and other members of the Royal Family is so central to those national occasions which do perhaps come closest to representing an expression of British identity, such as Remembrance Sunday, which Gordon Brown suggested in 2006 should be developed into a national day of patriotism to celebrate British history, achievements and culture, a 'British Day' equivalent to the Fourth of July Independence Day celebrations in the United States.

It is interesting to look at some of the other dates that have been proposed for a new UK Day to celebrate Britishness. Trafalgar Day (21 October) has been a popular option, given a recent boost when the coalition government let it be known that it was keen to replace the traditional May Day bank holiday with a UK Day in October to stretch the tourist season beyond the summer holidays. I myself have canvassed St Aidan's Day (31 August) as part of my campaign to give Britain a patron saint. As far as I am aware, the only suggestion of specifically linking a new UK Day to the monarchy has come from Andrew Rosindell, MP for Romford, who in 2011 proposed that the government move the May Day bank holiday to June to coincide with the Queen's official birthday (which is itself a movable celebration) and make it a day 'to celebrate all things British'.[55]

In my own contribution to the debate on Britishness, *Believing in Britain: The Spiritual Identity of Britishness* (2007 and 2008), I argue that the fact that the United Kingdom is organized and governed not around ethnicity, nationalism or some abstract political principle but rather around dynasty has a significant bearing on national identity. Allegiance to the monarch may not be a major factor in how the British see themselves nowadays, although, as we have just noted, it is now the key to becoming a British citizen, ironically perhaps since it is monarchy that makes the British subjects rather than citizens and in the eyes of some critics weakens the whole concept of citizenship in the United Kingdom. In all sorts of subtle and subconscious ways, however, monarchy still informs the nature of Britishness. This is particularly true in the metaphysical and spiritual sphere. Those great national occasions which come closest to expressing a shared collective sense of British identity

– Remembrance Day celebrations, royal weddings, ceremonies to commemorate significant national anniversaries and events and following major tragedies involving significant loss of life – share three characteristics. They involve religious services, they acknowledge in their different ways the transcendent and spiritual dimension of life, and they are graced by the presence of the Queen and other members of the Royal Family. It is the royal presence, almost as much as their liturgical context and content, that helps to establish their spiritual as well as their national atmosphere and resonance. In the words of Daniel Emlyn-Jones in a recent letter to the *Independent* following yet another secular republican blast from that newspaper: 'More than their endless charity work, business and political influence, the royal family enshrine the soul of our country. Without them, we simply wouldn't be British.'[56]

Could it be, indeed, that far from moving in a more secular direction, the monarchy might in fact best contribute to social cohesion, shared values and the development of a renewed generous capacious British identity in a multi-faith and multi-cultural society by being resacralized and emphasizing its sacramental and spiritual heart? This will be the argument of my next and final chapter.

9

The way ahead: a Christian monarchy in a multi-faith society

Before offering some concluding suggestions and observations about the future role and direction of the monarchy in the United Kingdom, it may be useful to summarize briefly the main findings and theme of this book so far.

The concept of sacred monarchy reaches back into primal religion and primitive society. That it still speaks to deep human instincts is clear from such diverse indices as the contemporary search for male identity on the basis of affirming 'the king within' and the huge popularity of the film *The Return of the King* and the Disney musical *The Lion King*. Sacred kingship has been a central element within the Judaeo-Christian tradition, as indeed it has in most of the world's great religions. The Old Testament witness is not unequivocal but it associates kingship with wisdom, prayer, just and merciful rule and the religious leadership of the people as well as with martial and administrative qualities. Jesus redefined kingship through his role as the servant-king and the sacrificial victim, but he is also celebrated in the Christian tradition as Christ the King, reigning in glory with his Father.

Within the British Isles over the past 1500 years there has been a noble tradition of Christian kingship. The throne has been occupied by saints as well as sinners, church builders, patrons of religious art and liturgy, and men and women of prayer who have pursued peace and justice. More recently, the Crown has allied itself with the cause of philanthropy, civic society and the active promotion of general welfare. For over 1000 years the coronation service has stood as the central defining symbol and sacrament of Christian monarchy, and indeed the supreme statement of the principles underlying the unwritten British constitution, through which kings and queens have been consecrated and set apart, taken a solemn oath before God to uphold justice and mercy, and had their rule set in a framework of transcendent metaphysical values.

At the dawning of the third millennium there is considerable doubt and debate as to the future of monarchy in general and Christian monarchy in particular. Most recent defences of monarchy and calls for its reform have advocated an essentially secular model. This book seeks to put forward the counter-cultural proposition that the monarchy still has a vital role and that this role is primarily spiritual. It involves symbolizing spiritual values, embodying the sacred, representing and defending religious faith against unbelief and secular materialism, promoting order in the midst of chaos, standing for the public good against private gain, and acting as a focal point for unity in a society which is increasingly fragmented and fissiparous. As an essentially sacred institution, the monarchy is particularly well placed to lead the recovery of our lost metaphysical imagination and the resacralization of our secularized society. This postmodern role involves recovering some of the main themes in pre-modern sacred kingship from the medieval and the primal eras. It also involves returning to Walter Bagehot's central definition of monarchy: 'It strengthens our government with the strength of religion ... constitutes the solitary transcendent element in the body politic ... and consecrates our whole state.'[1]

This sacramental and spiritual understanding of monarchy has underlain the reign of Queen Elizabeth II in an ever-more noticeable way. It also lies behind and informs many of the pronouncements of the Prince of Wales. In many respects both the current sovereign and her heir subscribe to and live out very clearly the principles of sacred monarchy that I have sought to describe and champion in this book. Those around them, and especially what are generally referred to as the chattering classes as opposed to the silent majority, are less easy with a spiritual model of monarchy and wish on the whole to fashion it in a more secular mould. In the remainder of this final chapter, I propose briefly to address the main areas of debate and offer my own suggestions as to how best the spiritual heart of the monarchy may be affirmed, enhanced and indeed harnessed to the task of helping to heal, bind together and inspire our wounded, fragmented and demoralized nation.

The Act of Accession and the coronation oaths

In the earlier editions of this book which appeared in 2002 and 2003, my first suggestion as to the changes needed to resacralize the monarchy ran as follows:

> First, the monarchy should be freed of its exclusive link with Protestantism. The United Kingdom is no longer a predominantly and definably Protestant country in the way that it was in the eighteenth and nineteenth centuries. The Crown should no longer be associated with anti-Catholic discrimination and prejudice. Roman Catholics have come in from the cold and now display conspicuous loyalty to the Queen – indeed, they are among her most loyal subjects. There is no good reason why there should not be a Roman Catholic on the throne. The Act of Settlement should be repealed, as should that part of the coronation oath which binds the monarch to upholding the Protestant Reformed religion.[2]

While I still feel that the Act of Settlement will and probably should eventually be repealed, I have changed my mind on the urgency of this matter and the desirability of an early repeal, partly as a result of being persuaded by conversations and comments in reviews occasioned by the above statement and partly because of the increasingly hardline attitude of the Vatican over the past few years towards Protestants. There has been a sea change in the attitude of the Church of England towards other denominations over recent decades – it is now unthinkable, thank God, that senior Anglicans would make the kinds of comments that their Victorian predecessors did about Queen Victoria attending and receiving the sacrament of communion in the Church of Scotland. By contrast, official Roman Catholic attitudes towards Protestants have hardened noticeably over recent years. It is now clear to me that the major source of discrimination in this area lies in Rome rather than in the provisions of the Act of Settlement. A Roman Catholic monarch would presumably not be allowed to receive communion in the Church of England or the Church of Scotland, nor to recognize the validity of Anglican or Presbyterian orders. It is very difficult indeed to see how he or she could validly be consecrated or anointed according to the rites of the Church of England. Until there is a change of attitude on the part of the Vatican and the Roman Catholic authorities, I do not see a case for amending or repealing the Act of Settlement.

I have also over the past ten years become more enthusiastic and positive about the Protestant foundation and character of the British constitution. Protestantism is often said to be in terminal decline and it often gets a bad press for its aura of gloomy stiffness and self-righteousness. It is sadly true that its most conspicuous manifestation today is the ghastly, narrow, judgemental and intolerant fundamentalism that has come to our shores from the United States. There is another, very different Protestant legacy that it is vitally important that we cherish, defend and promote – the tradition of open-ended, eirenic, gracious liberal Christianity that I have recently sought to define and reclaim in my book *Grace, Order, Openness and Diversity: Reclaiming Liberal Christianity* (2010). Its essence has been well expressed by Michael Gove, although sadly he puts it all in the past tense in an eloquent and mournful obituary to virtues which he observes 'now appear to have the potency of morris dancing and corn dollies, quaint reminders of long ago rather than objects of passionate attachment':

Protestantism was religion for grown-ups. It affirmed the spiritual without the need for ritual. It relished argument, lived in language, and celebrated a faith that had its beginning in the Word. Its spirit was democratic, with the Bible and church office open to all. Its polar opposite is not atheism, but the New Age faiths that celebrate feeling over thought and privilege a cast of gurus over the questioning congregation.[3]

It may be too late to save this Protestant heart of Britishness but it is certainly surely worth having one last try to keep its mature, open, tolerant, questioning spirit at the root of our national identity. The monarchy embodies the Protestant foundations of the British constitution. The oaths taken by each new sovereign at his or her coronation are the clearest expression of that embodiment. There is, I think, much to be said for recasting and expanding the first two coronation oaths which cover the broad principles on which Britain is governed and the values which are seen as being at the heart of the nation's life and well-being. In particular, there is a strong case for having the sovereign's promise to maintain and defend the traditions of tolerance and fairness which the Queen herself singled out in her Jubilee Address to Parliament in 2002 as being central to the character of the British people and nation. In an age of mission statements, and in the absence of a written constitution, here is a supreme chance for a solemn public declaration of the key core principles and values not simply by which the nation is governed but through which it defines itself.

It is the third coronation oath which, as it now stands, binds the sovereign to maintain the laws of God and the true profession of the Gospel, and to maintain in the United Kingdom the Protestant Reformed religion established by law. This part of the coronation oath has been changed more than once and there is certainly no reason why it could not be changed before the next coronation to make it more inclusive. I feel that it would be a mistake to remove any mention of the

Protestant establishment but perhaps this could and should be combined with a commitment to uphold the Christian religion and indeed, in the spirit of the proposed title and role of the next sovereign as 'Defender of Faith', to defend and safeguard the exercise of faith more generally in the context of an overall commitment to tolerance, peace and pluralism.

Supreme Governor of the Church of England

In the first edition of this book I suggested that there was a compelling case for abolishing the sovereign's role and title as Supreme Governor of the Church of England. I am now not quite so convinced that this case is, in fact, as compelling as I first thought, and I certainly do not wish to advocate, as some readers and reviewers took me as saying, any diminution or severance in the links between the Crown and established church. As I have already argued, there do seem to be significant benefits in the continuing existence of national established churches with a particular remit and mission to serve and minister to all people in the land and it is highly desirable that the Crown should have a close and visible relationship with them. There is certainly a case for a broader establishment, bringing in other denominations, and an overwhelming case for a hospitable establishment, to use the phrase coined by George Carey, which offers both a welcoming embrace and a sheltering wing to other faiths, and which seeks to keep religion in the public sphere and defend and protect religious minorities. The question is really whether the better model is that of the Church of England, with the monarch at its head and with a measure of state interference in its appointments and affairs, or the Church of Scotland, legally recognized as the national church with a special responsibility to make the ordinances of religion available to everyone in Scotland, yet having complete autonomy in the running of its own affairs and with the monarch as its defender, in terms of the commitment made on accession to preserve its Presbyterian government, but not as its head. The Church of Scotland's annual general assembly is attended and opened by the sovereign or her representative, the Lord High Commissioner, and there is a close and affectionate relationship between the monarch and the national church, which is maintained and expressed not least in the sovereign's regular participation in worship in the local parish church when she is resident in Scotland. There may be something to be said for a broadly similar relationship to be developed between the sovereign and the Church of England.

Perhaps the title 'Supreme Governor' is a little overbearing and archaic, although I am not really sure that it needs to be changed and, as several ecclesiastical and constitutional experts have pointed out, it is an aspect of the wider constitutional role of the Head of State and reflects the source and seat of sovereignty in our country in matters spiritual as well as temporal. I am strongly attracted by Paul Avis' argument about the desirability of having a layperson in a position of responsibility and leadership in the Church of England. In the first edition of this book I suggested that the sovereign's role be retitled 'Supreme Guardian'. David Edwards, picking up the Church of Scotland model, offered 'Senior Member'. Whatever the title, there is much to be said for a symbolic acknowledgement of the Church of England's role as a broad, capacious national church and, indeed, for a continuation of the practice of archbishops and diocesan bishops signifying their loyalty and allegiance to the crown on appointment as an expression of their commitment to minister to the whole nation and not just to the faithful few who are church members and attenders.

Quite apart from the maintenance of a title and constitutional role which binds Crown and church, it is also important that the sovereign should go on offering proactive leadership and encouragement to the established national churches especially in their particular and distinctive mission and calling. A good example of this was provided in Prince Charles' speech as Lord High Commissioner to the Church of Scotland's General Assembly in 2000. It signalled royal approval for one of the key principles of establishment, with its affirmation that 'the Church must continue to remain at the centre of modern Scottish society', while at the same time strongly commending discussions over possible union between the Church of Scotland, the Scottish Episcopal Church, the United Reformed Church and the Methodists as offering new opportunities 'for the pastoral and spiritual work of the Church'. The speech also specifically suggested that 'there might be ways in which the important contributions of other churches and faiths in Scotland can be embraced in your work for the good of all'.[4] It would be hard to find a more succinct expression of the case for a new model of ecumenical re-establishment with an inter-faith dimension to provide pastoral and spiritual care for the whole population.

Defender of Faith
In the context of such a wider, more open and more hospitable church establishment with a clear ecumenical and possibly inter-faith dimension, it seems anomalous for the sovereign to retain the title 'Defender of the Faith' with the rather exclusive connotations that it has come to have. Given the particular circumstances in which it was bestowed on Henry VIII, it seems ironic, to say the least, that the title has continued to be used by all British monarchs since and to have become particularly associated with the defence of Protestantism. Prince Charles' alternative 'Defender of Faith' is preferable in all sorts of ways, not least because it clearly links the monarchy with the promotion of the sacred and spiritual, and gives the sovereign a role that complements, and perhaps could even come to eclipse, that of philanthropist-in-chief which has been assumed by monarchs over the past 200 years or so. It is also a perfectly acceptable translation of the Latin *Fidei Defensor* and could continue to be represented on coins of the realm as *Fid. Def.* or simply *F.D.*

In practical terms, the sovereign's role as 'Defender of Faith' could be exercised through presiding over a new religious council, analogous in some ways to the Privy Council, and made up of leaders and representatives of the main churches and faith communities. This could have permanent statutory authority and a remit to advise on issues of community relations, religious discrimination and extremism, and the overall spiritual health of the nation. As head of the Commonwealth, the Queen already presides over a unique inter-faith family. The 2000 Home Office commissioned report on religious discrimination paid tribute to the Royal Family's 'public association with the positive development of the UK as a multi-faith society'.[5] At one level, the sovereign's role as 'Defender of Faith' would be to stand for tolerance, openness and embracing the other. But there is another deeper dimension to this title which implies a positive affirmation of faith over unbelief and of the value of the sacred over secular materialism. The importance of keeping religion in the public sphere and at the centre of national life has been emphasized particularly in recent years by the leaders of religious and ethnic minorities and by advocates of multiculturalism like Bikhu Parekh and Tariq Modood. In the context of an ever-more pluralistic society, where identity for ethnic minorities in particular is increasingly defined according to faith, there is an overwhelming case for the monarch, as head of state and embodiment of national identity, to assume the role of Defender of Faith as it has been construed by Prince Charles.

The Prince of Wales' conviction that the sovereign should adopt this particular title springs from his own overwhelming mission, about which he feels an almost evangelistic zeal, to promote religious belief and a sense of the spiritual and sacred against the prevailing tide of secular materialism and scientific reductionism. It also springs from his personal commitment to religious tolerance and pluralism, his particular desire to foster understanding between Islam and the West, and strong sense that as a future monarch he should represent and protect those of all faiths and strive for their integration and inclusion in British society. Perhaps his own understanding of this role was most clearly outlined in a remark he made about King Hussein of Jordan:

King Hussein had the kind of enlightened spirit which was in harmony with those who, in earlier periods of history, were able instinctively to respect the followers of other faiths for their piety and moral character, even if they did not accept them theologically.[6]

Here is a fascinating apologia for the monarch as fount of tolerance and respect for a wide range of beliefs, not from a position of latitudinarian indifference or secular laissez-faire but out of a real sense of the importance of religious faith. Clearly in a way that is not true of constitutional responsibilities like that of the Supreme Governorship, the assumption of this role by the monarch requires a more personal commitment, but its importance in the context of a multi-faith society, and in the face of the sensitivity of faith issues and the so-called clash of civilizations between Islam and Christianity in particular, is such that there seems to be an irresistible case for introducing it at the accession of our next monarch.

If we are to preserve, and indeed re-establish, the essence of sacred monarchy, then there must be a givenness about it and it must be linked into the constitution in a way that makes its spiritual dimension independent, insofar as it can be, of the personality of the individual sovereign. This is, of course, in part why the sovereign has carried the titles of Supreme Governor of the Church of England and Defender of the Faith. If these titles are to be changed, it is very important that we do not lose a sense of the sacredness and indeed the sacramentality of the office and institution of monarchy and an understanding that it is by virtue of their divine ordination to this office, rather than because of their own personal beliefs or whims or through any popular mandate, that sovereigns exercise their spiritual authority and discharge their sacred calling.

The shape of the next coronation

It is the coronation service which establishes the givenness of hereditary monarchy and asserts its sacred character and divine ordination. For this reason it is vital that the coronation does not simply become the swearing-in of a secular head of state but remains a religious ceremony that touches the transcendent and, in Edward Shils' and Michael Young's words describing the 1953 coronation, provides 'the ceremonial occasion for the affirmation of the moral values by which the society lives ... an act of national communion ... and an intensive contact with the sacred'.[7] The coronation must retain its sacramental character and its central element of the consecration and anointing of the new sovereign. It is not absolutely essential to this sacramentality that it remains embedded in an Anglican communion service. We should recall that the consecration of the monarch was itself long regarded as an eighth sacrament in the medieval church.

The next coronation should take place in Westminster Abbey and be presided over by the Archbishop of Canterbury. The historical resonances of this particular place and office are too important and powerful to turn our backs on. There may be a case for reviving the seventeenth-century practice of crowning the monarch of the United Kingdom in both Scotland and England, and the fact that the Stone of Destiny now resides in Edinburgh makes the Scottish capital an obvious location for a second coronation service. Whether coronation rituals should also be held in Wales and Northern Ireland is a much more debatable point. Northern Ireland almost certainly remains even today far too sensitive a location for such a ceremony and my sense is that Wales should rather host the investiture of the next Prince of Wales, as happened with Prince Charles at Caernarvon Castle in 1969.

There is no reason at all substantially to depart from the main elements of the 1953 coronation service: the recognition, the coronation oaths, the presentation of the Bible, the anointing, the investiture, the crowning, the benediction, the enthroning and the homage, although there may well be a case for dispensing with the celebration of Holy Communion for reasons already mentioned (p. 227–8).

There have been suggestions that the investiture of the monarch with the coronation regalia should be ditched as being the most archaic and irrelevant part of the service, full of medieval mumbo-jumbo. I believe that there is every reason for keeping the investiture in the next coronation service and for maintaining the atmosphere and language of medieval chivalry with which it is surrounded. Indeed, I have a sense that it may well speak even more powerfully now than it did to those who watched the 1953 coronation. Symbolism and metaphor are much in vogue in contemporary postmodern culture. The generation brought up on Harry Potter and the film version of *The Lord Of the Rings* are well aware of the potency of magic and the epic quality of the quest for justice, truth, service and sacrifice symbolized in precious objects. The medieval values of knightly chivalry and courtly etiquette provide the background for hundreds of fantasy computer games, videos and films. Television coverage of the next coronation will enable people both to marvel at the mystery and splendour of the symbolic objects and garb with which the monarch is invested and also to appreciate their significance and meaning in a way that has never been possible before. Let us not throw out these wonderful images at a time when we are rediscovering the value of the iconic and the symbolic.

At previous coronations the investiture of the monarch has been carried out exclusively by the Archbishop of Canterbury. There is perhaps a case for widening the participation in this element of the next coronation service. I wonder, in particular, whether children might be involved in investing the sovereign with, say, the spurs and armills. I have in mind what now happens frequently at the introduction of clergy to new parishes where they are presented by representative members of the congregation with a Bible, a baptismal bowl and a communion chalice. There may be ways in which, without diminishing the splendour and symbolism of the pageantry of this part of the coronation, it can be made more representative and inclusive of the nation as a whole.

Within a coronation service held in Westminster Abbey and

presided over by the Archbishop of Canterbury, there should be room for participation by those from other Christian denominations. The Moderator of the General Assembly of the Church of Scotland should, as in 1953, present the Bible to the sovereign. It would be a generous ecumenical gesture for the anointing of the sovereign with oil to be shared by the Archbishop of Canterbury and the Cardinal Archbishop of Westminster. Indeed, there may conceivably be a case for also involving a bishop or archbishop of the Orthodox Church in this sacramental act. The prayers and the blessing of the monarch should be shared by priests, ministers and pastors from all the major Christian churches in Britain. This has already become the norm for major state services and was handled in a particularly sensitive and generous way during the service in St Paul's Cathedral to mark the Queen's eightieth birthday in 2006. It may even be appropriate to introduce into the next coronation service a ceremony of laying on of hands in which representatives of all major churches take part and which would emphasize both the ecumenical nature of the coronation and the ordained nature of the royal office.

There is every reason, too, to involve leaders of the main non-Christian faith communities in the inauguration rites of future British monarchs and to enable them to acknowledge their fealty to and their sense of the sacredness of the new sovereign. Whether this element should be integrated into or appended on to the coronation service, or incorporated into a separate ceremony is a difficult question. My own view is that it would be better for the coronation itself to remain a Christian service and not be diluted into a multi-faith celebration. It is in fact significant that the leaders of the main minority faiths in Britain are not asking for the coronation to be turned into a multi-faith ceremony. Above all, they wish to see it preserved as a religious occasion filled with mystery and awe, and affirming a sense of the numinous and transcendent at the very heart of the nation. They are happy that it should retain its essentially Christian character and strongly oppose any watering down of its spiritual element.[8] The coronation has always been made up of a series of essentially separate and discrete parts and it would make considerable sense to detach the elements of recognition and homage, as happened in the past, and to incorporate them into a separate ceremony involving representatives of non-Christian faiths.

I would support the suggestion made by a number of senior clerics of reviving the old tradition of holding a ceremony in Westminster Hall following the ecumenical Christian coronation service in the Abbey. At such a ceremony, representatives from the main non-Christian faith communities in Britain could present the sovereign with their sacred Scriptures, garments and symbols, and offer blessings and prayers from their own traditions. This could be just one element in an act of homage focusing on the newly crowned and anointed sovereign's relationship with the people of the United Kingdom and Commonwealth and emphasizing the unifying and stabilizing role of monarchy as a focal point of loyalty and respect in a diverse and heterogeneous community of communities. At this ceremony, the monarch, wearing crown and robes, would be symbolically enthroned by leading members of the government, politicians from across the political spectrum and across the United Kingdom, Commonwealth prime ministers and senior officers in the armed forces.

Another important element of this separate post-coronation ceremony should be the paying of homage to the monarch by representatives of all those professions that make an oath of allegiance to the Crown – government ministers, Members of Parliament, bishops, civil servants, judges and magistrates, members of the armed forces and the police service. They could also be joined by representatives of those working in public services. At a time when there is increasing concern about the privatization of public services, this act of homage and allegiance would make an important statement about their political impartiality and loyalty to the Crown, and through it to the national good, rather than to politicians or the government of the day. The act of homage should also involve community leaders and representatives of health and social services.

There is a strong case for reviving the medieval practice of 'crown wearings' in which monarchs put on their crowns at special ceremonies which were held around the country, usually at significant feast days in the Christian year such as Christmas, Easter and Pentecost. Such ceremonies might have special significance in the weeks or months following the next coronation and it would be particularly good if they were held in more remote and deprived parts of the country. Writing about the shape of the next coronation in the journal *Political Theology* in the wake of the Bradford riots in 2001, I suggested:

> A ceremony of enthronement and homage in Bradford following the coronation of the next sovereign, and reflecting the themes of the Commonwealth, the monarch as Defender of Faith and guardian of the British tradition of tolerance and openness, and the affirmation of loyalty to the Crown by representatives of diverse ethnic and faith communities, might make a significant symbolic statement about common identity and purpose.[9]

My suggestion was taken up with alacrity by the Bradford *Telegraph and Argus* which devoted its entire front page to it under the somewhat misleading headline 'Crown Charles in City – Academic calls for Bradford to host next Coronation'. Bradford's Muslim Lord Mayor called the idea 'laudable' and the President of the Federation of Hindu Temples said, 'I think it is a wonderful idea. It would bring the community together and it would be such a positive step. I can imagine it doing a lot of good for all the people of Bradford.' David James, the Bishop of Bradford, was more circumspect in his reaction but did share with me his belief that it would 'be appropriate if the next monarch could tour the country and receive the acclamation of the people in several cities. I would be thrilled if Bradford were to be included.'[10]

What is vital is that those planning the next coronation and the other ceremonies that may accompany it do not lose heart and seek to diminish its metaphysical and magical elements. This is a time when more than at any other we need to be reminded of what one Anglican cleric has rather disparagingly referred to as 'the transcendent God of the state occasion'.[11] There should be lots of pomp, lots of Handel and lots of regalia. There should also be a weighty emphasis on the sacramental themes of sacrifice and consecration. In the words of Monica Furlong:

> The monarchy has borne and continues to bear an extraordinary weight of meaning, as if central to the identity of a people. If this meaning were to be expressed in a Christian ceremony of Coronation, one in which all the mainstream churches took part, but which gave recognition to the many subjects of a future monarch who are not likely to be Christian, this might speak, in as united a voice as our community and country are capable of, about the centrality of sacrifice and commitment.[12]

The emphasis on sacrifice in the coronation service is extremely important, all the more so for being so unfashionable and out of the kilter with the values of our 'me-first' consumerist culture. It serves as a reminder that monarchy is about duties more than privileges, and responsibilities more than rights. In the coronation the new sovereign is called and ordained by and before God to a life of sacrificial service, and to rule by example as well as by exhortation. He or she is also consecrated and set apart in a way that is difficult for us to understand and appreciate in our matey, informal, up-front culture. The 'otherness' of monarchy is an important part of its sacred quality. It is not just a matter of preserving the mystique and not letting too much daylight in on the magic. It is about maintaining an attitude of reserve, in itself a deeply Christian value, and a sacrificial posture which puts duty and discretion first and avoids the temptation of hanging out with the celebrity set and adopting their hedonistic values. The Queen's selfless espousal of that sacrificial posture throughout the fifty years of her reign testifies to the seriousness with which she takes her coronation and the strength she continues to derive from its sacramental quality. We owe it to our future monarch, as well as to the well-being of our nation, to ensure that the next coronation clearly embodies both consecration and benediction.

As a footnote to all this, may I just express the hope that broadcasters in general and the BBC in particular treat the next coronation as a solemn and significant act of national consecration and not as some super-celebrity event. My heart sank as I read the words of Piers Morgan about the impending wedding of Prince William and Catherine Middleton in 2011: 'It will be the biggest event in television history because there are no bigger celebrities in the world than the royals.'[13] I profoundly hope that this mentality does not infect the BBC and colour its coverage of the next coronation. Sadly, it will not be interpreted to us through the hushed and reverential tones of Richard Dimbleby or Tom Fleming, to my mind the best-ever commentator on royal events and himself a committed Christian who led the worship every week in a small Baptist church. Let us hope that it will be anchored by someone of equal gravitas.

Unity in diversity

For what will our next monarch be set apart, anointed, consecrated and blessed? First and foremost, to act as a focus for unity in an increasingly fragmented and polarized nation. The official definition of the sovereign's role, as expressed by the government, is to be 'the living symbol of national unity'.[14] Shils and Young expressed it rather less baldly in 1953:

> The monarchy is the one pervasive institution, standing above all others, which plays a part in a vital way comparable to the function of the medieval church ... the

function of integrating diverse elements into a whole by protecting and defining their autonomy.[15]

Thirty years later John Habgood, as Archbishop of York, reiterated the point with an even more direct coupling of church and Crown:

> There is not a single free nation in the world which has managed to hold a pluralist society together without some very powerful unifying factor. In Britain, we used to have a whole network of such factors mostly linked in some way to the Church and Crown. One of the effects of the decline of the national role of the Church has been to isolate the Crown as almost the only effective symbol of national unity.[16]

Among the most important ways in which monarchy promotes unity is by emphasizing the communal over against the individualistic. Writing about the development of sacred kingship, the sociologist Werner Stark has observed that:

> The societies in which the monarchical religion flourished were, by and large, communities … they were unities rather than diversities; they were collectivistic rather than individualistic; the whole was before the parts, both in reality and evaluation. This unity, this collectivism, this primacy of the whole needed to be made visible, to be symbolized, and its visible image, its commanding symbol, was the sacred king.[17]

Stark goes on to say that societies ditched their monarchs when they ceased to be communal and became associational. One might well reflect that it is a wonder we have held on to our monarchy so long in Britain when privatization and competitive individualism are so much in the ascendant. This is precisely why we need the monarchy. It cannot stand alone and Canute-like against the tide but it can symbolize, very effectively, something other than private gain and individual gratification. The crown symbol and designation 'royal' before an organization betokens a commitment to public service and to communal rather than private interest. A prime example is the Royal Mail, now so sadly threatened with privatization and an assault on its public service ethos. It is surely not coincidental that those professions which formally take an oath of allegiance to and act in the name of the Queen, such as the judiciary, armed forces and police, still tend to command respect in our society.

But does the monarchy really have the capacity to provide a focus for unity in an ever-more pluralistic and hedonistic society? Have not globalization and individualism fatally weakened collective and communal identities? Does contemporary pluralist Britain really want a centre or focus, let alone a spiritual one? These are all valid questions and I have to admit that most of the institutions which have traditionally expressed and inculcated a sense of shared and communal values, including political parties, trade unions, voluntary groups and churches, are in marked decline. What is there to suggest that the monarchy might buck the trend and provide the new 'big tent' that can shelter people of different races, faiths, class backgrounds and ages?

Let me make just three observations about the monarchy's potential ability to provide such a focus and to symbolize unity in diversity. The first is the extent to which both the Queen and the Prince of Wales have already themselves embodied and expressed a communal ethic. In the Queen's case it has been demonstrated both through her 'one-nation' perspective and in her very strong personal commitment to the Commonwealth and the principles underlying it. In the case of the Prince of Wales, whose overriding ideology has been characterized by James Morton as 'communitarian', it has been in the fostering through both speeches and philanthropic activities of an ethic of mutual obligation and co-operation and a sense of belonging.[18]

Second, I would point to the way in which royal events and occasions do still bring people together and produce a 'feel-good factor' which does inspire communal celebration and activity. This was demonstrated at the time of the royal wedding of the Duke and Duchess of Cambridge in 2011. The general atmosphere of rejoicing and the street parties held in cities and towns across the country confirmed Bagehot's observation that people 'care fifty times more for a marriage than a ministry' and that 'a royal family sweetens politics by the seasonable addition of nice and pretty events'. They showed that in the context of an overwhelmingly gloomy economic and international outlook, royal weddings and celebrations do cheer people up and bring them together in shared conviviality, as the comments of two of those who organized street parties in April 2011 testify:

> People sit down and they talk and that's what community is about – talking to each other and finding out about each other. It's that sort of spirit the country has lost.
> These parties bring out the best in people. Organising it has been the most enjoyable thing I've done for a long time.[19]

Even the *Guardian*, not noted for its pro-monarchist sympathies, grasped this important dimension of royal events. Writing on the day after the wedding, its columnist Jonathan Freedland speculated about what would live on in the nation's collective memory:

> When the Dean of Westminster invoked a 'mystical union', he surely got close to the essence both of the royal wedding and of something much larger. The literal reference was to the bond between Christ and the church, but he could just as easily have been describing the 'mystical union' that exists, and was reinforced in spectacular style yesterday, between Britain and the royal family.

For what we witnessed was the mysterious alchemy that somehow converts love of country into affection for the House of Windsor. The emblem of it was the banner waved by many in the crowds, the same one that has been on display in shop windows throughout the land: a Union flag, with a portrait of William and Kate at its centre.[20]

Certainly what struck me almost more than anything else about the crowds, the shop decorations and the street parties that greeted the royal wedding of 2011 was the extent to which the Union flag had been reclaimed from the far right and become a symbol of shared identity focused on royalty. Interestingly, this was conspicuous even in Scotland which just a week later elected the first majority Scottish National Party government in the Holyrood Parliament.

My third observation is about the difference between subjects and citizens and the potential that living in and under a monarchy gives to cement notions of belonging and shared identity. We have already noted that the new British citizenship ceremony has at its heart the act of pledging allegiance to the Queen. In the context of the wider debate over Britishness and national identity there has been much emphasis on the concept of citizenship over the past decade or so. It is sometimes argued that Britain has a weak tradition of citizenship because the existence of a hereditary monarchy has promoted a political culture where the emphasis is on being subjects rather than citizens. In fact, it seems to me that the fact of being subjects of the Queen and owing loyalty to the Crown may well create a more tangible sense of belonging and a stronger concomitant set of rights and responsibilities than the more abstract and less personal status of citizenship. Rather unfashionably I would, indeed, want to argue that we should be emphasizing the status of Britons as subjects as well as citizens, and that a dual approach, based on the personal, traditional and mystical ties of loyalty to the monarch as well as to the legal rights and responsibilities that go with citizenship, is more likely to promote a greater sense of shared Britishness and common identity than simply concentrating on the fashionable idea of the citizen.

I find myself writing this on the day after the outright victory of the Scottish Nationalists in the Scottish Parliament when commentators and leader writers are predicting the potential breakup of the United Kingdom. Whatever the result of the referendum that is now inevitable on the question of Scottish independence, I find it very significant that the ever-canny and politically astute Scottish First Minister and Nationalist leader, Alex Salmond, has indicated that he would be very happy with an independent Scotland retaining the Queen as head of state. Such a reversion to the seventeenth-century situation where England and Scotland shared a united crown but had separate parliaments and governments would, in fact, provide a new and potent illustration of the monarchy's ability to embody and encompass unity in diversity.

Stability, tradition and wisdom

Behind monarchy's embodiment of the principle of unity in diversity lies a deeper spiritual quality which reaches back into primal sacred kingship. Monarchs stand at the still, stable centre of things, holding their *fir*, or truth, and keeping the forces of chaos at bay. I am not here seeking to make the kind of wild claim that appears in a recent British Israelite publication, 'that the British Royal Throne represents the very last stronghold of the British world and the order of civilization that has prevented satanic dictatorship from total domination in the world'.[21] I am rather thinking in more universal and primal terms of a quality of monarchy which is still appreciated in so-called more primitive societies. It was nicely expressed in the remark made by a tribal chief during the Queen's visit to Ghana in 2000 that she 'symbolises unity in a world of insecurity. She is really something to cherish.'[22] Our own sophisticated and impoverished outlook has largely obliterated this almost shamanic sense of the monarch's role but it has not entirely gone. It is still acknowledged through the importance of ritual, as represented in the Court Circular, the Maundy Service and the Christmas broadcast. Part of the appeal of monarchy is its routine and dependability, qualities which are not to be scoffed at in a world of such change and uncertainty as ours. This is particularly important for those whose lives are dislocated or disordered. I find it both deeply moving and significant that a recent article by a nurse about the experience of being with terminally ill cancer patients at Christmas describes how important it is to carry on traditional family routines and singles out particularly 'sitting down to watch the Queen's speech'.[23]

Stability, tradition and continuity are other values particularly associated with monarchy. This is not just a matter of looking back and being conscious of the past, although having a sense of history is important and is perhaps especially to be championed at a time when there is so much uncertainty and fear for the future as well as so much emphasis on novelty and change for its own sake. It has been well said that a country's confidence in the present and the future is best measured by its ability to live at ease with its past. Christianity is a historical faith which sets considerable store by tradition while believing in a God who makes all things new. Monarchy is an important guardian of good tradition and a bulwark against passing fads and fancies. It stands for the long-term perspective and so points us to the God to whom we sing 'A thousand ages in thy sight are like an evening gone'. The 60 years of the Queen's reign stand in marked contrast to her prime ministers' brief sojourns in power. When short-termism increasingly rules in politics and other areas of national life there is much to be said for the long-term perspective represented by monarchy, and especially hereditary monarchy.

The quality of wisdom, traditionally associated with monarchy, is an important aspect of this long-term outlook. It is particularly needed today when so much policy is based on reading the runes of focus group surveys and opinion polls or the jargon-filled reports of narrowly specialized academics. Wisdom is a matter of discernment and sagacity, of taking the broad view rather than pandering to the latest whims of the spin doctors and the image make-over consultants. It does, in fact, have a lot to do with the steady and rather 'uncool' qualities of reserve and understatement that have characterized the Windsors.

I sense that in our very uncertain and troubled times, appreciation may actually be growing rather than diminishing for institutions and rituals which embody tradition, stability, continuity and wisdom. In the aftermath of the wars in Iraq and Afghanistan, there has been a striking revival of traditional solemn rituals associated with remembrance of those who have died in conflict, such as the three-minute silence on 11 November. New rituals have been developed, like the regular turn-out of the people of Wootton Bassett to honour the coffins of British service men and women as they pass through the town having been repatriated via RAF Lyneham. It was significant and appropriate that in March 2011, in recognition of this simple and dignified mark of respect for the war dead, Wootton Bassett became the first British town in more than 100 years to be given the prefix 'Royal'. It is a pointer to the enduring and perhaps even growing link between monarchy, popular ritual, patriotism and tradition.

Celebrating grace and recovering the symbolic and the sacred
Monarchy is at once the most personal and the most symbolic form of government and leadership. Its uniquely personal dimension makes it vulnerable to the intrusive prurience and gossip mentality of the media but also allows for the loyalty, identity and aspirations of a people to be to some extent focused on and expressed through a single figure. The personal aspect of monarchy can have a beneficial, almost redemptive aspect. As has already been pointed out, royal visits often leave those at the receiving end with a sense of benediction as if they or their community have been blessed as the result of even the briefest contact with monarchy. They also bring out the best in people. Shils and Young noted how feuding neighbours and family members were reconciled by the shared experience of watching the 1953 coronation. Another sociologist, Anne

Rowbottom, points to the happy, festive, friendly atmosphere which prevails at occasions graced by the presence of royalty. The use of the theologically loaded term 'grace' is highly appropriate here. It is as if there is a grace about royalty to which people respond by being kind and considerate to others, making sure that the young and the old get a good view, for example, as well as by offering gifts to the visiting royal in a ritualized form of exchange which takes us back to the world of primal religion. This is about mystery as much as magic, about sentiment as much as superstition. As Anne Rowbottom has observed:

> The idealisation of the person of the sovereign effectively shifts the focus of the public discourse away from the constitutional and political and on to the personal and symbolic. In doing so a situation is created in which, freed from political hostility and seen to be a person of great integrity, the monarch is able to provide a worthy focus for sentiments of national loyalty and identity. This not only strengthens the position of the monarch and the institution of monarchy within society, but makes available a set of symbols through which members of the society may construct and express a sense of belonging. … Royal symbolism facilitates the construction and expression of a sense of national, group and personal identity.[24]

Some will object that this is pure civil religion, and so in a way it is. It is the civil religion of ancient Israel which emphasized the public, communal aspects of God's dealings with His people and expressed His ultimate values and truths in symbolic form. As Anne Rowbottom says, 'ceremonies centring on the Royal Family represent one of the primary aims of a civil religion, that of allowing statements to be made about a community and its worth.'[25] We are uneasy about making any statements about worth and value nowadays, certainly of a metaphysical or all-embracing kind. They offend against the postmodernist canon that anything goes and that the only criterion of worth should be what works and feels good to me. They have also been hijacked and debased in our consumer culture where loyalty now means a little plastic card from the supermarket to thank you for shopping there and service means unctuous insincerity and box-ticking. Monarchy has traditionally stood for values like loyalty, service, duty and self-sacrifice, all of which are rather unfashionable. It perhaps also stands increasingly for another set of values – healing, wholeness, openness, tolerance and vulnerability – which we are beginning to see the need for in national as well as personal life.

It is in its symbolic embodiment of values that the greatest strength of monarchy lies. We live in an age which is rediscovering the value of the iconic and the symbolic. In contemporary Christianity there is a huge and welcome interest in symbols, in the power of the visual and the tactile, in the theology of imagination and the importance of poems and stories. Monarchy is especially rich in symbolism, visual imagery and story. Its appeal is to sentiment rather than to reason, to the imagination rather than to the intellect. It conforms to the Christian understanding of a sacrament as an effective sign and symbol which mediates and reveals the reality of divine grace. It also has the sacramental power to point beyond itself to those metaphysical values and mysteries which we have all but lost. This is why it is so important to retain the sacramental core of the coronation and, indeed, to resacralize the monarchy, devising new rituals and perhaps restoring old ones like the foot-washing in the Maundy service which speaks so powerfully of service in imitation of Christ. There may well be a case, as suggested by David Hope (p. 231), for introducing a symbolic act of service into the next coronation order.

Although we live in an increasingly secular society, it is also one where the quest for spiritual meaning and experience is growing. The important study by Linda Woodhead and Paul Heelas, *The Spiritual Revolution* (2005), showed how a decline in churchgoing and organized and institutional religion in contemporary Britain is matched by a rising level of interest and participation in alternative spiritualities. Far from moving in a more secular direction, I believe that the monarchy should be rediscovering and reasserting its spiritual heart. This is not a matter of conforming to the postmodern spiritual *Zeitgeist*. Far from it – monarchy nowadays is a profoundly counter-cultural institution and it should not be seeking to conform to passing trends and fads, although it would do well to remain in tune with the remarkable level of respect and indeed reverence that still exists for royalty at popular level and in what is often called folk or implicit religion, and to heed rather less the voices of the metropolitan secularists and sophisticates.

Ultimately, monarchy points beyond itself to the majesty of God. It encourages the God-given human faculties of reverence, loyalty and worship. This is the real sacramentality of monarchy. It derives its true sanction and authority from above rather than from below. The one title which must most assuredly remain alongside the royal profile on every coin of the realm, *Deo Gratia,* reminds us that the sovereign rules first and foremost by the grace of God. Hereditary monarchy is a lonely, noble, sacrificial calling. It could do with being more loved and cherished by the churches. What our sovereign needs and deserves most of all from us is our loyal and heartfelt prayer:

God save our gracious Queen,
Long live our noble Queen,
   God save the Queen!
   Send her victorious,
   Happy and Glorious,
   Long to reign over us;
   God save the Queen!

Notes

Introduction

1   B. Pimlott, *The Queen* (Harper Collins, London, 2001), p. 210.

2   See, for example, Melvin Oakes' letter to the *Church Times*, 6 April 2001.

3   *Daily Telegraph*, 26 December 2000; C. Longley, 'The Faith of the Queen', *The Tablet*, 6 January 2001. The full texts of the Christmas messages may be found on the official website of the British monarchy, www.royal.gov.uk.

4   P. Theroux, *The Kingdom by the Sea* (Hamish Hamilton, London, 1983), p. 257.

5   A. Nicolson, 'A Nostalgic Revolutionary', *Sunday Telegraph Magazine*, 1 November 1988.

6   *Guardian*, 24 December 2010.

7   *The Times*, 22 November 1997.

8   V. Bogdanor, *The Monarchy and the Constitution* (Clarendon Press, Oxford, 1995), p. 239.

9   J. A. Taylor, *British Monarchy, English Church Establishment, and Civil Liberty* (Greenwood Press, Westport, CT, 1996), p. 136.

10   P. Brendon and P. Whitehead, *The Windsors: A Dynasty Revealed* (Hodder & Stoughton, London, 1994), p. 241.

11   E. Shils and M. Young, 'The Meaning of the Coronation', *Sociological Review*, New series, Vol.1 (1953), p. 64.

12   R. McKibbin, 'Mass-Observation in the Mall', *London Review of Books*, 2 October 1997, p. 3.

13   A. Rowbottom, 'The Real Royalists: Folk Performance and Civil Religion at Royal Visits', *Folklore* 109 (1998),

pp. 77–88; 'Royal Symbolism and Social Integration' (unpublished Ph.D. thesis, Manchester University, 1994).

14 T. Nairn, *The Enchanted Glass: Britain and its Monarchy* (Vantage, London, 1994), pp. 235, 21.

15 Pimlott, *The Queen*, p. 637.

16 J. Paxman, *On Royalty* (Viking, London, 2006), pp. 283, 4.

17 *The Tablet*, 18 March 2000, p. 370.

18 T. Hobson, *Against Establishment* (Darton, Longman & Todd, London, 2003), p. 123.

19 K. Raine, 'Monarchy and the Imagination', in *Monarchy* (Temenos Academy, London, 2002), pp. 20–1.

20 R. Moore and D. Gillette, *The King Within* (Avon Books, New York, 1992), p. 110.

21 Ibid., p. 105.

22 G. Lindop, 'The Wheel Turning Monarch: An Ideal of Kingship in Early Buddhism', in *Monarchy* (Temenos Academy, London, 2002), p. 117.

23 S. Guppy, 'A Paean to Kingship', *Guardian*, 18 February 2008.

24 D. Baldwin, *The Chapel Royal* (Duckworth, London, 1990), p. 168.

25 *Life and Work*, March 1997, p. 12.

1 Monarchy in the Old Testament

1 J. Wellhausen, *Prolegomena to the History of Ancient Israel* (Meridian Books, Cleveland, Ohio, 1957), p. 253.

2 I. Bradley, *God is Green: Christianity and the Environment* (Darton, Longman & Todd, London, 1990), pp. 16-18.

3 H. Frankfort, *Kingship and the Gods* (University of Chicago Press, Chicago, IL, 1944), pp. 3, 12.

4 O. O'Donovan, *The Desire of Nations* (Cambridge University Press, Cambridge, 1996), p. 61.

5 *Sunday Telegraph*, 23 April 2000; *Kings and Queens of England and Scotland* (Andromeda, Oxford, 1996).

6 The only other coronation described in the Old Testament is that of King Joram, king of Israel from 852 to 841:

> The priest delivered to the captains the spears and shields that had been King David's, which were in the house of the Lord; and the guards stood, every man with his weapons in his hand, from the south side of the house to the north side of the house. Then he brought out the king's son, and put the crown on him, and gave him the testimony; and they proclaimed him king, and anointed him; and they clapped their hands, and said, 'Long live the king!'
>
> (2 Kings 11.10-12)

7   T. Ishide, *The Royal Dynasties in Ancient Israel. A Study on the Formation and Development of Royal-Dynastic Ideology* (Walter de Gruyer, Berlin, 1977), p. 183.

8   K. Dell, 'The King in Wisdom Literature', in J. Day (ed.) *King and Messiah in Israel and the Ancient Near East* (Sheffield Academic Press, Sheffield, 1998), p. 185.

9   R. Moore and D. Gillette, *The King Within* (Avon Books, New York, 1992), p. 236.

10 J. Eaton, 'Kingship', in R. J. Coggins and J. L. Houlden *A Dictionary of Biblical Interpretation* (SCM Press, London, 1990), p. 381.

2 Monarchy in the New Testament

1   N. Perrin, *Jesus and the Language of the Kingdom* (SCM Press, London, 1976), p. 15. This book, and Perrin's *The Kingdom of God in the Teaching of Jesus* (SCM Press, London, 1963), give a good run-down of the main controversies.

2   G. W. Buchanan, *Jesus: The King and His Kingdom* (Mercer University Press, Macon, GI, 1983), p. 41.

3   B. Lang, 'The "Our Father" as John the Baptist's Political Prayer', in D. Penchansky and P. L. Reddit (eds) *Shall Not the Judge of the Earth Do Right?* (Eisenbrauns, Indiana, 2000), p. 245.

4   O. O'Donovan, *The Desire of the Nations* (Cambridge University Press, Cambridge, 1996), p. 24.

5   Ibid., p. 117.

6   F. Matera, *The Kingship of Jesus* (Scholars Press, Chico, CA, 1982), p. 63.

7   Ibid., p. 149.

8   W. Meeks, *The Prophet-King. Moses Traditions and the Johannine Christology* (E. J. Brill, Leiden, 1967), see esp. p. 67.

9   O'Donovan, *Desire of the Nations*, p. 123.

10 'To the Christians', in *Oxford Book of Scottish Verse* (Clarendon Press, Oxford, 1966), p. 457.

11 G. Ramshaw, *God Beyond Gender* (Augustus Fortress Press, Minneapolis, 1995), p. 61.

12 B. Wren, *Praying Twice:The Music and Words of Congregational Song* (Westminster John Knox Press, Louisville, KT, 2000), p. 232.

13 *Opening Prayers* (Canterbury Press, Norwich, 1999), pp. 122–3.

3 Sacred kingship in Celtic, Anglo-Saxon and medieval Britain

1   J. Frazer, *The Golden Bough* (Macmillan, London, 1987), p. 20.

2   Ibid., p. 91.

3   J. Carey, 'Ideal Kingship in Early Ireland', in *Monarchy* (Temenos Academy, London, 2002), p. 51.

4   I owe this quotation and translation from *The Book of Ui Maine* to a paper by Dan Wiley on 'The Ideology of Kingship in *Aided Diarmata*' given at the Eleventh International Congress of Celtic Studies at University College, Cork, in July 1999.

5   Adamnan, *Vita Columbae*, Book 1, Chapter 9.

6   R. Sutcliff, *The Sword and the Circle* (Red Fox, London, 1992), pp. 23–4.

7   G. Ashe, *King Arthur's Avalon* (Fontana, London, 1990), p. 241.

8   I owe this reference to Dr Marion Bowman. There is an account of the thorn ceremony in A. R. Vickery, *Holy Thorn of Glastonbury* (West Country Folklore, No.12,

Toucan Press, Guernsey, 1979), p. 12. Anne Stallybrass'
comment was made in a letter to me dated 12 January
2001.

9   P. Cavill, *Anglo-Saxon Christianity* (Fount, London, 1999),
p. 43.

10 J. Cannon and R. Griffiths, *The Oxford Illustrated History
of the British Monarchy* (Oxford University Press, Oxford,
1997), pp. 19, 21, 24.

11 B. Ward, *High King of Heaven* (Mowbray, London, 1999),
p. 5.

12 S. Keys and M. Lapidge (eds), *Asser's Life of King Alfred*
(Penguin, Harmondsworth, 1983), p. 91.

13 Ibid., p. 137.

14 R. Abels, *Alfred the Great* (Longman, Harlow, 1998),
p. 220.

15 Ibid., p. 221.

16 Cannon and Griffiths, *British Monarchy*, pp. 121–2.

17 D. Baldwin, *The Chapel Royal* (Duckworth, London,
1990), p. 18.

18 R. W. Southern, *The Making of the Middle Ages*
(Hutchinson, London, 1967), p. 91.

19 E. H. Kantorowicz, *The King's Two Bodies* (Princeton
University Press, Princeton, NJ, 1957), p. 56.

20 Ibid., p. 49.

21 T. Aquinas, *On Kingship* (Pontifical Institute of Medieval
Studies, Toronto, 1949), pp. 41, 54.

22 M. Bloch, *The Royal Touch – Sacred Monarchy and
Scrofula in England and France* (Routledge, London,
1973), p. 22.

23 Ibid., p. 148.

24 P. Ziegler, *Crown and People* (Collins, London, 1978),
p. 183.

25 Quoted in L. Dakers, *Places Where They Sing: Memories
of a Church Musician* (Canterbury Press, Norwich, 1955),
p. 22. Another version of this prayer may be found in D.
Gray, All Majesty and Power: An Anthology of Royal
Prayers (Hodder & Stoughton, London, 2000), p. 39.

4 The coronation service

1 *Daily Telegraph*, 29 June 1994.

2 *The Times* Coronation Supplement, 11 June 1937, p. xii.

3 M. Enright, *Iona, Tara and Soissons: The Origin of the Royal Anointing Ritual* (Walter de Gruyter, Berlin, 1985), p. 75.

4 T. Silver, *The Coronation Service or Consecration of the Anglo-Saxon Kings* (Oxford, 1831), p . 22.

5 Ibid., p. 23.

6 J. Perkins, *The Crowning of the Sovereign* (Methuen, London, 1937), p. 60.

7 J. Cannon and R. Griffiths, *The Oxford Illustrated History of the British Monarchy* (Oxford University Press, Oxford, 1997), p. 29.

8 Ibid., p. 608.

9 W. Jones, *Crowns and Coronations* (Chatto & Windus, London, n.d.), p. xxix.

10 Quoted in G. Reedy, 'Mystical Politics: The Imagery of Charles II's Coronation', in P. J. Korshin (ed.), *Studies in Change and Revolution* (Scolar Press, Aldershot, 1972), p. 19.

11 W. Walsh, *The Religious Life of Queen Victoria* (Swan Sonnenschein, 1902), p. 16.

12 *The Times*, 12 May 1937.

13 K. Harris, *The Queen* (Orion, London, 1994), p.145.

14 E. Shils and M. Young, 'The Meaning of the Coronation', *Sociological Review*, New Series, Vol. 1 (1953), p. 67.

15 Ibid., p. 65.

16 Ibid., p. 79.

17 Ibid., p.67.

18 Ibid., p. 71.

19 Ibid., p. 80.

20 *Church Times*, 14 April 2000.

21 *The Form and Order of Service for the Coronation of Her Majesty Queen Elizabeth II* (Eyre and Spottiswoode, London, 1953), p. 4.

22 Ibid., pp. 6–7.
23 Ibid., pp. 8–9.
24 Ibid., p. 10.
25 R. Strong, *Coronation: A History of Kingship and the British Monarchy* (Harper Collins, London, 2005), pp. 487–8.
26 *Service for Coronation of Queen Elizabeth II*, p. 16.
27 Ibid., pp. 18–19.
28 Perkins, *Crowning the Sovereign*, p. 49.
29 *Service for Coronation of Queen Elizabeth II*, p. 23.
30 Ibid., p. 23.
31 Ibid., p. 24.
32 Ibid., p. 24.
33 Ibid., p. 25.
34 Ibid., p. 28.
35 Ibid., p. 29.
36 K. Martin, *The Crown and the Establishment* (Hutcheson, London, 1962), p. 19.

5 The Protestant project

1 O. O'Donovan, *The Desire of Nations* (Cambridge University Press, Cambridge, 1996), p. 238.
2 *The First English Prayer Book* (Arthur James, New Arlesford, 1999), p. 22.
3 Quoted in H .G. Reventlow, *The Authority of the Bible and the Rise of the Modern World* (SCM Press, London, 1984), pp. 136–7.
4 N. Sykes, *Old Priest and New Presbyter* (Cambridge University Press, Cambridge, 1957), p. 3.
5 J. Craigie (ed.), *The Basilikon Doron of King James VI* (Scottish Text Society, Edinburgh, 1944), Vol. I, p. 75.
6 Quoted in R. A. Mason (ed.), *John Knox and the British Reformations* (Ashgate, Aldershot, 1998), p. 174.
7 T. McCrie, *Life of Andrew Melville* (William Blackwood, Edinburgh, 1824), Vol. I, p. 92.
8 M. Lee, *Great Britain's Solomon* (University of Illinois Press, Urbana, 1990), p. 82.

9   J. Cannon and R. Griffiths, *The Oxford Illustrated History of the British Monarchy* (Oxford University Press, Oxford, 1997), p. 356.

10 W. Stark, *The Sociology of Religion* (Routledge & Kegan Paul, London, 1966), Vol. I, pp. 65–6.

11 A. Nicolson, *Power and Glory: Jacobean England and the Making of the King James Bible* (Harper Perennial, London, 2004), p. xviii.

12 T. Corns (ed.), *The Royal Image* (Cambridge University Press, Cambridge, 1999), p. xv.

13 K. Raine, 'Monarchy and the Imagination', in *Monarchy* (Temenos Academy, London, 2002), p. 14.

14 Quoted in M. Pittock, *The Invention of Scotland* (Routledge, London, 1991), p. 10.

15 Quoted in G. Reedy, 'Mystical Politics: The Imagery of Charles II's Coronation', in P. J. Korshin (ed.) *Studies in Change and Revolution* (Scolar Press, Aldershot, 1972), p. 31.

16 Corns, *The Royal Image*, p. 267.

17 Ibid., p. 65.

18 Quoted in Pittock, *The Invention of Scotland*, p. 2.

19 N. Figgis, *The Theory of the Divine Right of Kings* (Cambridge, 1896), pp. 5–6.

20 R. Filmer, *Patriarcha and other Political Works*, ed. P. Laslett (Blackwell, Oxford, 1949).

21 J. B. Torrance, 'The Covenant Concept in Scottish Theology and Politics and its Legacy', *Scottish Journal of Theology*, 34 (1981), p. 238.

22 John, Third Marquess of Bute, *Scottish Coronations* (Alex Gardner, Paisley, 1902), p. 173.

23 F. Prochaska, *Royal Bounty: The Making of a Welfare Monarchy* (Yale University Press, New Haven, CT, 1995), p. 6.

24 Pittock, *The Invention of Scotland*, p. 5.

25 O'Donovan, *Desire of Nations*, pp. 240–1.

26 R. S. Churchill, *The Story of the Coronation* (Derek Verschoyle, London, 1953), p. 74.

27 C. Hibbert, *The Court of St James* (Weidenfeld & Nicolson, London, 1979), p. 167.
28 I owe this point to the Methodist historian, Henry Rack.
29 P. Scholes, *God Save the Queen* (Oxford University Press, Oxford, 1954), p. 215.
30 Prochaska, *Royal Bounty*, p. 11.
31 S. Piggott, *Female Virtue and Domestic Religion Recommended by the Example of our Late Illustrious Queen Charlotte* (1818), p. 2.
32 Prochaska, *Royal Bounty*, ch. 1.
33 H. More, 'Daniel', *Sacred Dramas* (1782), p. 241.
34 *The Times*, 25 October 1809.
35 *The Times*, 26 October 1809.
36 *The Day*, 26 October 1809.
37 Stark, *Sociology of Religion*, p. 67.
38 C. Buchanan, *Cut the Connection* (Darton, Longman & Todd, London, 1994), p. 138.

6 Duty, discretion and dignity – the Victorian Legacy

1   J. Brooke, *King George III* (Constable, London, 1985), p. 361.
2   W. Walsh, *The Religious Life of Queen Victoria* (Swan Sonnenschein, 1902), p. 184.
3   F. Prochaska, *Royal Bounty: The Making of a Welfare Monarchy* (Yale University Press, New Haven, CT, 1995), p. 80.
4   Ibid., pp. 113–14.
5   Walsh, *Queen Victoria*, p. 257.
6   Ibid., pp. 257.
7   Ibid., p. 10.
8   Ibid., p. 258.
9   Ibid., p. 214.
10 Ibid., p. 29.
11 A. Ponsonby, *H. Ponsonby, Queen Victoria's Private Secretary, His Life from His Letters* (Macmillan, London, 1942), p. 118.
12 Walsh, *Queen Victoria*, p. 33.

13 Ibid., p. 32.
14 Quoted in A. Leak, 'Listening to Them but not Liking Them – Queen Victoria's bishops', *Church Times*, 19 January 2001, p.17.
15 Ponsonby, *Life*, p. 178.
16 I. Bradley, 'Partial to Presbyterianism', *Life and Work*, January 2001, p. 15.
17 Walsh, *Queen Victoria*, p. 260.
18 A. Leask, 'Listening to Them', p. 17.
19 M. Lutyens (ed.), *Lady Lytton's Court Diary* (Rupert Hart-Davis, London, 1961), p. 114.
20 O. Chadwick, *The Victorian Church*, 2nd edn (A & C Black, London, 1980), Vol. II, p. 336.
21 Ibid., p. 33.
22 R. Williams, *The Contentious Crown: Public Discussion of the British Monarchy in the Reign of Queen Victoria* (Ashgate, Aldershot, 1997), p. 222.
23 J. Wolffe, *God and Greater Britain* (Routledge, 1994), p. 155.
24 Walsh, *Queen Victoria*, p. 161.
25 W. Bagehot, *The English Constitution*, World's Classics edn (Oxford University Press, Oxford, 1928), p. 35.
26 Ibid., p. 34.
27 Ibid., p. 35.
28 Ibid., pp. 39, 40.
29 Ibid., p. 47.
30 Ibid., p. 53.
31 D. Cannadine, 'The Context, Performance and Meaning of Ritual: The British Monarchy and the Invention of Tradition, c.1820–1977', in E. Hobsbawm and T. Ranger (eds) *The Invention of Tradition* (Cambridge University Press, Cambridge, 1992).
32 Wolffe, *God and Greater Britain*, p. 155.
33 Williams, *The Contentious Crown*, p. 180.
34 Quoted in Prochaska, *Royal Bounty*, p. 134.
35 Wolffe, *God and Greater Britain*, p. 223.
36 Walsh, *Queen Victoria*, p. 259.

37 Ibid., p. 127.
38 Quoted in Prochaska, *Royal Bounty*, p. 135.
39 F. Prochaska, 'But the Greatest of These – Civil Society and the Welfare Monarchy', *Times Literary Supplement*, 15 January 1993, p. 15.
40 Prochaska, *Royal Bounty*, p. 209.
41 *King George VI to His Peoples 1936–51. Selected Broadcasts and Speeches* (John Murray, London, 1952), p. 3.
42 Prochaska, *Royal Bounty*, p. 230.
43 J. Reith, *Into the Wind* (Hodder & Stoughton, London, 1949), p. 169.
44 C. Stuart, *The Reith Diaries* (Collins, London, 1975), p. 197.
45 Ibid., p. 201.
46 *King George VI to His Peoples*, p. 9.
47 Ibid., p. 21.
48 P. Brendon and P. Whitehead, *The Windsors. A Dynasty Revealed* (Hodder & Stoughton, London, 1994), p. 91.
49 Cannadine, 'Context, Performance', p. 132.
50 See, for example, A. Wilkinson, *The Churches and the First World War* (SPCK, London, 1978) and my own *The Power of Sacrifice* (Darton, Longman & Todd, London, 1995), pp. 197–203.
51 Brendon and Whitehead, *The Windsors*, p. 27.
52 Ibid., p. 63.
53 D. Marquand, *Ramsay Macdonald* (Cape, London, 1977), p. 774.
54 H. Nicolson, *George V* (Constable, London, 1952), pp. 671–2.
55 Brendon and Whitehead, *The Windsors*, p. 68.
56 Ibid., p. 68.
57 Ibid., p. 88.
58 Ibid., p. 95.
59 *The Times*, 11 May 1937.
60 Prochaska, *Royal Bounty*, p. 230.

61 B. Pimlott, *The Queen* (HarperCollins, London, 2001), pp. 31–2.
62 Ibid., p. 46.
63 Ibid., p. 59. The text of this broadcast may be found at http://www.royal.gov.uk/ImagesandBroadcasts/Historic speechesandbroadcasts/Wartimebroadcast1940.
64 http://www.royal.gov.uk/imagesandbroadcasts/the queenschristmasbroadcasts/christmasbroadcasts/christ masbroadcast1952.

7 The past 60 years

1 Quoted by Paxman, *On Royalty*, p. 258.
2 *Daily Telegraph*, 15 October 1999.
3 *The Times*, 18 April 1996.
4 *Daily Telegraph*, 7 October 1994.
5 C. Longley, 'Siege of the House of Windsor', *The Tablet*, 13 November 1999.
6 *New Statesman*, 20 July 1956.
7 *Reynolds News*, 12 November 1959.
8 Lord Altrincham, *Is the Monarchy Perfect?* (John Calder, London, 1958), p. 11.
9 K. Martin, *The Crown and the Establishment* (Hutchinson, London, 1962), p. 168.
10 *Daily Telegraph*, 26 December 1998.
11 *The Times*, 10 April 2001.
12 J. Morton, *Prince Charles – Breaking the Cycle* (Ebury Press, London, 1998), pp. 14, 203.
13 Ibid., p. 76.
14 C. Longley, *Chosen People: Anglo-American Myth and Reality* (Hodder & Stoughton, London, 2002), pp. 20–1.
15 *Established Certainties? Reflections on Church, State and the Formation of Englishness* (Christian Socialist Movement, 2000), p. 7.
16 'Defenders of the Faith', *The Times*, 30 December 1996.
17 'A Time to Heal', *Temenos 5* (spring 2003), p. 15.
18 'The Sacred in Modern Life'. Speech to the Investcorp Dinner, 10 July 1996.

19 Ibid.
20 'A Reflection on the 2000 Reith Lectures'. BBC Radio 4, 17 May, 2000. This, and all other speeches and articles quoted, are on the Prince of Wales' website at www. princeofwales. gov.uk/speeches.
21 'Thought for the Day', BBC Radio 4, 1 January 2000.
22 'Seeds of Disaster', *Daily Telegraph*, 8 June 1998.
23 'Of Cabbages and Princes', *The Times*, 9 June 1998.
24 *Higher Calling* (Journal of Values in Higher Education), 4 (June 2000), p. 17.
25 'Royal Authority, Both Temporal and Spiritual', *The Times*, 12 June 1999.
26 *The Times*, 17 June 1999.
27 *Daily Telegraph*, 26 February 2000.
28 H. Carpenter, *Robert Runcie* (Hodder & Stoughton, London, 1996), pp. 220–5.
29 Anniversary Reception for Prayer Book Society, 29 April 1997.
30 *Worship Material for the Queen's Golden Jubilee* (Churches Together in Britain and Ireland, London, 2002), p. 19.
31 'Losing Faith in Coronations', *Guardian*, 7 June 2003.
32 P. Brendon and P. Whitehead, *The Windsors. A Dynasty Revealed* (Hodder & Stoughton, London, 1994), p.141.
33 C. Buchanan, *Cut the Connection* (Darton, Longman and Todd, London, 1984), p.143.
34 K. Harris, *The Queen* (Orion, London, 1994), p. 240.
35 Brendon and Whitehead, *The Windsors*, pp. 220–1.
36 Ibid., p. 249.
37 Ibid., p. 232.
38 *Spectator*, 29 August 1998.
39 *Church Times*, 12 September 1997.
40 *Church Times*, 14 April 2000.
41 P. Heelas, 'Diana's Self and the Quest Within'; L. Woodhead, 'Diana and the Religion of the Heart', both in J. Richards, S. Wilson and L.Woodhead (eds) *Diana:The Making of a Media Saint* (I. B. Taurus, London, 1999).

42 A. Billings, *Why We Made a Saint of Diana* (Centre for Practical Christianity, Kendal, 1998), p. 4.

43 E. Norman, 'The Dogma of the Queen of Hearts', *Church Times*, 28 August 1998.

44 Richards, Wilson and Woodhead (eds), *Diana*, pp. 128–9.

45 G. Bennett and A. Rowbottom, '"Born a Lady, Died a Saint": The Deification of Diana in the Press and Popular Opinion in Britain', *Fabula* 39 (Walter de Gruyer, Berlin, 1998), p. 207.

46 J. Wolffe, *Great Deaths* (Oxford University Press, Oxford, 2001), p. 6.

47 Richards, Wilson and Woodhead (eds), *Diana*, p. 51.

48 Bennett and Rowbottom, *Born a Lady*, p. 208.

49 Ibid., p. 208.

50 R.McKibbin, 'Mass-Observation in the Mall', *London Review of Books* (2 October 1997), p. 5.

51 T. Hames and M. Leonard, *Modernising the Monarchy* (Demos, London, 1998), p. 19.

52 *Guardian*, 12 June 2000.

53 *The Times*, 25 August 2000.

8 Current debates

1 Quoted in *Wake Up!* (Kingdom Foundation, Irvine) (January/February 1999), p. 157.

2 *Guardian*, 5 April 2011.

3 *Wake Up!* (January/February 1999), p. 158.

4 Christians Together in Highlands and Islands news release, 11 December 2008; H. M. Cartwright, 'The Act of Settlement and Its Relevance Today', lecture given in Inverness, 19 January 2009.

5 A. Hilton, 'The Price of Liberty', *Spectator*, 8 November 2003. See also leading articles in the *Daily Telegraph*, 20 November and 27 December 1999, and letters to *The Times*, 31 December 1999.

6 *Church Times*, 27 October 2000.

7 S. Reid, 'The Act of Settlement is Just Fine', *Guardian*, 25 September 2009.

8   *Church Times*, 30 May 2003, p. 17.
9   *The Christian Standard*, 5(2) (summer 2000), p. 2.
10 *The Bulletin* (National Council for Christian Standards), 4(2) (autumn/winter 1999), p. 8.
11 *The Bulletin*, 4(1) (summer 1999), p. 3.
12 This point was well made in a letter to *The Times* by Elizabeth Young in November 1999.
13 J. Dimbleby, *The Prince of Wales: A Biography* (Little, Brown, London, 1994), p. 528.
14 Ibid.
15 Ibid.
16 *Sunday Times*, 26 June 1994.
17 Dimbleby, *Prince of Wales*, p. 528.
18 'Faith and Nation' (Evangelical Alliance, 2006), p. 166.
19 E. Shils and M. Young, 'The Meaning of the Coronation', *Sociological Review*, New Series, Vol.1, 1953, p. 68.
20 *Church Times*, 30 May 2003, p. 21.
21 *Church Times*, 6 September 1996, p. 11.
22 *Church Times*, 15 January 1999.
23 C. Buchanan, *Cut the Connection* (Darton, Longman & Todd, London, 1994), p. 150.
24 *Wake Up!* (January/February 1999), p. 157.
25 *Daily Telegraph*, 23 January 1999.
26 *Faith and Nation* (Evangelical Alliance, 2006), p. 166.
27 *Religious Discrimination Project: Interim Report* (Religious Resource and Research Centre, University of Derby, 2000), p. 84.
28 *Daily Telegraph*, 10 and 12 April 2000.
29 R. Strong, *Coronation* (HarperCollins, London, 2005), p. 499.
30 W. Carr, 'This Intimate Ritual: The Coronation Service', *Political Theology*, 4(1) (November 2002), p. 15; *Church Times*, 20 September 2002.
31 *Guardian*, 23 June 2003.
32 Quoted in K. Harris, *The Queen*, pp. 373–4.
33 *The Tablet*, 2 February 2002, p. 19.

34 P. Avis, *Church, State and Establishment* (SPCK, London, 2001), pp. 29–30.

35 C. Buchanan, *Cut the Connection*, pp. 151, 146.

36 I. Bradley, 'National Churches that Stand for Communal Values', *Guardian*, 15 October 1990; 'A Force for Gentleness in National Life', *Church Times*, 16 July 1993; *Marching to the Promised Land: Has the Church a Future?* (John Murray, London, 1992), pp. 22–3, 32, 212–7; *Believing in Britain: The Spiritual Dimension of Britishness* (I. B. Tauris, London, 2007), pp. 130–5, 215–17.

37 Lecture given at Lambeth Palace, 23 April 2002.

38 T. Hobson, *Against Establishment* (Darton, Longman & Todd, London, 2003), pp. 3, 5.

39 This point is developed more fully in Bradley, *Believing in Britain*, pp. 204–7. See specifically J. Sacks, *The Persistence of Faith* (Weidenfeld & Nicolson, London, 1991); T. Modood (ed.), *Church, State and Religious Minorities* (Policy Studies Institute, 1997); B. Parekh, *Rethinking Multiculturalism: Cultural Diversity and Political Theory* (Palgrave, Basingstoke, 2000).

40 P. Avis, 'Establishment and the Mission of a National Church', *Theology*, (January/February) 2000, p.8.

41 *Established Certainties? Reflections on Church, State and the Formation of Englishness* (Christian Socialist Movement, 2000), p. 7.

42 M. Percy, 'The State of the Church We're In', *Affirming Catholicism*, 23 (1997), p. 5. See also the same author's editorial in *Modern Believing*, 40(2) (April 1999), p. 3.

43 W. Storrar, 'From Braveheart to Faint-Heart: Worship and Culture in Post-modern Scotland', in B. Spinks and I. Torrance (eds) *To Glorify God: Essays on Modern Reformed Liturgy* (T & T Clark, Edinburgh, 1999), p. 76.

44 *Independent*, 8 May 1998, p. 3.

45 Ibid.

46 *The Times*, 19 November 1999.

47 T. Hames and M. Leonard, *Modernising the Monarchy* (Demos, London, 1998), pp. 21–2.
48 Ibid., p. 30.
49 Ibid., pp. 30–1.
50 Ibid., pp. 33–4.
51 Ibid., p. 22.
52 V. Bogdanor, *The Monarchy and the Constitution* (Clarendon Press, Oxford, 1995), p. 239.
53 *The Times*, 10 April 2001; *Independent*, 11 April 2001.
54 J. Paxman, *The English* (Penguin Books, London, 1999), p. 240.
55 *Guardian*, 5 February 2011.
56 *Independent*, 14 March 2011.

9 The way ahead: a Christian monarchy in a multi-faith society

1 W. Bagehot, *The English Constitution* (World's Classics edn, Oxford, 1928), pp. 35, 39, 40.
2 I. Bradley, *God Save the Queen* (Darton, Longman & Todd, London, 2002), p. 194.
3 'Britain Gives Up On the Reformation', *The Times*, 4 August 1998.
4 Lord High Commissioner's address, 23 May 2000.
5 *Religious Discrimination Project: Interim Report* (University of Derby, 2000), p. 80.
6 Speech at King Hussein's memorial service, 5 July 1999.
7 E. Shils and M. Young, 'The Meaning of the Coronation', *Sociological Review*, New series, Vol. 1 (1953), p. 67.
8 These remarks are based on an interview with the director of the Religious Discrimination Project, Professor Paul Weller, on 23 October 2000.
9 'The Shape of the Next Coronation', *Political Theology*, 4(1) (November 2002), p. 41.
10 *Telegraph and Argus*, 3 June 2003. Letter from David James to author, 6 June 2003.
11 A. Billings, *Sex and Religion* (Centre for Practical Christianity, Kendal, 1998), p. 3.

12 M. Furlong, *The Church of England: The State It's In* (Hodder & Stoughton, London, 2000), p. 244.

13 *Guardian*, 4 April 2011.

14 *The Monarchy in Britain* (Central Office of Information, 1983), p. 10.

15 Shils and Young, *Meaning of the Coronation*, p. 71.

16 J. Habgood, *Church and Nation in a Secular Age* (Darton, Longman & Todd, 1983), p. 30.

17 W. Stark, *The Sociology of Religion*, Vol.1 (Routledge & Kegan Paul, 1966), p. 136.

18 J. Morton, *Breaking the Cycle*, pp. 265–6.

19 Caroline Brewster from Maidstone and Terry Phillips from Cardiff quoted in P. Barkham, 'Let Them Eat Cake', *Guardian*, 5 April 2011.

20 'A Nation Still in Thrall to the Mysterious Alchemy of its Royal Love Affair', *Guardian*, Royal Wedding Supplement, 30 April 2011, p. 1.

21 *Crown and Commonwealth* (B. I. W. F. Journal) (Spring 2001), p. 10.

22 *Daily Telegraph*, 9 November 1999.

23 *Marie Curie Supporter News*, Winter 2000.

24 A. Rowbottom, 'Royal Symbolism and Social Integration' (Ph.D. thesis, University of Manchester, 1994), p. 7.

25 A. Rowbottom, 'The Real Royalists: Folk Performance and Civil Religion at Royal Visits', *Folklore*, 109 (1998), p. 86.

Index of names